Alzheimer's
Not just a memory

By Angela Hogarth

Alzheimer's
Not just a memory

Angela Hogarth

Design©Tricorn Books
www.tricornbooks.co.uk

This is a work of nonfiction. The events are portrayed to the best of Angela Hogarth's memory. While all the stories in this book are true, some names and identifying details have been changed to protect the privacy of the people and institutions involved.

ISBN 9781912821204

Published 2019 by Tricorn Books
Aspex
42 the Vulcan Building
Gunwharf Quays
Portsmouth

Printed and bound in the UK by CMP Poole

I dedicate this book to our beautiful daughters,
who have been my rock. Your dad would be very proud.
So am I. Love you both millions.

Mum xx

Special thanks
To Marilyn, who has always been there for me.
To Fiona, who has dedicated her life helping
those going through this journey.
To friends, who stay by my side. You know who you are.
To the Joseph Carey Psychic Foundation, who through their teachings
and healing have given me a sense of belonging.
My homeopath who has seen me through some difficult times.
To all who have gone through or are going through this journey.
My heart goes out to you.

To Derek.
They call it the long goodbye.
Until we meet again.
All my love, Angela x

A note from the author

It was never my intention to write a book. I don't even know how it came about. I guess I just wrote things down in journal form as a kind of therapy. The hardest part was reading it back. The result – this book – is based upon my journal, so reflects my feelings at the time in all its raw detail.

I can't believe how the system doesn't work and has made our lives so much more difficult. More and more people are diagnosed with this evil disease each day and still there are no facilities for the younger generation being diagnosed. When are those in power going to listen? When are the carers going to get help? This evil disease is not going to go away.

I was 44 years old when my husband was diagnosed. I hadn't a clue about Alzheimer's. Now it's all I know.

I hope that this book helps those who read it and are in the same situation. You are not alone.

Angela Hogarth
October 2018

Contents

Introduction

I cannot remember for sure when things began to change. The doctors ask me this question all the time, and in all honesty I reply that I don't know. I can only remember markers in my life that guide me to the answer.

We were leading a normal family life, we both had good jobs and a nice house which Derek had built for us. We did everything together as a family and considered ourselves a tight unit. We enjoyed holidays together, running the girls to and from after-school clubs. Derek loved his football and working in the garden.

There were no signs that Derek was ill. In fact, in all the years I have known him, he has only been ill once. He was borderline workaholic and hated taking time off work as he was self-employed. He always insisted that we couldn't afford for him not to work. He would only have a couple of weeks off a year.

The early signs were his hearing. Then later he would hit his head with his hands. When he walked out of work we were left with only my part-time wage. Not enough to run a house, let alone a family.

This journal is an account of when my hard-working husband's health began to deteriorate and the effects it has had on our family life.

2008

March 2008
We have begun to wonder if Derek is going deaf, as he won't respond to us when spoken to. He said it was because we spoke too quietly, but I booked him an appointment at the doctors for a hearing test. He has come back with great joy to say that there is nothing wrong with his hearing.

April 2008
It's time to get the books together for the accountant, as Derek is self-employed. Derek does this job and I take them to the accountant. I am shocked to realise that Derek has not done any book work for the previous year at all and I have to learn how to do it very quickly. I explain to the accountant that if there are any errors it is my fault, as I have had to do the books this time.

Derek is also getting confused about bank accounts. We have two accounts, one current and one business, but this appears to confuse him, so we have changed one of them to a different bank. I have power of attorney for this one, so I can sort out any problems.

Derek is suffering from osteoarthritis and the doctor has decided to refer him to a critical pain clinic to see if they can help. Unfortunately, we have missed this appointment – something I have never done before. I feel so bad for not turning up. I am juggling two jobs, a family and trying to remember appointments. I have written to the hospital to apologise and explained the situation at home. I have said that Derek's memory is not so good and they have given us another appointment.

June 2008
June 2. We arrived at the critical pain clinic and Derek was examined by a consultant and asked lots of questions about his health. Until my dying day, I will never forget the way he was in that consulting room. He was like a caged animal, that's the only way I can describe it. He was edgy and very nervous. The consultant noticed that there was more than osteoarthritis going on and said that right now Derek needed sorting out in other ways. He said that at a later day we should go back to his clinic, but in the meantime he was referring Derek back to his doctor for further investigations.

July 2008
July 22. Derek has been referred to a mental health team. This involves going over Derek's medical history to try to find out why his memory is failing and why the antidepressants aren't working any more.

They have changed his antidepressant to 37.5mg of Venlafaxine a day. It is hoped that this will improve his mood and therefore his memory.

August 2008
Derek's boss has contacted me to ask after him. He says that he is worried about him and wonders how he can help, since he is finding it difficult to follow instructions. I have asked

him to write down instructions for Derek to follow. Derek has become quite tearful at times. To see a grown man this way is upsetting enough, but when it's your husband it seems that much worse.

September 2008
The mental health team have noted that Derek is muddling his words and forgetting them when he speaks. Blood tests taken in July have shown that he is anaemic, so he is now on iron tablets. He also gave a stool sample. He has lost a lot of weight, but his appetite is still very good.

We have been trying to get Derek to take Fridays off work to give him a longer weekend to help him relax more. But he always says that we can't afford it and he has to work a full week. We made a pact that I would give up one of my part-time jobs so that I could be home too. We have been going out on bike rides and I think it has done us both good to spend time together. The Venlafaxine dose has been increased to 75mg.

October 2008
When I came back from work, Derek was there. He had walked off a job, after he apparently made a mistake fitting a lock in an oak door. Words were said and Derek packed up his tools and walked off, refusing to go back.

Derek has been referred to SWACAS age cognitive assessment services. We have been going to the mental health clinic every six weeks, but I didn't feel that we were achieving anything – same questions every time, lots of tears (mainly mine, as I feel so frustrated and want answers). We have had a home visit which lasted a couple of hours. His medical history was taken and his problems discussed.

We only have my part-time wage, but this doesn't seem to bother Derek. Earlier this month his Venlafaxine dose was increased to 150mg. At the end of the month it is now 225mg.

November 2008
Derek has gone to the psychiatric hospital for a two-and-a half-hour appointment. He has seen a psychiatrist who has booked him for a further appointment next week.

We met the psychiatrist for a neuropsychological assessment. This has been quite a harrowing ordeal. I guess I thought we would get some answers. I was taken into a room with the psychiatrist and I told him how things were at home with Derek – about his forgetfulness, his inability to hold a conversation without losing interest, how I have had to take over the running of the house, and be both mum and dad to our daughters. I told him how Derek goes to bed in the afternoon, or early evening if there's nothing on TV, how his speech is muddled, his lack of understanding of how little money is coming into the house, and his lack of concern about not working. He has also started breathing very heavily.
The psychiatrist met with Derek and examined him. He then met with me again and has advised that Derek has a chest X-ray and MRI scan.

December 2008
I had a phone call at work to tell me that the chest X-ray has come back clear. This is good news. On the 23rd Derek has his MRI scan.

2009

January 2009

I have received a phone call from the psychiatrist office to say that he has the results from Derek's scan. We have made an appointment to see him on Friday. This must be one of the worst parts of being ill – waiting for results. Every possible thought is going through my head. At least we will know what we are dealing with and maybe get some normality back in our lives.

Derek has not slept well. He has been very anxious, as have I. Friday is here and I am not feeling too well. In fact, if it wasn't for the hospital appointment I would have stayed in bed.

January 9. We arrived at the hospital at 2pm. We met with the psychiatrist who advised that on reading the notes he had no answers for us. The scan showed that his brain has shrunk, but that the fluid around the brain had not. He said that he had not seen a result like this before and therefore had no explanation. He asked if we had any questions. I said that he has told us nothing that couldn't have been said on the phone, so why the appointment. Yet another knock down. I am not sure how much longer I can cope with this situation.

In the evening, I received a call from the hospital to ask if I was OK, as I had been so upset and angry when I had left. They told me that in case I hadn't heard correctly Derek's scan had shown an abnormality which needed further investigation.

We are now waiting for an appointment at a Brighton hospital. We were referred there a month ago, but so far have heard nothing. This is being chased up on Monday. We were told that we would receive a phone call on either Monday or Tuesday with an appointment date.

***

There seems to be no consistency to Derek's illness. He complains about being cold all the time, and often says that he can feel a chill running down his spine.

***

January 15. Today is Thursday and there is still no phone call. I phone the Brighton hospital to find out what's going on. They gave me a date for Derek's appointment – 4 March. We are still in January. It has been classed as a routine appointment, but how can that be so when we have already been told that there are abnormalities in the scan? I am now losing trust in the psychiatric hospital. I had said that we had an appointment on Friday for the Chapel Street Clinic, but since we were seeing a new consultant I didn't think we needed to attend. The hospital agreed and said that they would cancel the appointment, but they forgot to do it. I am now at a loss as to what to do. Do we just accept that we now have to wait six weeks until we see the neurologist from Brighton? Or do we go back to our doctor to ask her to chase this appointment and bring it forward?

February 2009

19 February. We are waiting for our March appointment. I have obtained a copy of Derek's scan to take with us to Brighton because I am worried that when we get there they won't have a copy of it. Derek is complaining of pain behind the left eye and back of the head, which is quite worrying.

28 February. We had an appointment with Chapel Street Clinic, which wasn't very helpful at all. They asked if we had heard from the DVLA. I asked what she was on about. She had assumed that we were there to find out if Derek should still be allowed to drive. This was the first I'd heard about it. Derek was asked about his mood on a scale of 1 to 10 on a good day and a bad day. The whole session was a complete waste of time. I have asked that we are not sent there again because it is of no benefit to Derek.

March 2009

3 March. We received a phone call from Brighton to say that Derek's appointment has been cancelled because the neurologist is unwell. They said they'd contact us with a new appointment. I am so angry.

4 March. I tried to call Brighton, but I only got through to an answerphone. I have left a message saying that we had waited three months for this appointment. This evening I got a call from Brighton to say that an appointment had been made for Derek to see the neurologist on 6 March.

***

Derek has never managed the art of using a mobile phone, but as long as we could get hold of him when he was at work, a mobile was a good thing. Recently, Derek has been asking the girls how to use his mobile and how to text. He even asked me at one stage. We tried to show him, but he found it too confusing and got angry. The nurse from the hospital advised us that if Derek was finding things like the remote control difficult, to take them out of the equation. Also, he has been running out of credit, more so than when he was at work. I have tried to explain to him that he shouldn't use the mobile to make day-to-day calls because it is using up his credit. I have looked at his phone to see who the calls have been to and there is a random number on it. I have asked him who the number belongs to, but he says he doesn't know. I wonder if it's his friend who visited recently. Although Derek is very cagey about his phone, he is always playing with it and has said that some numbers need to be taken off it.

6 March. We had our appointment with the neurologist today. We were very impressed with him. We had to start at the beginning, when we noticed changes in Derek's health. He has done so many tests, which I have to say have been done before. I asked if he had seen Derek's scan – he hadn't. So I got my copy out and he put it into his computer. He asked us what we had been told, and we told him. He then went on to explain in great detail what the scan meant. No atrophy has been found, but he could see a problem. His words were that he was not a betting man, but if he was he would say that there were early signs of Alzheimer's.

The most important thing to do now is to change Derek's mood and change the antidepressants. If his mood changes and his memory improves, then we may be looking at another matter.

The next step is to wait for an appointment with the psychiatrist; another scan will be done at Brighton in June; and in July we will meet with the neurologist again.

***

My daughter asked me if I had found out who the mystery phone number belonged to. 'Why don't you phone it?' she said. Anyway, her boyfriend offered, on the pretence of ringing the wrong number. A lady answered called Jen. This happens to be an ex-girlfriend of Derek's. I just couldn't believe it. I am very angry and have been stewing for a day. I can't hold in my anger any more and have confronted Derek. He said that she is a friend of my family's, which I know, and understand. She often visits his mum. But this does not excuse why her mobile number is on his phone. He says that they have got friendlier again, but that there is nothing in it. Maybe not, but it has left me uneasy. Part of me is wondering if this is to do with his mental state, or maybe he is not as unwell as we thought.

***

26 March. We have been to the hospital to see the psychiatrist. We were separated so that he could do some tests with Derek and I could talk to the nurse about any worries I have. I told her about the phone calls and about Derek's need to relive his past.

The psychiatrist wants to give Derek another lot of pills to help his moods, on top of his high dose of antidepressants. I pointed out that maybe this wasn't a good idea as after more than 12 years of antidepressants it was time to stop them, since some of the side effects can be depression and memory loss. So we agreed to drop his dose to 150mg a day for three weeks, followed by 75mg a day for three weeks, then no pills for three weeks. We were then to go back to see the psychiatrist. I am praying that this works, with no repercussions.

27 March. Derek is very down and has now gone to visit friends from his past. Yesterday he made two visits to see his mum.

We received a letter from Brighton to say that an appointment has been made for Derek on 5 August. I am really annoyed that we are having to wait that long to see the neurologist again as we were told that June would be the next appointment for a scan. I phoned the hospital and left a message, as it seems impossible to speak to anyone straight away. They did phone me back to inform me that the appointment was for the results of the scan. I had to tell them that we had had no date for the scan as yet, but they reassured me that we would get an appointment soon. This would come from a different department.

***

31 March. I came home from work and started making a cup of tea. Derek was listening to the MP3 player that I had bought him for his birthday. He then burst into tears. I asked him what was wrong and he said it was the music he was listening to. This is not like him to show emotion over a piece of music.

***

The last couple of days I have been starting to think that maybe things were getting back to some normality. Maybe Derek is not as bad as we thought? Maybe the tablets were the cause of the depression? Then my bubble was burst.

April 2009
3 April. Donna is having boyfriend troubles and, just for caring about it, I bear the brunt of it. Anyway, she has not spoken to me in two days. Her problem, but it hurts me because I was only trying to help. Derek has received a text on his phone from Donna, asking him if he could pick her up from her boyfriend's house or should she get the train. Derek does not know how to text, even though we have shown him many times. I asked him if he wanted me to text her back, which he agreed to. I asked Donna if she would get the train back with her boyfriend, since I didn't want her to travel alone. I also didn't want Derek to have to drive to the other side of town to pick her up. Derek then went off on one, saying that he should have answered her question, not me. I pointed out that he would get no thanks from Donna for going out of his way to pick her up, as he always complains that she hardly speaks to him. Derek said that she says 'thank you'. A no-win situation. That is a contradiction. Derek gets annoyed with me, so I tell him to go to bed. Louise is upset too, because she says that she has tried to teach her dad to text, once spending an hour with him. She says it's like watching the film *50 First Dates*!

May 2009
After a gradual reduction in Derek's medication he is now into his third week of no antidepressants. There is no drastic change, but he has been working more in the garden, whereas before he was sleeping in the afternoons. He sometimes gets tearful and he still has some anger towards me, but my patience isn't too good with him. I guess some part of me is angry with him. Is he as ill as we think?

The scan date has at last come through. It is for 1 June at Brighton. The results will be on 5 August. No other appointments are booked until then.

Derek's brother phoned and asked if Derek is at home. I said he wasn't and he just said 'bye' and hung up. He didn't even ask how we were or how things were going. I am not sure what I have done to deserve this.

Derek will make himself a cup of tea, but forget to make me one. He washes up his cup and leaves everyone else's. He also goes out and doesn't tell us where he is going. I have to renew the insurance for his bike and they have asked me if he is still a carpenter. I say no and that he no longer works. They ask why and I tell them that he is off sick. They ask me what is wrong and I tell them. They say they will make a note on his records. When I tell Derek this he is very angry. He says that he is retired now and that is why he doesn't work!

June 2009
We travel to Brighton for Derek's second – and hopefully last – scan to identify what is wrong.

Derek is in the scanner for about 30 minutes this time. We now have to wait until 5 August for the results, although I have phoned the hospital to see if there is an earlier appointment. They said that the results were available three weeks after the scan and that our GP would get them. But we haven't seen Derek's GP for a while and I don't want to make an appointment only to find out they can't understand the results, as has happened before.

It seems that every day now Derek is crying. When I ask what is wrong, he says that his head is all jumbled.

I made an appointment for Derek to see the psychiatrist, as I felt that maybe he needed to be on antidepressants. Unfortunately, the appointment was cancelled because the psychiatrist was on holiday. An appointment was made for the following week, but that was also cancelled because he is away for two weeks.

I called for a meeting with Derek's nurse, the clinical nurse specialist, and Derek's brother and sister to discuss his illness. I first phoned his sister to ask her to the meeting. She didn't want to come, but said that if their brother came, she would. I phoned their brother and he really surprised me – he said he did want to come. The meeting was arranged at the Unit for 8 June.

7 June. I attended a meeting for partners with dementia with Derek's nurse at the hospital. This was a meeting I needed to go to. I was so nervous, but I went and met some really nice people who were going through or had been through the same experience as me. Although I found it helpful, I also found it distressing to have to listen to what the end outcome of the disease would be like.

8 June. The family meeting. I am not sure if I can put down in words how I feel about the outcome of this meeting. Devastated may be a good start. I don't think this meeting was ever about Derek in their eyes, more like 'let's tell Angela how we really feel about her'. Basically they ran me into the ground. I was accused of not making them feel welcome in my home, for leaving them on the door step and not inviting them into the house, the expression on my face in photos taken when the girls were small. For taking Derek off antidepressants too quickly, for not visiting their mother. I was shocked to hear how they felt about me and how they accused me of confiding in my 'many friends' rather than in them. They said my children were not kids – aged 17 and 13 – when I told them how Derek's illness was affecting them. They complained about Derek only being allowed to watch the small TV in the kitchen. I was even asked if I showed any love towards him.

***

On Tuesday I went to work as usual, but I am afraid that as soon as I walked through that door I was so upset I burst into tears. One of my work colleagues told me that her mother went through a very similar thing when her dad was ill, and that when asked to help they said they couldn't. The family became divided. I was also told that this often happens in these situations.

***

Between the clinical nurse specialist and myself, we have decided not to give Derek any antidepressants at the moment, as there are a few good signs when he is not on them, such as no night sweats and more energy. He also isn't walking around like a zombie. I have been advised to look out for warning signs and to stay in contact with the nurse.

I haven't told Derek what happened at the family meeting, although surprisingly he did ask. But I don't think he needs to know, as I am sure it will upset him.

***

Towards the end of June I am getting desperate to know what to do about Derek. Not a day goes by without tears and on one Monday afternoon he sat on the conservatory floor and cried, not knowing what to do, saying that the pain in his head was so bad. He has also been waking up at around 5am and, I believe, forgetting to eat lunch.

I phoned the clinical nurse specialist and she said she would get us an appointment to see the psychiatrist. When she phoned back she said there would be a prescription in the post for Mirtazapine. He is to take 15mg at night for the first two weeks, followed by 30mg if everything is OK.

After a couple of days, Derek told Louise that the pills were making him feel worse. I think this was probably physiological.

July 2009

Derek's mood seems to have improved. He sleeps well and isn't in a rush to get up in the mornings.

Work have been brilliant throughout my ordeal and today asked if Derek would like to do some odd jobs around the centre so that he isn't left on his own so much. It also gives him the opportunity to interact with the clients. This may be a positive move for him and hopefully help him. I hope he takes them up on the offer.

I have joined a chat forum for those with Alzheimer's and their carers which has helped a little, as last weekend I thought my world was ending. August is fast approaching and although I don't want to wish the summer away, I am eagerly awaiting the appointment on 5 August so that we can start Derek's treatment.

August 2009

5 August. Because my dad took us to the first appointment to see the neurologist, I was not confident in finding my own way there, so we purchased a satnav. I set it all up and set off for our long-awaited appointment. After the first half hour of travelling the satnav took us a different way to the one my dad took, but I trusted it even though I didn't see any signs at all. I started to feel nervous and I didn't want us to be late. As it turned out, we got there in good time and had to wait an hour as they were running over time.

We entered the neurologist's office and sat down to be given the long-awaited news. Although not 100% sure, Alzheimer's is the verdict. We may only get 100% assurance with an autopsy.

I guess I wasn't that surprised. Deep down I knew that was going to be the outcome.

We have been told that there is a trial that Derek could go on and also medication called Aricept. I have mentioned to the neurologist that Derek is unable to make day-to-day decisions, let alone decide about his treatment. So he told me that it was up to me to make the decisions.

We were taken into another room to see a nurse and talk over options. The trial drug consists of going to Brighton every 13 weeks to have a drug given intravenously for an hour, then tests and scans over two days. Every six weeks we would have to go to Brighton for tests. The downside is that one in three get a placebo, one gets a lower dose and just one gets the full dose.

I decided that Aricept was maybe the way to go, but Derek came out of the meeting saying that he didn't understand what was being said.

The next day I phoned the psychiatric hospital and got a prescription for Aricept. Following Derek's diagnosis, I have to inform the DVLA in case Derek is unable to drive. We are awaiting the reply.

It is Donna's birthday and Derek's brother and wife have come to the house to give her a present. My dad is with us, but not mum as she is unwell. Derek's sister-in-law is very giggly and both are holding a conversation with my dad mostly. We are all in the kitchen and Derek's sister-in-law makes a silly comment about how dark Louise's eyes are and that she must have her grandad's eyes. She then said, 'Oh, but your mum has dark eyes, doesn't she?' like I wasn't in the room. When they leave they say to Derek, 'Derek, you are always welcome around our home any time.'

September 2009

Louise is worried that she is going to be kicked out of the youth theatre as she hasn't sold the allocated five tickets for the next performance. I contact the theatre to advise them of the situation at home. It was a very emotional phone call as it meant having to admit to outsiders that we were having problems at home. The kindness we receive is second to none, however, and I am told that the youth theatre is 100% behind us and our tickets were paid for. They are glad that I have made them aware of the situation so that they can keep an eye on Louise.

***

Louise and I went to watch the Youth Theatre performance. Donna went out with friends. I was going to pick up Donna on the way home.

We got home quite late at night and went to open the front door to find that the lock had been dropped and we couldn't get in. We tried ringing the doorbell and phoning Derek's mobile and home phone, but still we could not wake him up. I drove around to my sister's house, but all her lights were out and I didn't want to wake her so we went back home, and rang the phone and doorbell. In the end, we were banging on the front door. Eventually we woke Derek up and with some confusion he managed to open the front door. It comes to something when your husband is unaware of you being home or not. I said to the girls that you have to laugh or you would cry.

***

I started a spiritual and psychic awareness course. I wasn't going to mention this because at the end of the day this journal is about Derek. But then I realised that you need to know about the family's part in this and how we cope.

***

At the end of September we were given an appointment at the psychiatric hospital to see the psychiatrist. He told us that he had a form from the DVLA to fill in about Derek driving. He asked me if I thought he was OK driving. I replied that I didn't want to comment on this because at the end of the day I have to live with him and if his licence is taken away I don't want to get the blame.

Aricept was increased to 10mg – the maximum dose. Hopefully this will work, but I have since learnt that the success rate is only 40%.

October 2009

It is Derek's mum's 90th birthday on 3 October and I was asking Derek what he thought we should buy her. He started talking about a get-together arranged on her birthday in the afternoon for her family. Not that this was mentioned to me. This was the last thing I needed, to meet up with Derek's brother and sister.

3 October. Although I had a chest infection and Louise had a cold we decided that we would go to the so-called family party. But Derek wasn't sure what time it started so he tried to phone his brother and sister. No reply. So he went down to his mum's house and everybody was already there. Derek came home to tell us that it had started and then went back to the party with us following him later on.

When we got there, Derek's ex-girlfriend was there. No surprise! I was so proud that the girls came with me, as neither of them wanted to go. We walked up to Derek's mum and wished her a happy birthday. Derek's sister poked her nose in and said to Derek's mum, 'Do you recognise the girls? They're Derek's girls.'

We went in and sat next to Derek's aunt and uncle who talked to us the whole time, making us laugh. The aunt said she was making us laugh to pass the time. She was like a guardian angel sent to protect us from the wolves.

I have never felt so unwelcome. Photos were being taken and someone said they wanted a photo taken of the Hogarth family, but we were not included. Not even the girls.

As the girls and I left, Derek's sister had to have the last word, saying 'Thanks for coming, I realised you did it for Derek.' I said, 'Yes, for Derek, not for the rest of you.'

On the way home, my girls were in tears. I am so proud of them. At least we know where we stand.

***

The next morning Louise said to me, 'Can't we change our surname to Bailey? I don't want to be a Hogarth.'

***

I woke one morning to Derek sobbing and saying, 'She's gone!' I thought at first that he meant his mum had died, but it was our beautiful rabbit Daisy who we had had for seven years. She had just died in her sleep. We were all very upset about this, but Derek took the news the worst. He went into his shed and made a wooden coffin for her.

November 2009

Derek's dose of 10mg of Aricept seems to be upsetting his system, with diarrhoea and having to wee a lot more. I made an appointment for him with the doctor, after having spoken to the psychiatric hospital about this. A wee sample was done and a blood test was taken.

At this point I had taken the girls away for a couple of days to Glastonbury, as I felt that we needed a break. I labelled Derek's food and left notes on the two appointments he had, and phoned him each day to make sure he was OK. This sounds like I am trying to apologise for leaving Derek at home, maybe I am, but I had also told the psychiatric hospital that I was doing this.

We almost didn't go to Glastonbury. We looked around Street and Clarks village, went to Chalice Well and had a meal out – a mini holiday.

Unfortunately, the journey home was not so good. All was fine until we hit Eastleigh. The traffic was at a standstill due to a major accident and a woman jumping off a bridge. We decided to come off the motorway and take the backroads home. Big mistake. We then got held up in a large fire. At first we thought it was a firework display, but it turned out to be a car scrapyard on fire. We had to crawl past it, which was very frightening as we could hear the horns of the cars going off and the popping of petrol tanks. A journey which should have taken two hours took six in the end.

**

Derek's blood test and wee sample came back clear, which possibly means that Derek is having side effects from the Aricept.

Just before we went away I did think that maybe Derek was getting a little worse. But I am never sure if it's just me being oversensitive.

**

The day after we came back from Glastonbury Derek was involved in a car accident. That morning the car had broken down and Derek took me to work and picked me up when I finished. After we got home from work, Derek received a text from Donna asking to be picked up from the dentist. I then received a phone call, which I ignored thinking it was Donna being impatient. But the phone rang again and when I answered it I could hear police sirens and Donna said they had been in a car accident. My car was in the garage, so I ran across the road to a neighbour to ask if she could give me a lift. There had been two accidents along that road. Derek had pulled over to let the emergency services through and a car from nowhere had ploughed into the side of the van Derek and Donna were in. Thank god they were not hurt, just very shaken. I phoned the police because the van was not driveable and in my panic didn't know what to do. We were told to go to the local police station within 24 hours with driving documents. That evening the car driver who went into the van phoned me up and accused Derek of pulling out in front of him. The next morning we went to the police station. Donna and Derek gave statements, but Derek could not remember the details and was contradicting Donna's statement.

Derek was very confused and very shaky after the accident.

The van was a write-off. As Derek had no way of getting to his mum's to give her dinner, which he had been doing for some time; I phoned his brother to say that he could no longer go. That weekend we went into town shopping and then for a meal as a treat. In the short time we were out Derek had to go to the loo four times and while having a meal Derek broke down and cried.

On the Sunday, Derek was very confused about doing his mum's dinners, saying he had to do them. I explained that it had been sorted, but he was going to tell his brother that he couldn't do them. Derek got very upset and said that they would say he had to catch a bus to his mum's and that there would be an argument. I wasn't sure what was going on in his head or whether someone had been saying something to Derek. I will never know the answer to that one!

Anyway, I phoned up Derek's brother to explain the situation and to verify that he would not be doing his mum's dinners until further notice. Derek's brother's reply was, 'Where's Derek's van?' He then went blabbering on about nothing to do with Derek. They just don't get it, do they?

***

Derek went back to the doctors to see about the results from the tests. She agreed that Derek was having side effects from Aricept.

The doctor advised that he come off Aricept for two weeks and see how he goes, and then try another drug called Reminyl.

I phoned the psychiatric hospital to let them know what was happening. They said it wasn't a good idea to come off Aricept as there was no going back if Derek's condition got worse over the two weeks the medication was stopped. I was quite annoyed, as having told the hospital in the first place that Derek was having problems they had told him to see his GP. Then when the GP gives the advice, they say it's wrong. We are in the middle and don't know which way to turn.

The outcome was to halve the Aricept to 5mg a day and see what happens.

I also told the hospital that Derek seems to be getting worse and they said it could be the result of the accident and that we went away without him. I also asked if the antidepressants could be changed as the ones he is on don't seem to be working. They said that they would arrange a home visit with the psychiatrist. That was two weeks ago and we are still waiting.

***

I have applied for a free bus pass for Derek while he waits for his van to be sorted. Hopefully he will use it. Derek has not seen his mum for almost three weeks. I have offered to take him to see her, but he says he doesn't want to go. I find that very strange.

As I am unwell again I said to Derek, 'Why not ask your brother to take you to see her?' But he says he couldn't ask him to do that.

While having to deal with Derek's Alzheimer's and depression, I also have the turmoil of dealing with my mum's possible cancer. My mum had cancer about four years ago and was feeling very positive that she had beaten it, but sadly in August she was to learn that it had returned. But this time, not in a good place. Although my mum is quite positive, my dad, who is also having to sort out two of his sisters who are ill and having to go into homes, is very tearful, which breaks my heart. He is such a strong man. I know that he feels he won't have mum for much longer.

I feel helpless. I don't understand why so many bad things are happening to us.

It is 3.30am and I have written the last two pages as I could not sleep after seeing my dad get upset again and knowing he's not sleeping. I am worried about him. I also have not been well again. Some virus I picked up, it seems, that's all I do at the moment.

I know that I am going to have to make some changes, but as yet not sure what or how. Just that we have got to have a better life.

***

We have received a letter from the DVLA to say that on medical grounds they will issue Derek with a licence on a yearly basis. But to be quite honest I don't want him to drive. I am not saying that the accident was his fault, but I don't think Derek is aware enough. But the DVLA and doctors think otherwise.

December 2009
Derek is getting more tearful and I can feel his low moods are pulling me down. I phoned the psychiatric hospital to see when Derek's next appointment will be and they said they have no meeting rooms available and they would phone us on the day and visit at home. This is no good to me as I cannot take any more time off work. The hospital said to leave it with them and they would sort something out. Ten minutes later they phoned back to say how would I feel being transferred to the over-65 mental health team, with a nurse and social worker. I said that would be great.

One week later we get a phone call from the over-65 team and we were visited by a community nurse.

28 December. Derek has now been taken off Aricept for a week and then another drug will be tried.

2010

January 2010

Our appointment at Brighton on 6 January is cancelled due to the heaviest snowfall in 30 years. We are re-scheduled for 3 February. The prescription for the new drug Galantamine was posted to us, but due to the snow we have had no post for a week.

14 January. I have a double funeral to attend – my two aunts. A very sad day. I went with my dad, as I didn't want Derek with me. Mum didn't feel well enough to attend.

15 January. The nurse was due to visit Derek at home. This appointment was cancelled by the nurse and re-scheduled for the following Monday. I think that the nurse was surprised to see how low Derek's mood was. She said she would come and see us again the following week.

This appointment was yet again cancelled by the nurse and rescheduled for the following Monday, but I was unable to make it so I cancelled and said I would reschedule once we came back from Brighton.

***

The new drug, Galantamine, arrived, a low dose of 8mg. But already Derek is having an upset tummy. I phoned the nurse and with the psychiatrist's advice we are told that he should stop this drug. But Derek doesn't want to stop taking it and he says it will help him to not get worse.

February 2010

3 February. A meeting with the neurologist's nurse, a lovely lady who spent over an hour with us, but as usual I got upset. I often wonder if I will ever get a grip on this!

I explained that Derek was told to come off Galantamine because of the upset tummy and she said that was not a good idea and another drug could be given to counteract this. I explained that we were always given different advice and we were in the middle trying to decide which was best. The nurse explained that this was because Alzheimer's was associated with psychiatry and it should be neurology. This is an ongoing battle that two departments have. Not much help to us. The nurse explained that we could be just referred to the psychiatrist, but they would like to keep Derek as a patient at Brighton. I agreed that we definitely wanted to be under the watchful eye of the neurologist, as he is the best.

The nurse suggested that Derek had respite, maybe with a member of the family. I said that wasn't possible as my mum has cancer and it would be too much. And I was not speaking to Derek's family. I wouldn't give them the satisfaction of asking for help.

The nurse said that she strongly advised respite, if only for the girls' sake, but I have seen the outcome of respite and it would make Derek worse. What kind of a person would I be to do this at the early stage of the disease? I have got to be stronger and not let this situation destroy mine and my children's lives.

One thing that did surprise me was that Derek told the nurse that I had a lot to deal with at the moment with my family, so he is aware of this situation. I am confused as to how this disease works, it's almost like playing tricks on him as to what he can and cannot understand on a daily basis.

I had a brilliant idea. I asked Derek if he could make me a trunk-type box to keep my memorabilia in, something to keep him occupied and for me to keep as a keepsake of his workmanship. But he fretted about the wood type, how big to make it, not having the correct tools, and how much time it would take. I was sad that he found it too challenging a task, especially as he once built a rocking horse. I just wanted something to remember him by which could be passed down through the family.

Another blow. My dad has had a breakdown and is now in hospital. I didn't see that coming. All the stress of losing two sisters and the return of my mum's cancer was too much for him. I cannot go and visit him at the moment as I don't feel strong enough mentally to cope, which sounds really bad.

I also don't have Derek to talk to about how dad is as he gets too confused. I cannot go to the hospital with Derek as it is a mental health ward and I don't want Derek to see what the patients are like or how ill dad is.

March 2010
10 March. Last Friday Derek's nurse came for a visit. I explained about Brighton, mentioned respite and was shocked to hear that this was not an option for Derek as he is under 65. I replied that I hope Derek does not get any worse in the next two years then.

I asked when Derek was going to be reviewed by the psychiatrist as Brighton wanted this done and that was over a month ago. The nurse said she would chase this up and was coming to visit again in three weeks and we should have heard from the psychiatrist by then. I said that I wouldn't hold my breath. I also said that I feel we have been forgotten because they know there is no cure.

***

Meanwhile, Derek decided to build another rabbit run. Not that we needed one, but it gave him something to do. But even that became a challenge. He told my mum that I told him to build it, which is not so.

Derek complains of aches and pains more and is always cold.

Still not heard a word from the psychiatrist. Friday the nurse will come and she said we should have heard from him by then. I will bide my time until Friday, then I will phone Brighton.

21 March. A very trying day. I shouted at Derek as he couldn't understand the simplest of instructions. We were trying to fix a camera into a bird box for him to watch on TV, but I got angry with him and landed up crying. In the afternoon, I went out for a drive with mum and Louise. I needed to be away from Derek, but I felt mean that I didn't take him with us. I hate the way this disease is turning me into a horrid person with no compassion.

***

It seems that the government is spending money on TV ads to make people aware of dementia. I wish they would put more money towards helping the carers to cope with this disease.

***

Derek has said that when the better weather comes he will be gardening and keeping busy in the garden. But in the last few days the weather has been fine, Derek has been wandering around the garden looking lost, not knowing what to do. I am starting to get angry now as no help is out there for us and Derek seems to be getting worse. Or are my tolerance levels very low?

26 March. The nurse turns up as promised. She asked if we had heard from the psychiatrist. I said no, but was not surprised as I already said I didn't think he would contact us. The nurse phoned and made an appointment for the following Monday afternoon. Apparently they hadn't heard from Brighton. That same afternoon the nurse phoned me up to say that the psychiatrist was double-booked on Monday and cancelled. But there was an appointment on a Tuesday, but I work so that was no good to us.

I phoned Brighton and asked if they had sent a letter to the psychiatrist and they confirmed that they had on 3 February.

The nurse at Brighton said I should phone Derek's nurse to ask for help. I phoned and left a message.

Derek told the nurse that only Louise talks to him and that we all chat together and he just sits there like a zombie. That made me feel like shit. How many times do I have to try a conversation with Derek with no response, no output or opinion, before my soul is destroyed?

Today I feel like shit and have no faith in the mental health system.

April 2010

Half term and I decided to take the girls for a day out in Brighton. We were looking forward to walking round the Lanes and having a great day. Just as we were leaving Derek wanted to know why he couldn't come which made me feel bad. I said we were just shopping, but he said it would be better than staying at home. So we missed our train and asked a friend of Donna's if he wanted to come and take Derek around the Sea Life Centre. We caught the later train, but Louise was disappointed that Derek came with us as she wanted some girls' time.

***

At last I managed to get hold of Derek's nurse. She gave us an appointment to see the psychiatrist on Monday 26 April.

***

The weekend of 19 April I was feeling unwell and spent the weekend in bed. On the Monday I received a text from my brother to say he was stuck in Kenya due to flight disruptions and was being put up in a hotel. I tried to phone mum to tell her he was OK but no one answered the phone. I decided to pop in on the way to my psychic course, but the curtains were drawn and no one was opening the door. The next-door neighbour called out and said that the paramedics were outside in the early hours. Mum had collapsed in the night and was in hospital. I went to see her and they let her out that morning. Her insulin level had dropped, which caused her to collapse.

The next day I went into work, but was very tearful. I had to go to the doctors and was told I had another chest infection – more antibiotics!

Mum came to stay with us and I was off sick from work for the week.

***

On Friday the nurse called round. Derek is now on a new medication which I found out about from work, They are patches which you change every day, called Rivastigmine.

***

The past week has most probably been my lowest of all. I felt very low with no one to turn to. It helped having mum to stay as another adult to talk to. I was sad to see her go home. Even mum was surprised at how Derek was, with conversation very difficult and him not understanding what was being said. She said that her heart goes out to me and the girls and she wishes she knew how to help us.

Out of desperation, I have asked the nurse about respite for Derek, not something I wanted at this early stage, but I don't think I can cope without a break. A manager from a local care home, has offered to call round for coffee with Derek to get him used to her. And then hopefully Derek can visit her.

***

The visit from the psychiatrist went better than I thought. He was surprised at how quickly Derek had deteriorated. When Derek goes to the higher dose of the new drug they will change his antidepressants to anti-anxiety drugs, which might help him. I have also asked for help at a local carers' support group which also gives counselling.

26 April. I went to my psychic course and I broke down afterwards. My teacher had a long talk with me and she said anytime I need a chat just call her and I can go round to hers for a coffee and chat. Without friends I don't think I could cope.

May 2010
7 May. The CPN was due at 2pm. I got home at 2.10pm and Derek said the nurse had been and gone. I was so angry that she hadn't waited ten minutes for me. I phoned and left a message to say I needed to talk over some things with her. When she phoned back she said, 'Didn't Derek say I was calling back later?' If the nurse doesn't understand Alzheimer's, there is no hope!

***

Louise was doing a performance at the youth theatre and parents were allowed to watch. But she didn't want Derek to come. This made things a little difficult as we had to be careful not to talk about it in case he was hurt at not being included.

***

Had a meeting with carers' support at the Westgate Centre which was very helpful. I was told about carer's support money for Donna's driving lessons and that I could carry a special card that would inform anyone if I was in an accident that I was a carer; also to have my name flagged up on the computer at the doctors to inform them that I am a carer.

When I told the nurse about these things, she didn't know anything about them.

June 2010
Had social services out to see if we can get any help with Derek's respite. She filled out the forms but not once did she ask what Derek's illness was.

Went to look around a respite home in Havant. It was two houses joined, the people were friendly, but I would like it to have been more spacious, more open. Anyway, the following day Derek went there for five-and-a-half hours. When I left him there I cried my eyes out. It was like taking the children to school on their first day.

When I picked him up they told me that he was more alert than the others there and he ate a good dinner and pudding. I must admit it smelt a bit like wee in there. Anyway, Derek said he wasn't going back, but when Louise asked him how his day was he said 'OK'.

***

Louise wanted to know why I didn't pick a day for Derek to go to respite when she wasn't at school so she could be at home without him being there. I think that it is so sad she feels that way. I guess I underestimated what a big effect this is having on her.

***

Derek has now been given mood boosters to see if they will improve his mood. Not sure if they are working, but he doesn't seem to cry much now.

25 June. I went to a carers' meeting at a garden centre in Birdham. First of all I got lost. When I found the place I walked into the café and didn't recognise anyone so waited outside for my friend Susan to turn up. Anyway, there were six of us, but the problem was Susan and I were the youngest. One lady was about 80 and the other two were caring for their son and daughter. One had bipolar, the other had been in a car accident and had brain damage. But at the end of the day, they still had their husbands to share this with. Call me hard-hearted but I feel that this is not the same as what I am going through. I don't think I will be going to any more of those meets.

***

Derek seems to be in more pain with his arthritis so I will have to get an appointment with the GP to see what's going on.

***

It's Donna's boyfriend's birthday. We had bought him a present and a card, but Derek had also bought him a card and signed it from just him. I don't think I will ever get my head around how this disease works. It's almost as though Derek thinks he is living on his own.

***

My dad is now home after a three-month stay at the psychiatric hospital. The rest of his recovery will be at home. Unfortunately, mum is not coping too well with dad's illness. We went to see them yesterday and mum was upset because she was looking forward to going out and at the last moment dad didn't want to go. Mum feels trapped and although she wouldn't say it, I know she is desperate for my dad to get better because she doesn't know how much longer she has left.

July 2010

2 July. A young carer was due to come and see Louise, but unfortunately this was cancelled by the carer and rescheduled.

22 July. Derek started at the day centre. I had to take desperate measures. Derek staying at home all day every day with very little or no contact with the outside world wasn't great. But there is no place who cares for under 65s. I decided to book Derek into my place of work at £30 a day.

The young carer came to see Louise and offered her some help and maybe some singing lessons.

***

As much as I ask Derek what he has been doing while I have been at work, his answer is always 'Pottering in the garden'. Well, one evening during the week I took a look around the garden and nothing had changed. I realised that after all the times I had asked him to cut down plants which had become too overgrown and to deal with the plum tree that has some kind of blight, nothing had been done. I found the pruners and started cutting while Derek was watching TV. Louise came to help me but it wasn't long before Derek came outside. He wasn't happy. He moaned that he would have done the jobs in his own time. But the thing is, I had a job to reach the plants now, so if left any longer I would have had to pay someone to cut them down. Derek tried to put the tools away when we still needed them and stood over us all the time we were in the garden.

I always thought that when the summer came, Derek would be pleased to be out enjoying his garden, but it has come as a shock to realise that sadly he is unable to look after the garden as he used to.

27 July. Derek's rabbit had to be put to sleep. He had problems with his back legs. I phoned the vet and made an appointment for 9.30am. I explained to the receptionist that my husband had Alzheimer's and may be upset, so she advised that I came with him so we changed the appointment to 3.30pm as I was working. But I felt annoyed with myself for not having the compassion to think that Derek would need me to go with him.

Derek was borderline obsessed about his rabbit and I was worried about how this would affect him, but so far all is OK. I wanted to have his rabbit's new run, as the run I have for my rabbit is falling apart. But no, he wants to sell his run so I guess I will have to buy it off him with his money!

30 July. Today was a very stressful day as I had social services around again. Apparently the lady who came round in June was just a helper and only partly filled out the form on my behalf. It now needed to be filled in by a social worker. She was a lovely girl who had compassion and seemed to understand the situation.

I was telling her how we were going to London for a couple of days as Derek has never been to Madame Tussauds. But Derek then turned round and said he had been before and it was just dummies and he really wanted to go on the London Eye. He sounded like a child and I felt annoyed that he was so ungrateful for me sorting out this trip.

I also had the British Red Cross round to do a carer's assessment. I found it more like a counselling meet. The lady was very helpful, but unfortunately time ran out as I had to take Donna to the doctors so the form was only half filled out.

***

I have been left an inheritance which has been a lovely gift. But it comes with a kind of grief as my brother and sister also have the same and they are lucky that they have their partners to decide together what to do with it. I will put mine into savings and one day it will help me achieve my dreams.

August 2010

A year has passed already since the diagnosis. Derek, Louise and I travelled to London on the train for a short break. When we first got there I wondered why we had come. The transition between home and city life was very daunting. I realised that Derek and Louise were relying on me to find our way around and take charge of everything, although I relied on Louise as well. We went to the Natural History Museum first. I hailed a taxi – a first for me. The museum was crowded and lots of walking was required. Derek said he enjoyed it, but there were times when I saw him just staring at the floor! The second day we went to Madame Tussauds, the London Eye and the aquarium. In the aquarium Derek wandered off and we panicked. He had gone to the next floor looking for us when we were still in the loo. That was a scary moment and a reminder that he should carry ID with him.

Derek was a little hard work as he couldn't hear us most of the time and we had to be ever watchful in case he got lost.

We went on the London Eye because Derek wanted to go on it. For me it was my worst nightmare, but I couldn't not take him on it because I don't see him ever doing a London tour again. So in a way I am glad that we went on it for him.

I will see if I can get Derek a hearing test as he seems to hear less of what we say. Maybe it was the hustle and bustle of London, but Derek did seem more confused when we were away.

***

After London, the four of us went on a two-night break to Warminster. We did a lot of sightseeing in the three days we were away. The pressure was not so intense as Donna was with us and I didn't feel the need to constantly look out for Derek, although Donna said when we got home that Derek was constantly looking for me and asking where I was.

While we were away Derek had a couple of strange turns. I asked what was wrong but he wouldn't answer me. When we got through to him he couldn't explain what was wrong. I decided that when we got home I would take him to the doctors for a check-up.

***

We got home on the Saturday and on Sunday morning Derek said he only had two of his antidepressants left. The prescription was 19th July for 28 days. I realised that Derek had been overdosing, taking 90mg a day instead of 45mg. I phoned NHS Direct who said I was to take Derek to the doctors in the morning and ask for blood tests and a blood pressure test. We also talked about his painkillers and the nurse suggested Derek have patches for his pain.

Monday morning I phoned the doctors and by 9.15 we were seen by a doctor. We had not seen this doctor before, but she was brilliant. She phoned the toxicology department to find out what to do about the overdose. It was decided that no plan of action was needed, but Derek's medication was now to be administered by me. I asked for an appointment to be made for a hearing test for Derek and for him to be referred to the pain clinic again so they can help his pain. Apparently the patches contain morphine and could make Derek more confused. I have also gone out and purchased a pill dispenser.

***

Derek had another strange turn at the centre. I had taken the day off work to go to Brighton with the girls, dropped Derek off at the centre and apparently he had a dizzy spell before dinner.

The following Monday Derek slept all day on the settee, I took him to the doctors and they said he had a urine infection and put him on antibiotics for a week. When the results came back from the hospital it was all clear, which I do not understand.

September 2010
Derek is still complaining of lower stomach pain, but on the 2nd I went to work because we were short staffed. I phoned mid-morning to check on him and he was upset because he was at home on his own and had been sick. I came home and phoned the doctor who came out to the house. Blood samples were taken and a rectal examination was done. I was very worried because the pain in his stomach was still evident and I seem to remember that his dad had cancer of the stomach, although that was unconfirmed because Derek can no longer remember.

After the doctor went I was still not satisfied so I called NHS Direct. Although they were helpful they thought that maybe it was a sickness bug!

During the night, Derek was acting very strangely, getting up and turning on the main light, patting my head and talking nonsense. I was worried so I phoned the out-of-hours doctors. I spoke to a very helpful doctor who had the results of Derek's blood test – all was good. The doctor suggested that maybe Derek was constipated or it was the result of the combination of drugs he was taking.

In the morning I phoned both Derek's nurse and doctor to see what they thought. His psychiatrist was on holiday, but the nurse was waiting to speak to his replacement. The doctor said maybe taking Derek off some of the drugs would be a good idea, but it would have to be the psychiatric hospital's call.

I feel so lonely as I don't know who to call. I can feel myself getting low, and selfishly I was disappointed as I had planned to go out for the day with Donna, and I have now had to stay in to keep an eye on Derek. I was so looking forward to going out.

I just want this hurt to go away, the feeling of being trapped, it seems that when I look forward to something, something else comes along to ruin it.

***

I have had a very stressful week. Derek so far has seen seven doctors and had one chest X-ray. Still I am no further forward in a diagnosis. It could be a gut problem, kidney stones, an ulcer or bladder stones, take your pick. A urine test shows white blood cells, pus and blood. We saw Derek's doctor yesterday and he's agreed it probably wouldn't be a good idea for Derek to go into hospital as he would be too confused and this could make matters worse.

10 September. Today Derek had his worse four upset tummies, with yellow poo. I am waiting for the doctor to call back. Derek has been in bed all day again, tomorrow I was supposed to be going to London to see *Phantom of the Opera*, but it's not looking good. Donna has taken the day off work so she can be with Derek, but my gut feeling is to stay home as it's my responsibility to look after him.

***

Yesterday I popped to the local shop and met Derek's brother and sister-in-law. They barely said 'Hello' and didn't even ask how Derek was. I really had to stop myself from having a go at them.

***

I am thinking of taking Derek to A&E as I do not want another weekend like last weekend. I feel angry that it has come to this.

Our GP phoned to say they were not letting this situation go on beyond Monday and there was no point taking Derek to A&E because nothing would be done over the weekend.

I cancelled my trip to London to see *Phantom of the Opera*. I was looking forward to that!

13 September. We had an appointment to see the GP for some signing of legal papers. I asked her what was happening to Derek. She suggested Derek have a scan as well.

16 September. A letter came from the hospital asking me to phone to make an appointment for a scan. The earliest appointment was Friday 17 September, or have to wait another week. Unfortunately this means I miss my psychic class again, which makes me very sad. I phoned the hospital to ask if the appointment for the endoscopy would be soon, but they had received no record of a referral. I was mad. I phoned the doctors who said a referral was made on the 9th. I complained to the doctors, they said they would fax the details to the hospital. I then phoned the hospital back and they informed me that there was a six-week waiting list and that was an emergency waiting time.

I phoned Derek's nurse, but she was out. Then I phoned the social worker who was calm about the situation. The social worker wanted to contact the Red Cross carers for me to chat to as I was so upset. I said no, because at the end of the day if the NHS was any good the system would not upset me and many more like me. It's OK for them to say, 'Oh Angela you must look after yourself, carry on doing your things that help you to relax.' THEY ARE JUST NOT LISTENING. I CANNOT DO WHAT I WANT TO DO BECAUSE I HAVE TO RUN ROUND SORTING EVERYBODY ELSE OUT.

***

I am also worried about Donna, who was upset at work. They are setting up a one-to-one meeting for her to talk about why she has time off work. She just won't talk to me or open up, and it's doing my head in.

***

Another GP phoned me on the 16th and suggested we put Derek in for another type of investigation. I can't remember the name of it but she is hopeful that the scan will give us the information we need. She is phoning me back on Monday afternoon.

***

I am on holiday from work, and have arranged to meet up with Susan. I haven't seen her over the summer, so time to catch up.

Monday, our GP phoned as promised. She has made an appointment for Derek to see her on Thursday, just to check him over again.

***

Monday, Derek woke up with an upset tummy and being sick. I phoned the doctor again and spoke to the GP. She said that for some reason a stool sample had been overlooked and that she would also chase up the endoscopy appointment.

I had to cancel meeting up with Susan, which I was upset about. Yet again my plans are changed.

I also took Derek's Alzheimer patch off as a last desperate measure to stop the upset tummy. I contacted the nurse to tell her that I had done this. Meanwhile she was going to check that it was OK to do so.

***

Wednesday, the stool sample was taken to the doctors. I spent the day researching the drug Rivastigmine. First I contacted the Alzheimer's Society who advised me to contact NICE.(National Institute for Health and Care Excellence) They in turn told me to contact MHRA (Medicine and Health Care Products Regulatory Agency). Although they were unable to speak to me about an individual case, the gentleman I spoke to told me step by step how to obtain the required information to download. For that I thank him for his time and effort. The 30-page document shows side effects of the drug Rivastigmine, Now I won't even pretend to understand a drug analysis report, I am a little confused on the dates, e.g. report run date 10 Aug 2010 data lock date 9 Aug 2010, self-explanatory, but period covered 1 July 1963 to 9 Aug 2010, earliest reaction date 1 June 1998?

Total number of reactions 998, adverse drug reaction 445, deaths 18.

Reactions include diarrhoea 15, abdominal pain and vomiting 36, gastrointestinal disorders 147, 2 fatal. Others mentioned are agitation 32, confused state 48, peripheral coldness 1, cough 1, all of which I can associate with Derek.

I then phoned the local pharmacy to ask if it was possible to have a reaction to a drug a few months after taking it and she confirmed that it was possible.

22 September. Our wedding anniversary. I didn't tell Derek, as I didn't feel the need to acknowledge it, but Derek realised when a card came through the post addressed to us both. Derek was very tearful that he had forgotten, and I was angry and said we had nothing to celebrate. Yet again Derek's illness has brought out the worst in me. I hate how this illness has made me into a selfish person with so much hate. If Derek had acted the way I have I would be so hurt. I feel under a lot of stress and at times I just want to run away.

On Thursday the nurse phoned to say the psychiatrist said it was OK to stop the patch, but I had already done that anyway.

Derek asked me what tablets he was taking for his head. I tried to explain that he is no longer taking anything because it was making him ill. He was sad because he said that he will get worse quicker, but I tried to explain that there was no guarantee that the drug would slow down the process and at the end of the day was it worth it when it was making him ill? I was surprised that he understood about the drug.

I went to the doctors and logged in to find that Derek had been booked in with another doctor. I complained and eventually we got to see our GP She phoned the hospital to see if the stool sample results were available, but they were not so I will phone tomorrow. Scan results were all OK.

A hospital appointment came through for 29 October to see a gastroenterologist for a consultation.

Stool samples came back OK.

October 2010

Went to Center Parcs for a break. We had a great time and it was not as stressful as other weekends away, such as London. I think it did us all good.

When we got back a letter was waiting from the hospital cancelling the October appointment. Another appointment was made for 12 November with a Dr in gastroenterology. Later that week we get another letter for Derek to attend hospital on 27 October to have an endoscopy. At a guess, I would say the NHS do not know what they are doing!

***

The social worker came round to check if Derek was OK and to say we are a step nearer to having a carer.

***

I went to a Joseph Carey Psychic Foundation show on 9 October and had a reading done. It was mentioned that maybe Derek's problem started after the death of his father. I guess that I also wondered if that may be the case or maybe it was to do with me. Maybe the responsibility of having a young family when he was in his forties was too much to deal with, or maybe I am not the loving wife he thought I was and he wanted more? Having said that, I know deep down how much Derek loves me and would do anything for me. I guess sometimes I should stop and remember this. He used to say I was the best thing that ever happened to him.

I now feel very sad and the tears are falling while trying to write.

Going back to my reading, the reader suggested that Derek try fish oils and new era biochemic tissue salt – all natural. Hopefully this may help.

The only tablets Derek are taking are Mirtazapine 45mg.

Derek is still having upset tummies so as a last resort we have changed the Mirtazapine to a morning application to see if that will make a difference.

15 October. The nurse came to check on Derek. She had finally managed to contact Brighton hospital to find out about his long-lost appointment. Brighton told her that we were given an appointment in May and we hadn't turned up, so they have taken us off the list and if we want to go back we would have to be re-referred by the psychiatrist. Well what can I say? If we had received the appointment we would have turned up of course, so I told the nurse that we won't bother with Brighton anymore as there is no way Derek will be on one of their trial drugs. End of.

I often ask myself why do I come up against brick walls at every turn? I can't believe how much we have to fight to get things moving in the right direction!

27 October. Derek has a hospital appointment for an endoscopy. We arrive at the hospital for the 3pm appointment. The waiting area is full. After about an hour of waiting we were called in to see a nurse. She filled out the required forms and said there was a waiting time of an hour. I said we had already waited an hour and she said there was another hour to wait as they had an emergency that day so appointments were running late. At 5pm we were called in. I had to go in with Derek for obvious reasons. This was not a pleasant experience. The camera was thicker than I expected. There is no way I could have swallowed something that big. I was OK until Derek started to retch, then the tears started falling. The nurse asked if I was OK. I felt silly for being so emotional. I guess that's why you usually go for an endoscopy on your own.

We go back to the hospital on 12 November for results.

31 October. We had a small party to celebrate Halloween. It was great having local kids ringing the doorbell for trick or treat. I don't think Derek liked the noise or fuss we made, but I still want to keep things as normal as possible for the girls, and I love Halloween.

November 2010
2 November. We had a visit from Crossroads, a carer service. She asked a lot of questions and Derek was getting very annoyed. He was clenching his fist and his face was like thunder. The lady asked if Derek was capable of washing and dressing himself. With that

Derek was so angry he turned round and said, 'I am not a baby!' I was so embarrassed I laughed and Derek turned to me and said I was just a joke to him. I guess that he will never understand or know how much I hate having to have a stranger in our house looking after him, or how I feel about an intrusion into our lives, because of his illness.

Deep down I know I have to set up carers for Derek as there will come a time when I will need their service.

With Crossroads there is a 48-hour emergency service, so if for any reason I was unable to get home or had an accident, a carer would step in. They will also take Derek shopping or give help with gardening, or go for walks, which will be good for Derek.

The only difficult thing to sort out was if for some reason I was taken ill or in an accident, I had to give names of people who the carer could contact, to look after Derek. I didn't want to put my mum and dad down as they have enough to deal with now, and I didn't want the girls to be left in a situation. Derek's family are non-existent in my eyes, so we had to say social services. I hope to god it never comes to this and I live to regret my decisions, but I really feel my hands are tied.

On this same day I was told that the centre I work at is closing down and I will be made redundant at the end of the month. Just when you think things can't get any worse. I have not told Derek, and I didn't want his family to know. For some strange reason I felt that it would make me look like a failure!

The next day my friend Anna came round to cut Donna's hair. We have been friends since the age of 16. I wanted to tell her about my job, but Derek was hovering around us all the time. I kept giving him jobs to keep him out the kitchen – empty the rabbit litter tray, take the rubbish out, etc. I was feeling very stressed, and claustrophobic, so I started to tell Anna about the carer that Derek was going to have. He got annoyed and went into the sitting room and started kicking the furniture. This was a new thing. I wasn't proud of myself for winding him up, and sometimes I think if he got better would he still love me or even like me anymore for I am not the person he married anymore? I don't even like myself.

***

Christmas is approaching and I wanted to give the girls something special, so I booked a two-day trip to London, to see *Wicked* in April. I feel like shit not taking Derek, but I know the girls need some time away from him. It will do us all good. I am very excited.

12 November. We went to hospital to see a gastroentorologist. We had a fair wait, but not as long as last time. When we were called in the doctor's phone rang and he took the call, which I thought was very rude. I wonder what he would have said if my mobile rang and I answered it?

I asked if the endoscopy showed up anything and the doctor looked at me and I thought he said, 'Have you daughters?' Then it registered that he said, 'Are you Derek's daughter?' 'No!' I replied, 'his wife!' For the second time I had been mistaken for Derek's daughter. This makes me angry, as why is it now that the medical profession think I am Derek's daughter?

Anyway the results were good, no problem with the stomach. The next thing offered was a camera up his back passage, but I said to the doctor that things had settled down more now and I truly feel that the problems were caused by the cocktail of drugs he was taking. The doctor agreed and we have left it that if things take a turn for the worse then we are to go back to our doctor and they will contact the hospital for further investigation.

14 November. I was out for the day. While I was gone, Derek received a phone call from his sister to say that his uncle had died. This made me angry that his sister had not thought through the consequences of her actions. Why tell Derek something like that when he was at home on his own?

17 November. As if that wasn't bad enough, at 2am, I heard the phone ringing. At first I thought I was dreaming, then it stopped, then rang again. I shot out of bed thinking it was my parents calling. When I reached the bottom of the stairs it stopped then started ringing again. On answering, a lady asked if I was Mrs Hogarth. I said, 'Yes.' She said that my alarm was ringing. Confused I asked what she meant. She said the button I wear around my neck. 'Oh!' I said, 'you need my mother-in-law, you have the wrong number.' So I gave her Derek's mum's number, but told her that she no longer answers the phone, so I also gave her his sister's number. I was unsure as to what to do, but I didn't want to phone any of Derek's family. I trusted that the careline would contact the family, so I went back to bed.

18 November. In the morning I told Derek and tried to phone his brother, but the phone was engaged. Derek started to get very agitated and wanted to go and see him. In the end I told Derek to go and see his brother as I couldn't get hold of him by phone. I went and had a shower. By the time I went back downstairs, Derek was back home, he said he kept banging on his brother's door but no one answered. I found his mobile number, dialled and gave the phone to Derek to speak. But understandably Derek got confused as to what to say. My fault I know, I should have spoken to him, but I just couldn't bring myself to do it.

Out of desperation I phoned his sister and told her what had happened. She said she had heard the phone ringing but hadn't bothered to answer it because she thought it was work related. Well I was lost for words, why would someone phone up for work at 2am? And she knows her mum has careline so when the phone rang why didn't she wonder whether her mum was OK?

Anyway, it turned out that Derek's mum was OK. She must have activated the call button in her sleep. The careline tried to contact her through the intercom, but she was confused as to where the voice was coming from. They tried to phone her but to no avail as the phone is left off the hook because she doesn't know how to use it. So in other words she has no contact with the outside world. Is that how a 91-year-old with Alzheimer's is supposed to live? I don't think I will ever understand Derek's family's mentality.

The nurse was due a visit at 2pm later that day. At 1.50pm we get a phone call to cancel it. An emergency came up. I have lost count how many times this has now happened. It makes me feel second best.

***

A couple of things have happened over the last week, which one day we will look back and laugh at. But at the moment it causes more tension. One being that when our delivery of food arrives Derek puts it away which is good, until we can't find a particular item. For example, I ordered pantliners, couldn't find them, checked on the shopping list and yes they were delivered. But I just can't find them, maybe they are in the freezer?!

Secondly, I went to clean my teeth before bed and found Derek's toothbrush head on my toothbrush and my toothbrush head in his toothbrush box. So not sure what was going on there. Did he use my toothbrush, instead of his? When I questioned him he didn't know what I was talking about.

***

I am aware that Derek does not sleep a deep sleep any more and last night his legs seem to be jumpy. I remember the medical profession asking me if he was jumpy at night, but at that time he wasn't, so I don't know what it means. I will have to ask the nurse when she turns up next.

***

Although I try to make everyday living as normal as possible, I think that maybe I try to block out what is happening. Sometimes truth rears its ugly head and I break down. Like today at work a lady who has Alzheimer's and isn't that old was very agitated and angry. She kept saying 'No!' to everything and 'Shut up!' and saying she was stupid. Well, this upset me today and I found it hard to deal with her as she is a reminder to me of what's to come.

It also reminds me that if I show compassion towards Derek I will fall apart. See, even while writing this down I start crying. I hope to god that I will not regret how I behaved towards Derek, but unless you have lived through this you would have no idea what I am talking about.

37

27 November. After not feeling too good all week due to a virus/cold I thought I would have a lie in, but at 8am someone was knocking on the door so I had to get up. It was Donna and the door was double locked so I needed to unlock it. Then the phone rang. It was mum. She had been ill in the night and they had to call a doctor. She asked me to pick up a prescription for her, so I drove to her house, picked up the prescription, took it to the chemist, took the medication back to mum, then went to Tesco to get their weekly shop. I asked dad to come with me, but he didn't want to. Four weeks before Christmas on a Saturday morning is not a good time to do a food shop. I was waiting at the checkout and a little boy in a trolley was giving me a lovely smile which made me feel good at first, then I felt tears well up. It was a reminder of how happy I was when the girls were little. I seem to be very fragile with my emotions at the moment.

Tempers were a little fraught today. I was looking for a needle file which I knew I had, but as usual I couldn't find. I went down in the shed with Derek to look. We couldn't find them, but there is lots of junk down there so I said at some point this shed needs sorting out. Derek got angry because there were boxes in the shed from work, and he said he wanted them out. He got angry because I said they were staying until I knew what to do with them. He was shaking his fist up to my ear. I thought he was going to hit me. In fact, yet again I wanted him to hit me. Why?! Later he wanted a cuddle, but I walked away. I wish I could show my feelings, but I can't get too close. I am afraid I will fall apart.

December 2010

Heavy snow fell so we were confined to home. I decided to go for a walk around the village with the girls and a sledge. We found our own slope with no one around. We had such a laugh, it made us feel normal.

5 December. My birthday. The previous day my sister came round for all of 30 seconds to give me a birthday present from my mum and dad as mum is very unwell. She also handed me a card from herself saying she hadn't gotten round to getting me a present. I was upset and said to her not to bother. I felt hurt that she didn't have time for me.

The girls wanted to do something for my birthday, Donna had booked the day off work, and we decided to go bowling. Donna paid. We then went for a meal at the Beefeater. When it came to paying the bill I went to get my money out and the girls gave me £10 each, but I didn't feel that they should pay, so I paid the bill. When we got home Derek said how he enjoyed the day etc. I don't think he realised it was my birthday treat!

9–10 December. Started my new job. I found the atmosphere very tense and was feeling very stressed, with not being able to be more organised with preparing work due to lack of work space. By the end of the first day I was ready to pack it all in.

The second day was not much better. As I came home from work Derek asked me to top up his phone for him. I asked how he had managed to use up his credit as I didn't think he used his phone. He replied he had phoned Jen, a previous girlfriend. I asked why he felt he needed to contact her. He said she was a friend. I don't know how Derek got hold of her number, because it was not logged on his phone.

The thought of Derek contacting an ex-girlfriend is eating away inside of me. I can feel myself getting more and more angry. I feel I have no one to turn to.

***

Louise and I went to do my mum's food shopping. I also had to call into the florist to order some flowers to be delivered for mum's birthday on Tuesday from dad. I phoned dad from the florist to ask how much he wanted to spend. Dad was asking if I had got the shopping yet as if there was an emergency. No matter I gave up my day off to sort out shopping and a birthday present. He was more worried about the shopping. I know it's part of his illness but I feel like I am drowning in other people's illnesses.

Louise and I delivered the shopping round to mum and dad's, and took mum for a ride so she could deliver some Christmas cards. I told dad that the flowers were being delivered on Tuesday lunchtime. He then said they would be going out for lunch, so I had to cancel the delivery and now I have to pick up the flowers and deliver them. More time taken out of my supposed 'me' time. This sounds so selfish and if I didn't feel so stressed this would not be a big deal. But I could have gone to Susan's on Tuesday, except I just can't fit her in as well as the homeopath at 10 and picking up flowers at 12.

When Louise and I went to mum and dad's, mum was crying and saying she can't deal with dad anymore. I am afraid that she is giving up the fight to deal with her illness. Louise also got upset and I am so sorry that my daughters have to deal with all this pain.

Going to visit mum and dad is like going from one hell to another.

***

That night I went to bed at about 11pm. The main bedroom light was on so I turned my bedside light on, as Derek was fast asleep. I went to turn off the main light, went to say goodnight to Louise and went back into my bedroom. Derek was out of bed fully dressed. He thought it was morning.

The following day Louise and I were thinking of going out and she said to me, 'Not to nanny's though.' Usually she would have wanted to visit mum and dad.

***

Today I confronted Derek about the phone call he had made to his ex-girlfriend. I asked him again how he got her number. He said she must have given it to him. It was written on a piece of paper which Derek gave to me. I shredded it and deleted the number on his dialled list. I told him that if he contacted her again I would leave. Like I would, but I feel very let down. Would Derek have contacted her had he been well? I will never know.

Also today I was sorting out Derek's wardrobe for dirty clothes and turned around with a pile of jumpers in my arms and he was standing right behind me. I screamed so loud. He was downstairs when I went upstairs, I didn't even hear him come up the stairs. This is the third time he has made me jump like that.

***

Our next-door neighbour came round for coffee, and he was saying how upset he was when he saw Derek the other day. They were having a banter about Man United football, and Derek had no response to his banter as though he didn't know what he was on about.

***

The nurse came today. I asked her about Derek twitching in bed and about his hands being shakey. She said it could be the Alzheimer's doing it, and also the creeping up behind me is a sign of insecurity, looking to see where I am all the time.

***

Next year when Derek is 65 we will have a new consultant who is also dad's consultant. Maybe she can advise that Derek have another scan.

19 December. Tomorrow is a busy day. Louise has to be in rehearsals, Donna has her driving theory test, I need to go to a new work venue to see about shelving and Donna has a hospital appointment. I asked Derek to top up the car with oil, as he has done this before so I thought it would be OK. I just glanced out of the kitchen window and saw Derek with the screenwash bottle in his hand. I ran outside saying, 'Please say you haven't topped up the oil with screen wash?' He had. More stress. I phoned up the RAC and they said not to drive the car and that it would need an oil change. I phoned the local garage and left a message on their phone. I'm not sure how I am going to fit in all my running around without a car.

20 December. Mum was taken to hospital in an ambulance. She was too ill to go to her appointment at the hospital, and has landed up staying in there. Her insulin levels were very low and she has some kind of blockage.

Picked up Louise from Youth Theatre. While getting tea I found her sitting on the stairs crying. She wouldn't tell me at first why she was upset, but it turned out that the girls at Youth Theatre were talking about their dads and how they make them laugh, and how much they love them. Louise said it made her sad as she feels that she hates her dad as she is always angry with him. I explained to her that she doesn't feel hate for her dad, only for the illness. I feel so very sad for my girls.

22 December. This was a bad day for me. It started just before 10am when I got a text at work from Louise to say she has to be at rehearsals at 10am and not 2pm as first thought. So I had to leave work and go home to pick her up and take her to Havant.

Derek and I went to visit his mum with Christmas presents, not a nice experience as she kept asking me who I was. We then went to dad's to see if he was OK. He had turned the heating off because he was worried that he would run out of oil, but bless him he had managed to do washing and drying and hoovered around the house. He seems to be coping well without mum there. Friends of dad's were visiting him so we all had a cup of tea and a chat. We were talking about jobs and I was saying that there were more jobs about than people say there are and dad turned round and asked why I hadn't got a better job. Talk about being kicked in the teeth, that really hurt. Maybe I will put it down to his illness!

I also met dad's CPN nurse who came to check on him. She asked me if I was the daughter who did reiki. I said, 'No, the one who has a husband with Alzheimer's.' She said, 'Oh, I want to give you a big hug.' That made me sad.

Between myself and dad's nurse I think we have persuaded dad to come and stay with us from Christmas Eve, which would be good.

From dad's, I took Derek back home, then went to the hospital to take some things up for mum. She wasn't looking so well today, and she hadn't been given anything to eat or drink because they didn't know what was happening, if she was having an operation or not!

Got home at 8pm to find that the washing machine has broken down. Louise had got upset again at the Youth Theatre and she had a meeting with the leader of drama and a few close friends so she could tell them about home and what's going on.

I am not looking forward to Christmas at all. I feel so down I need a break from all this sadness. I booked a second day away in London with the girls, as I felt one night away is not enough. I don't even know who will look after Derek, I just know I need to get away and my girls feel the same.

23 December. Mum came out of hospital, which meant that they could come and stay with us, for Christmas Day and Boxing Day.

***

I must admit I found Christmas Day a bit stressful and a little sad. I had bought Derek a few presents, one being a puzzle book which he got very engrossed in, and a jigsaw, which he didn't find too interesting. But the biggest disappointment was the solid silver SOS talisman I had bought him. He showed no reaction at all. On the other hand, mum and dad gave him a ticket to see a '60's show and Derek was very tearful at such a gift.

41

Christmas night I didn't feel too well, and was sick. Maybe it was due to stress.

28 December. Derek and I went into Chichester. We'd just parked the car and the temperature gauge lit up on the dashboard. There was also steam coming from the bonnet. Derek didn't seem perturbed by this. I knew I had to wait for the engine to cool before I could do anything.

We went and did some shopping, then phoned my brother to ask what type of water I could put in the radiator. He said bottled water would be OK but I must put antifreeze in when I get home. So I bought some bottled water, went back to the car, lifted the bonnet, but didn't know where the radiator was. I looked in the manual, then a young man came and parked next to me and asked if we were OK. I said, 'No, not really, I don't know where the radiator cap is.' We had been told to only touch the caps that were yellow when we purchased the car and none of them were the radiator. Luckily he found the cap and said the radiator was empty, so we topped it up with bottled water and managed to get home OK. I will have to phone the garage tomorrow to get the car fixed, as I need it to run Louise back and forth to rehearsals.

***

Derek seems to be getting worse, he doesn't seem to understand the simplest of instructions, and when he talks it's in a kind of mumbled way.

2011

January 2011

I do not think that Derek was aware it was New Year's Eve. He went to bed early. Louise was unwell so she was in bed and I was sat on the sofa with Donna and her boyfriend. I stayed up until 11.30pm then went to bed. I never was a great fan of New Year's Eve. Whilst lying in bed Derek was making involuntary movements with his legs.

I feel alone and I sometimes can feel panic as I no longer know what the future will bring. I can only feel sadness. It's not fair that Derek is being taken away from me. The girls will grow up and live their lives to the full and have everything to look forward to. Me, I have no one to share my life with. What did I do that was so wrong?

***

My mum is going into hospital on Wednesday for the operation, but I phoned today and she had been up all night being sick again.

5 January. As I was about to go to work I noticed Derek had got his coat out. I asked him where he was going. He said to his sister's. I was surprised. Derek insisted that he had told me, but he hadn't.

My job changed venue, and it took me half an hour to get there and I got lost. It's a much better hall, but still no room for art things. Looks like I will have to get rid of all the boxes stored at home.

Left work early to take mum to hospital. She looks so ill and she was upset and said she just wanted to get back to normal. I stayed with her until she went in. They said it would be a couple of hours.

Came home and Derek was still out.

Two or so hours later the hospital phoned to say mum would be staying in overnight and tomorrow as they were putting her on antibiotics. They said everything was OK.

Louise and I had our tea. Derek was still not home. I took Louise to Havant for the show, and just as I got home my phone rang. It was the hospital saying that mum was going to be put on a different ward as there was no bed available. I asked if everything was OK and whether the stent was put in. They said no, a stent was taken out, but they did not replace it. The doctors would speak to mum in the morning to discuss other options.

By 6.10pm I was worried about where Derek had got to, so I phoned his sister to ask if

43

he was still there. When she answered, she said they were just bringing him back home. I said that his tea was waiting, and didn't realise that he would be gone for so long. She said she had told Derek that she would give him his meals. I replied, 'Yes, you told Derek, but Derek cannot remember to tell me. In fact I didn't even know he was coming to you until this morning.' She said that Donna knew, as she was home when they picked Derek up. 'Yes,' I replied. 'I knew only this morning but didn't think Derek was going to be at yours all day.' She was talking to me in her high almighty voice so I told her to stop talking in her sarcastic voice, and put the phone down.

I was so upset, I asked Donna if I had done the right thing. She had no comment, which upset me more. I just had to get out of the house. I drove around for a while, then went to see dad. I was scared to come home! I truly hate the way Derek's family make me feel.

When I got home I told Derek how I felt. He started going off on one about how my brother used his chop saw and hadn't brought it back. I explained that he was using it to do his kitchen over Christmas and hadn't had time as he was running around for mum, dad and auntie and anyway he had said he could use it.

***

I have decided to write Derek's sister a letter. It's the only way to get rid of the anger I feel for Derek's family. Went to work but was too upset so they sent me home.

A letter to Derek's sister

I thank you for having Derek for the day yesterday, but I feel I should explain my reaction on the phone. I am most certain that you are unaware of the deterioration of Derek's health, mainly because you have had little contact with him. He has the terminal illness Alzheimer's, which is different to your mum's illness. I know you said that you had read books on Alzheimer's but have you read about Alzheimer's in the under 65s? There is a difference.

This illness gives Derek short-term memory loss, along with many other traits. He also has clinical depression, so two major illnesses which we as a family are trying to cope with. Myself and the girls are also having to cope with my mum who has secondary cancer and in hospital, and my dad who has had a breakdown. With all of this stress I am sure you will agree it can be too much at times to cope with. I also have to keep working so Derek is left at home quite a lot which doesn't help his condition.

I am not asking for sympathy or any help from Derek's family, as you have all made it obviously clear how you feel about me and the girls. I do ask that if you feel you would like to invite Derek over for the day – which would give him and us a break, and help us as a family – that you would please give some consideration as to telling me what is happening, as at the end of the day not only am I Derek's wife but his carer too.

Derek cannot relay a message. Neither of us know how long we have left with Derek, but in some ways we have already lost him, and with no medication suitable we have to take each day as it comes. If you would like to help by inviting Derek over for the day, that would be great, but please go through me and don't rely on Derek passing on a message.

Thank you.
Angela

MUM

Not sure how to start this, as after a lack of sleep and a few days of going back and forth to hospital, my mind is mixed up, but I will write as best I remember it.

Dad and I were visiting mum on the ward, and while we were there they were taking swabs for MRSA. They found traces of the bug in her nose, so they moved her to a side ward, which in a way was a blessing.

That night we all stayed at the hospital, my sister and her husband, my brother and his wife and myself. We watched as mum was on many drips of saline and antibiotics. One of the main worries was that her blood pressure was low.

The last few days have been a blur and I guess with a lack of sleep it's difficult to remember what happens next. The conflicting messages we as a family got from doctors made it hard for us to understand what was truly going on.

On the night we all stayed with mum, one of the doctors came into the room and told us that mum would not make it through the night. Mum told him she wasn't going anywhere.

The next morning mum saw the same doctor and said, 'See, I am still here!'

The biggest threat is the jaundice, low blood pressure and, although the max amount of fluid has been put into mum, she is still dehydrated.

An operation was scheduled for today, Wednesday, at midday, but that is no longer an option. It is a case of making her comfortable until she passes.

Dad seems to be coping OK. We keep a watchful eye on him. I know feelings are running high and everyone is on overdrive but I phoned my sister to say I had a phone number for one of the nurses who said we could call her any time, and also to say should we phone mum's hospice nurse. My sister told me that my brother had not long left mum and he had got a smile out of her and she was breathing a lot better and seemed brighter. I said to my sister that sometimes people make an improvement just before they pass and she asked in a most hurtful way when did I become an expert. I hung up on her. I have a habit of doing that just recently. I could say that maybe she didn't mean it, but I truly feel resentment from her and I don't know why.

On one of the evenings, I went to bed tossing and turning and couldn't sleep, so I got dressed and went to the hospital and stayed all night. At about 6.45am I came away from the hospital feeling very giddy and light headed. I don't know how I managed to drive home, but I really frightened myself. I was exhausted. I went straight to bed and stayed there all day.

15 January. Mum is still with us. When I went to visit she was talking and drinking and she ate a whole jelly pot. Thoughts went through my mind, maybe they have made a mistake, maybe she will recover.

Mum asked how the girls were and said she had dreamt that she had died. She said it was the future. I said we all die in the end. She asked if the doctors had told me that she was dying and I said no. But I am not a good liar so I am not sure how convincing I was. She held my hand and said she loved me and I promised to look after dad.

***

I may have to change Derek's carer as when she came on Tuesday Derek said he didn't want to walk to Emsworth again and go to the same coffee shop. But I gave him some bread to feed the ducks at the local pond and off they went for a walk, eventually as she insisted talking to me for half an hour. On their return they had walked to Emsworth, gone to the same coffee shop, looked around the charity shop, bought a bin bag full of puzzles and games for her grandchildren and Derek got to carry them home all the way from Emsworth. To me that seems unacceptable.

I received an invoice today for Derek's care. There was a separate invoice for £12.80 for a trip to Bognor and Emsworth which I wasn't asked permission about. I phoned up to question the invoice and to say about Derek's carer shopping during the time looking after him. They were very apologetic about it and asked what I wanted to do. We are now going to have a male carer, who we will meet on Thursday.

18 January. I am worried about my pent-up anger and how it has made me feel. Today I lost my temper in KFC of all places. I am not proud of the fact. I threw the KFC at the assistant because after going through the drive-in we found we were short by two portions of chips. I went in to complain and they asked me to wait my turn, so I threw the bag on the counter and said, 'What's the point of a drive-through when I then have to park up and get the order sorted?'

Then when I got home Derek said he was going to his sister's tomorrow, so that annoyed me because I thought she was winding me up by asking Derek without asking me. As it turns out, Derek had phoned her, but I had already got angry and Derek had phoned his sister to say I didn't want him to go. She then phoned me to say Derek said I said he couldn't go to hers, all a little confusing and a lot of upset over a small matter.

19 January. Today I took the car to the garage to have a full oil change and new filter, as a result of Derek putting screen wash in with the oil before Christmas. The plan then was to pick up dad, take him to the dentist and then to the hospital to see mum.

I texted my brother to ask how mum was today, but he did not text back. So I phoned him. His words were, 'I think she has gone.'

My mum died on the 19 January. It's now 6pm and I am waiting for Derek to come home to tell him the news. Not sure what his reaction is going to be.

I told Derek about mum. He cried at first, then he went to comfort me but I didn't want comfort from him. I wanted to stay detached. I guess that's because I have had to sort things on my own; I have become independent which in some ways is a bit scary because it feels like I have lost my emotions.

I am not sure if it has sunk in about my mum's death. Derek goes about his normal day as if nothing has changed.

I so want to talk about mum but it's not my girls' place to compensate for Derek. I guess I will just deal with it the best I can.

***

My brother and sister have done most of the funeral arrangements. I am not sure if mum had said anything to them about not asking too much of me, but I am grateful as my head is not in a good place at the moment.

Derek said we should invite his brother and sister to the funeral. I had to be blunt and say they were not welcome. I hope they don't turn up, I have been a bit deceitful in not writing in my diary the date of the funeral so Derek cannot tell his family.

I purchased two copies of our local paper, one for dad to see the write-up about mum. I was so upset when I saw my name had been left out of the write up. They had forgotten me. My name is Angela and she was my mum too. The error was with the funeral directors, yet another kick in the teeth for me. WHY ME?

27 January. Today we met Derek's new carer. I am not good at making guesses on people's ages, but he is younger than I expected. He is from Poland and seems very nice. I feel happier with him.

28 January. Today we meet Derek's new nurse. She seems OK. We had a long chat. She wanted to know about Derek's case by talking to me rather than reading about him. I got very emotional and she asked me if I had seen a doctor. I asked why. So they can put me on antidepressants. Is that all the medical profession know?

Ironically, dad's new nurse is going to be Derek's old nurse. Talk about small circles!

February 2011
6 February. Dad received a sympathy card from Derek's brother. Not sure what they thought they would achieve by doing this, but enough said on that matter.

7 February. Today is my mum's funeral. It's 5.44am and at the moment I am feeling calm. I hope I can hold it together. It seems like mum's been gone for ages, but in other ways she is still with us.

***

The funeral went well. Lots of people attended. As a whole I think I did well. It's now one week on that I am finding it difficult to cope. I want to scream, shout and run away all at once. Friday would have been mum and dad's 50th wedding anniversary. We all got together and had a Chinese takeaway.

I just can't get my head around the fact that mum has gone and I feel so alone. I am starting to question the meaning of life and what I have to look forward to. If I didn't have the girls I do not think that I could cope any more.

25 February. Somewhere between mum's funeral and today we have had visits from a social worker and today the nurse. With due respect, the new nurse does ask questions in more detail to find out how things are, but at the end of the day they all talk. In all honesty, what else can they do? They have no magic wand to make life better again and at the end of the day they go home to their cosy lives.

The nurse thinks I am depressed; maybe she is on commission to put me on pills. She says she can feel the tension in the house – she should try living with it. Derek told the nurse that I am always shouting at him. Maybe I am, I am no longer aware of it.

***

My feelings are all over the place and part of me questions whether I still love Derek. Maybe his brother was right and my lack of love for him has made him ill? I hate what this illness has done to us as a family, how it has questioned me as a person, am I really the hard-faced cow who has no compassion or sympathy for those who are sick? I just don't know. I would never have spoken to Derek in the tone that I do now. When I read about how those people deal with this illness and how they show love and compassion I wonder why I can't be like that. I am scared that one day I will regret the way I am towards Derek, but I don't know how to change

March 2011
14 March. Not such a good weekend. Dad came to stay but he doesn't seem to be getting any better. He talks about the same old thing – how he has no money, can't afford this and that, which is not the case. I also feel sorry for him because he is so lonely.

I would like to do more to help him but to be quite honest it's as much as I can do dealing with Derek.

The only thing that keeps me going is that hopefully one day I can live my life without having to deal with this mental torment. I find it very hard, having no close contact with adult family members who are not having mental health problems.

I am trying to busy myself booking up trips to the theatre and short breaks away. This is all I can do to keep myself sane and give me some purpose to life. I don't even know who's keeping an eye on Derek, I just know I need to get away.

Today Derek's birthday present arrived. Myself and the girls bought Derek a water feature for his 65th birthday. He seemed quite pleased with it, although still not as emotional as when mum and dad gave him theatre tickets for Christmas.

15 March. Today we purchased a new electric kettle, as I woke up this morning to the smell of gas. Derek had not turned the gas off after he had made himself a cup of tea.

We went to the garden centre to buy some flowers for the garden, but it was hard work getting Derek to understand what to do. His memory and understanding has deteriorated.

16 March. Derek's birthday. He is 65 today, the supposedly magic number if you have Alzheimer's.

Derek did not show any emotion to the fact it was his birthday. I decided that it would be better to order a takeaway instead of going out. When it was delivered I said 'Happy birthday!' No response. While Derek was washing up I set up the birthday cake, lit up the candles and called Derek in. We sang happy birthday. He looked at the cake then went back to the washing up, then turned on the TV without blowing out the candles.

Just to point out Derek always washes up. It's almost an obsession. He has been known to take our plates before we have finished, it's as though it's a race.

17 March. Today I broke down at work. I would have been OK if it wasn't for Marilyn asking how things were at home.

Derek is in a real mood today. I was embarrassed for the carer as Derek would hardly speak. He was moody and very down. I don't know what is wrong with him. Maybe it's me. I think maybe he hates me, he looks so angry.

I have asked Louise to ask him what's wrong, hoping that he might speak to her. Derek told her he was feeling down.

I found out about a care centre who looks after people with Alzheimer's. They look after about five people maximum, take them out for the day and give them a cooked meal. I am going to visit the lady this evening.

This looks hopeful. I was very impressed with the lady who runs the Alzheimer's day care home in Waterlooville. She is an ex-nurse who has set up this business looking after people with Alzheimer's, taking them out for the day, giving them a cooked meal and activities in the afternoon. Because she only has a maximum of five people it's not got that overwhelming feel of a club. I am going to set up this arrangement with social services as I think it will do Derek good.

***

Had a couple of very bad days, couldn't stop crying and felt there was no way out. I think maybe it was losing my mum and also Derek's situation. I woke up one morning and heard Derek talking about a fat cow. I assumed he was talking about me. That really hurt me more than I can say.

On Tuesday I am going to see a life coach. Hopefully she can help me. I don't want to go to the doctors as they will only put me on antidepressants.

The life coach experience was a little upsetting as I knew it would be, but she did pick up about the wall I had built up around me. However, I am still not ready to bring that down yet, if ever. I need it to protect me.

27 March. Derek and I went to the Kings Theatre to see the *Solid '60s Silver Show*. Mum and dad had bought Derek tickets for Christmas. At the start of the show Derek was emotional and thanked me for bringing him. I reminded him that mum and dad had given him the tickets for Christmas, and he said that he didn't know. Conversation in the interval was hard work. I was asking Derek questions about some of the artists but he said that he didn't know. Now that was hard, because Derek used to know everything about the sixties.

28 March. Derek's first day with Ann the care worker in Waterlooville. The morning started off with Derek putting on his work clothes saying he was going to cut the grass. I explained that he was going to Ann's today and he needed to put on better clothes. He was not happy but he did go and get changed. When we arrived, Ann made Derek a cup of tea and had bought him a paper to read, which I thought was a nice touch. Ann said they had a good day planned. They went to a museum in Southsea then had coffee, came home for lunch, then she had bought seeds for Derek to plant.

When I picked up Derek from Ann's, Derek was very chatty telling me about a painting she had on the wall, but when Derek got in the car it was like he was a different person. I asked him about the day and what he had for lunch, but he said he could not remember. It is as though when he is with me he shuts down.

While Derek was with the carer I decided to take the old conservatory chairs to the tip. One problem, I couldn't get all the chairs into the boot of the car, so I decided to saw them in half. That was a game and a half. A next-door neighbour came along and offered to help. Then a taxi driver who was waiting for his fare got out of his car and helped. Between us we managed to saw the chair in half, and we had a right laugh doing it. It's nice to know that there are people out there willing to help.

When Derek got home he asked what had happened to the chairs. I said we took them to the tip, but had to saw them up. He immediately went down to the shed to check his saws.

Today I also went to see dad, and to sort out some more of mum's things. Dad looked a little tearful. I feel so sad when I go around to their house. I wish there was more I could do for dad. It's almost as though he has given up. I wish I could spend more time with him and keep my promise to mum to look after him, but I am scared that I will not cope with looking after two sick people.

30 March. Derek said that his sister was taking him out on Friday. I asked Derek what time he would be home as I needed to know if he was having his tea out or not because I was going out that evening. Derek was confused, so with great trepidation I phoned his sister to find out. She said that they were not going now because Derek said he had an eye test. 'That's next week,' I said. So she replied, 'Oh well, I will have to wait for my husband to come back home in case he has made other arrangements.' Anyway, later that evening she phoned back to say they would go Friday. I asked what time and she said they hadn't decided yet, but about 8.30. She still can't grasp the concept of having to make arrangements through me. I told her Derek gets very confused and she agreed that on the phone he was, but she told him to calm down and then he was better. She really is a pathetic person with no idea of what she is on about; she clearly chose to ignore the letter I wrote to her, what more can I do?

31 March. This morning when the alarm went off Derek got up and dressed very quickly. I asked him what was wrong and he said he was going out with his sister today. 'No,' I said, 'that's tomorrow!'

April 2011
1 April. Derek went out for the day with his sister. The day out didn't seem to lift his mood much. I expected him to come home full of info on the day's activities. He even got confused about the meal he had, not remembering when and what he had to eat.

4 April. A meeting at the psychiatric hospital. Not my favourite place to visit as it brought back memories of dad being there, but Derek is also a patient so we went and met a very nice doctor. She spent an hour and a half with us and she did a memory test on Derek, while I waited in another room. Then she came out to talk to me. I couldn't help noticing that her eyes were tearful and she had a tissue in her hand. I wanted to hug her and say it's OK, we are OK.

Derek's score was lower and she said that the part of the brain that was probably damaged was the part that understands and hears you speak. Also the speech was affected, which we already knew, but yes the Alzheimer's had got worse. I asked what would be the next stage and she said it could be that Derek s coordination may be next, e.g. putting on his clothes back to front, inside out, etc.

The sad thing is Derek is well aware of this disease, but the doctor says that as time passes Derek will become unaware of what's happening, which will be a blessing in disguise.

This made me very sad and yet again I cried. I was very strong at the beginning of the meeting but by the end was upset.

***

Derek had his first eye test in a couple of years and the optician said that Derek's eyes had got worse, especially the right eye. New glasses were required and distance glasses needed to be worn all the time. The eye test was OK. Derek seemed to manage that, but when it came to choosing glasses Derek got very confused and at one point put a new pair of show glasses into his glasses case, getting the glasses mixed up.

5 April. The car went in for an MOT at a cost of £300. Due to the work needed to pass the car, the paperwork said the car was dangerous to drive pre-MOT state. This made my decision a little easier. I had to get rid of the car, our prized possession, a PT cruiser. Yes it was ten years old and yes it was costing me money, i.e. petrol, oil, repairs and the pending road tax due at the end of the month at £235, but I feel I have no other choice.

The following weekend I went looking for cars. Now this was strange because when buying a car I usually would have either my dad or Derek for back up and advice, but this time it was down to just me. But as Louise said, single parents have no help so I guess it's no different.

I decided to go for a Ford as they are cheaper in repairs and a diesel engine means less fuel and £30 road tax, already a saving of £205. An 08 reg, so hopefully I made the right decision. I feel as though someone above has helped guide me to this decision.

After paying a deposit, that night I had a terrible night with an upset tummy, no sleep, tears, all because I was worried about getting rid of the PT cruiser. I was also due to take the girls away for a few days to London. I was in a right state, then I got a text from my friend who said they were travelling up north to buy a new car, as they could no longer afford to run their current car. Strange as it may seem, that made me feel much better, it put everything back into perspective.

12–14 April. The long-awaited break away with the girls to London. Everything put into place, social worker to visit on one day, the carer to visit the other two days, salad made, quiche made, cold cooked chicken bought, day planners written out, all ready to go. So why do I feel so sad? Derek walked us to the station, he was a little tearful, and I felt guilty leaving him behind, but we all needed a break big time.

The train journey was relaxing. I read my book while the girls listened to their iPods. We went straight to the hotel and booked in, then took a taxi to Covent Garden and had a lovely meal, did some shopping then walked to the London Eye. We watched the street entertainers and a very talented painter, we then purchased some snack food for supper and caught a taxi back to the hotel. The porter opened the taxi door for us which made us feel special and important. We had a girly night in with a picnic supper.

I phoned Derek to see if all was OK. He seemed confused. He didn't know who I was to start with, then he said the carer hadn't turned up, but I tried to explain that he wasn't due on that day and the social worker came instead.

The following day we went to see the show *Wicked*. It was magical, the best show ever.

On the last day we went to Ripley's Believe it or Not!, another great place to visit. We were sad to be coming home, as the few days away gave us some normality.

When we arrived home, Derek was out with his carer so we had a cup of tea and relaxed a little.

When Derek got home he didn't seem too bothered about us being there, all he was worried about was his TV mag and why wasn't the football on. Right up till bedtime all Derek kept on about was when is Saturday, the next morning same thing.

25 April. Easter. I am fed up with social services. No money has come through to help with Derek's respite care, something to do with being 65 and a different department now being involved. Or maybe that's a cop out for not giving us any money. Anyway, because the last bill was £105 for just three sessions of care I had to make the decision to cut down on the respite.

Derek will now only go once every other week for respite. The social worker advised that no back payment would be made for the care so anything I paid out I would lose. I have no faith in the system. Right from the start they insisted that we get respite, but when I finally find somewhere there's no money coming in to pay for it. I would complain if I knew where to complain to. I am just sick and tired of having to fight.

Dad came for Easter which was nice. There is improvement in him for sure. We had a roast dinner in the garden with wine and Christmas pudding, dad's favourite. On the Monday we went to Southsea, played crazy golf and had lunch in a pub. Dad had some of his sense of humour back which was nice to see.

28 April. Still waiting for the social worker to get back to me about Derek's payment for day care. Just phoned again but the social worker is not in her office. If this carries on I will just cancel Derek's day care.

After many phone calls I still cannot locate the social worker, so I phoned Worthing who deal with payments of care. They had no record of Derek pre-65 or otherwise so now I am very confused as to what forms were filled out last year. Oh, and apparently if the carer at Waterlooville is not HMRC status then they will not pay her anyway. This system stinks big time!

May 2011

1 May. Long weekend. Royal wedding on Friday and Bank Holiday Monday. Yet again for the third week running my dad has come to stay. My sister is away on holiday and my brother is busy, that leaves just me again. I don't mind having my dad to stay but it seems as though my weekend is taken up with meals and washing, ironing and cleaning. I feel myself falling into a vicious circle.

***

As much as I love my dad and the fact I promised mum I would look after him, whose looking after me? There I have said it now, this is why I am so angry. There is no one to look out for me. Both my brother and sister have partners who can give them support. Me, I have no one. When dad comes round to stay he just sits and stares out of the window; he moves from armchair to dinner table, back to armchair. He says he can't do anything, and that he is just like Derek. I said to him that he didn't have Alzheimer's, and his response was 'Nearly'. That made me very angry.

There is no conversation between dad and Derek, and so this afternoon when Donna is at work, Louise at drama, it's just me and Derek and dad at home and I feel trapped.

I am losing hope that dad will get better. In fact I am not sure he wants to get better, it seems that he has no incentive to do so.

3 May. Derek had an appointment with the GP about the pains in his legs and hands. While we were in with the doctor Derek had a funny turn. He became very hot, grey looking and very giddy. The GP got Derek to lie down and she took his pulse. I asked what was wrong and she said that with Alzheimer's can come problems with blood pressure and strange turns. If it continues they will investigate. She said when they happen Derek should lie down until he feels better. I explained that Derek is left on his own a lot and she replied that I couldn't be with him 24/7. That made me feel tearful.

Derek is now waiting for an appointment at the hospital for X-rays.

On this same day I was taking dad to the doctors for his introduction as he had moved to our surgery. When I went to pick dad up my mobile rang. It was the social worker–hurray! She said she tried to phone home, but my phone was out of order. But I used it before I left home! Then she said she had left me a message. I didn't receive it. She has the paperwork for us to sign, I advised her that I have had to cut down the care hours, and that when I phoned Worthing to ask about the paperwork, Derek's name was not on the system. She said she wasn't sure what I meant, so she is phoning back this afternoon and hopefully calling round for papers to be signed.

I also ordered a skip to be delivered today, as over the weekend we have managed to clear out the greenhouse, little shed and some of the large shed. There was too much for a trip to the tip, so a skip it is.

The social worker turned up with the paperwork. We filled it in, signed it etc., so that shouldn't take too long now. The social worker also advised us that we could now apply for attendance allowance as Derek has reached 65.

***

The day the skip was delivered, I was at work in the morning. When I got home, Derek had moved the skip items to various places, including down the side of the house. I just couldn't believe that he had done this. It was hard work trying to get him to understand about what to put in the skip.

***

Applying for attendance allowance was a pain. First I phoned to ask if they could send someone out to help fill out the forms. They said there was an eight-week waiting list. I said that was fine. They then asked if I had access to the internet, since it would be easier to complete the forms online. So I went on the website, logged in and started to fill out the form, but when it came to turn to the next page my computer would not let me, so I phoned them up. They explained that you can't do it on Google Chrome, which is what I have. I had to apply on Internet Explorer, which no matter how I tried I could not find, so I gave up. Another phone call later and I had the forms sent to me.

11 May. Had a phone call from the social worker to say she couldn't get hold of the carer, and that she needs a letter from her to say what kind of care is offered, the prices etc., so she can send them with the forms we filled in a week ago. I phoned the carer straight away and she said she would email the letter that very same day.

13 May. Derek picked up his prescription from the local chemist while I was at work. When I got home I noticed that they were a different drug called Citalopram and only 20mg. I phoned the chemist thinking they had got the prescription muddled up with someone else's, but they assured me that the prescription was correct and that they were an antidepressant. So I then phoned the doctors who said yes, that was correct as per the telephone consultation, which we never had. I then had to wait for the duty doctor to phone me back. Meanwhile I phoned Derek's nurse, who advised me that these tablets were to be taken alongside the others as advised by the doctor at the psychiatric hospital. It was five weeks ago that we last saw this doctor. I can't remember what I did yesterday, let alone five weeks ago. Apparently this was also discussed during the recent phone call with the psychiatric hospital, which I never received.

***

Louise and I went to Glastonbury with my brother's wife, and daughter for a short break. Donna stayed home as she couldn't get the time off work. We had a lovely time.

Donna phoned me to say that Derek's sister called into the garden centre to tell her that she was taking Derek out for the day, but they left the message with a work colleague who couldn't find her. When Donna got home there was a note put through the door for her, so they must have known that I was away.

June 2011

Half term and Louise was at home with Derek. I was at work. Louise phoned me to say the home phone had just rung and when she'd answered it the person pretended that it was a wrong number. Louise dialled 1471 and the number was Derek's sister. She actually pretended that she had the wrong number just because Derek hadn't answered.

The more I think of Derek's family the more I deeply detest them.

***

Derek had been out with his carer to Chichester Cathedral to see the birds nesting on a large screen. This was Derek's idea to go, but when he came home, his carer said Derek was in a very bad mood. He had a right go at the carer, all over the fact that he had wanted to park outside his sister's house, but there was no room. So the carer asked Derek to go into his sister's to see if they could park on her drive. But Derek refused to go and ask. This resulted in Derek being in a bad mood. Whether this had anything to do with the phone call I do not know.

Derek said something about his sister wanting to go with them so I really don't know what's going on, but what I do know is still Derek's family refuse to come through me with regard to Derek. They really don't get it.

3 June. Today I took the decision to take more control of Derek's contact with his family.

After much looking I found Derek's mobile in one of his jacket pockets. I changed the sim card, so he has a new number, and put his old sim card into an old phone.

That way I can see who contacts him behind my back. I have also changed the home phone to ring twice then go to answerphone, but already that has caused a problem as Donna was waiting for a call from the doctors and didn't get to the phone on time, so I think that I will have to think again on that.

***

I have received a letter from disability living allowance to say that we are not entitled to a larger payment for Derek. I am annoyed about this because this means Derek cannot go to the carer once a week. So I phoned Derek's social worker to say we were not entitled to more funding. Her reply was that the paperwork had not been sent off yet as she was still waiting for the carer's letter. The social worker said she would send me via text her email address so I could forward it on to her. Three days later no text. So I sent a text to the social worker to say I hadn't received her message. Her reply was she had sent it, so someone is not telling the truth. I am angry that after weeks of waiting for funding the paperwork is still on the social worker's desk, and I am just piggy in the middle having to sit and wait for them to get their act together.

If it takes this long to sort out funding for two extra days a month, I hate to think what would happen if Derek had to go into respite!

June 17. I have had enough of toing and froing from carer to social worker. I phoned the social worker to find out what's going on. Sadly she is not available on the two numbers I have for her so with a bee in my bonnet I phoned Derek's nurse to see if she can help. But guess what, she is not working on this particular day so I phoned the Chichester clinic where Derek's social worker works and asked to speak to someone above Derek's social worker, but he's not in the office either. So I leave a message.

***

Monday comes and I drop Derek off at the carer in Waterlooville and she asks me to guess who's been on the phone to her. Derek's social worker! Hopefully funding will be sorted out soon, but I won't hold my breath.

21 June. I went for a reading with a lady in Southsea. I don't usually make a habit of having readings done, but in the last year it has been my third, which most probably says a lot about my state of mind. I just need to know there is an end to this shit we are dealing with and that there is still a life out there for me, although some days I wonder that.

I was told that I needed to get more help with Derek and that he should go to the doctors for a check-up which I have now booked for next month. The reader was quite adamant that there was more going on with Derek than the Alzheimer's. The reader also said she could see me writing a book/journal which would be published – for that we will have to wait and see!

Today would have been my nana's birthday, and the day I decided to spread my mum's ashes. So all my family met at the spot my mum had chosen and spread her ashes.

***

I feel I should describe how I feel at this moment in time, but as I think I have said before I worry that I have not grieved for my mum and I worry how this will affect me later on in life. One thing I do know is on the odd occasion I have nothing on my mind or nothing to do I feel myself being very tearful and low.

23 June. Today my friend Jane sent me a clipping out of a newspaper about a guy of 45 with Alzheimer's. On reading this article I question yet again how a family living with a member with Alzheimer's seems so loving towards the person with the disease, when I find myself wanting to detach myself from Derek. Why is this so?

***

We have been having problems in the garden with rats, and all poison left down doesn't seem to work. So I called the rat man in to deal with the problem. He came today and put down a lethal poison to hopefully end our problem. When Derek came home from being out with his carer, I asked Derek not to go down between the two sheds as there was poison there for the rats and I didn't want anything disturbed. Approximately ten minutes later I asked Louise where dad was. She didn't know. I looked down the garden to see Derek between the two sheds. I just couldn't stop myself from shouting at him, asking what he was doing. He replied that he was looking at the tomatoes, which are in the greenhouse not between the two sheds. I was so very angry with him. I felt like shit for shouting at him. I then went upstairs and cried my eyes out. I later went out as I was ashamed that I had shouted at him.

I am getting worried that I am losing my grip on life. Today at work they decided to have a staff meeting on Monday 4 July at Waterlooville at 11am. I had already said that I had to bring Derek to his carer at 9 30am at Waterlooville, which means I would have an hour-and-a-half wait in Waterlooville for the meeting or I go home in-between. Which means six trips to Waterlooville in one day on a day that's supposed to be for me to relax! What a laugh, relax being the opposite word.

I was so close to tears when this was mentioned. I have thoughts going through my head at the moment about whether I should give up work? Seems a bit extreme, but it's not the first time I have thought of this.

***

Met up with Susan today. If I haven't mentioned her before, she is a lady I met at the psychiatric hospital when they held support groups for the under 65s with mental health problems. This support group no longer exists, but Susan and I remained friends. We are the same age and her husband has Pick's disease which has resulted in him being put in a secure unit. We jolly each other along, keep in touch by text and the occasional meet up.

When I first arrived, Susan said to me, 'You won't be angry with me or hate me if I tell you something?' I wondered what she was going to say. She continued, 'I have met up with an old ex-boyfriend and we are seeing each other.' 'Why would I hate you for that?' I said. 'You lost your husband in every way possible, he will never return home and at the end of the day you are still young and have a life to lead. Anyone who feels the need to criticise you cannot even begin to understand the situation you have been living in.' Susan then said how nice it was to feel the love of a man. I wasn't going to mention this side of my relationship with Derek because it's a private matter and I didn't feel it was relevant to his illness, but on reflection I have been honest throughout this journal and maybe this fact is important. Truth is, Derek and I have not had a sexual relationship in five years, and when Susan had said the same about herself and her husband, it was a kind of release to know that I was not to blame for this as previously thought. Maybe I needed to write this down to release this tension in my head? Also if this journal ever gets printed those going through the same situation can also identify with this.

***

Also today Derek fell over while coming back from the shop. He grazed his knee and hand but luckily nothing else. I am writing this in because it may have just been an accident or it could have been his coordination.

28 June. I am taking Derek for a walk along Wittering beach to see how he is in a different environment and without lots of shops, just open sea air.

We had a good time, although things didn't go as planned. When we got to Wittering the tide was up so we walked a little way along the path. We couldn't see the Isle of Wight as it was very overcast, then came the thunder and we landed up in a storm, but we bought sandwiches and ate them in the car.

July 2011
1 July. For the past week I have been feeling very tearful, low and in turmoil. At one point I wondered if maybe I was having a breakdown. I am finding it harder to pull myself out of this low mood. Today I broke down at work and felt I had nowhere to turn, the feeling of deep despair just washed over me. The last thing my work colleagues need is having to carry me. I feel so stupid at breaking down yet again, but I feel so emotionally drained.

I was told that maybe my work place is draining my energy, which I feel could be very true as the clients are very negative. I feel hurt when they question the work I set and even though I spend many hours preparing work, they don't appreciate it.

I am thinking of giving up work for maybe a year to concentrate on Derek and dad, as I don't spend enough time with either of them. I don't get paid a lot in my job and have worked out that I could use some of my savings to compensate for loss of wages.

I feel that I am losing control of time and things are spiralling out of control. I need to get my head back into a better place.

2 July. Today dad asked me to take him food shopping, but I contacted my brother to ask him to have dad for the weekend as I can't cope at the moment. Dad then said he needed to go to a hospital appointment on Wednesday at 2pm, but I said I don't get home till 1.30pm. He said he would have to cancel again. I asked him to ask my sister to take him. Whether he will or not is a different matter.

***

Turns out dad got the date wrong for his hospital appointment, so panic over. While I was over at his I took a look around the garden and felt so sad that it had turned into a jungle. The fish pond was dark green with one dead fish floating on top, pots of soil which were once planted with flowers were placed around the patio left there by mum ready to plant in the spring. I didn't appreciate just how much hard work mum and dad put into the garden, until mum's death and dad's breakdown. I truly want to help but my inner self warns me to take care of myself and at the end of the day dad could employ a gardener,

4 July. Meeting at work. I went with the letter in hand ready to hand my notice in. After the meeting I was called to one side and they expressed their concerns for my health. They asked what I wanted to do and I replied that I would leave because it's not fair when they are a new business and need the staff there.

They kindly said they didn't want to lose me, and that they were willing to give me a month off work to get my head together and decide what to do.

I couldn't ask for anything more. I bet there are not many work places out there who would have been that generous.

So I have one month to decide my future, my biggest worry is if I do give up work will I become depressed being at home 24/7?

5 July. Derek and I had doctors' appointments. Derek's was in the morning to have a general check-up, urine sample checked. All OK, and now booked in for an ECG and full blood tests.

My appointment followed in the afternoon with the same doctor.

I walked into the room and broke down. I asked for help. She was very sympathetic and replied that I was too young to be dealing with this. Derek is too young to have this disease. When looking at my notes the doctor said she could see I didn't want antidepressants. I replied that I didn't know anymore, I just wanted to feel better. She asked if I wanted some counselling. I replied that I did. With regards to the antidepressants, the doctor said that if I started taking them, it would not make the problems go away and at some point I would have to face these be it now or later. She advised that taking St John's wort can help as it has some properties that are in antidepressants, but natural. I asked her to write me a prescription for antidepressants just in case.

7 July. Derek had an ECG – all OK – and blood test. Now waiting results.

Dad phones up to say that his washing machine has broken down, but I can't get there today as Louise has dancing Wednesday and Thursday I have friends over. Friday I am on my course and Saturday I am working all day, so I say I can come over Sunday. But dad says he has run out of underwear. I explain that I can't physically get to him until Sunday and that he should phone my sister. I feel bad about letting him down, but I am one person and have many people relying on me. Sometimes the pressure is too much.

10 July. Today Derek's annoying habit of continually jingling change in his pocket got the better of me. On two pairs of his jeans I have sewn up the pockets. This may sound a bit extreme, but if anyone lives with someone with this very annoying habit you will know exactly how I feel.

***

I am feeling better this week, whether it's because I have four weeks off or that I genuinely just feel more positive. It is quite possible that my five-week healing course may have brought out the feelings I have kept suppressed for so long .

***

Into my second week off work, not sure if it's a good idea to not work as I think I need some structure to my life.

19 July. Phoned the social worker to ask about Derek's funding. 'Oh, I was meant to phone you last week!' was her reply. Because of the government changes, delays in funding are long. As far as I can work out the paperwork we filled out in April has still not reached the funding panel. In desperation, I told the social worker that if funding was not imminent I would have to stop all care for Derek as I am off sick from work and without pay, so I need to make cuts because I am not sure if I will continue to work.

The social worker said she would phone me Thursday.
I'm sure Derek is getting worse. I went in the garden to see if l could get him to move a plant and to trim the plum tree. He said he would do it later, then sat in the conservatory for the rest of the day looking out at the garden.

Derek's understanding of words is, on a bad day, zero. He seems to be understanding less and less which is very worrying.

I had an idea to contact an ex-next-door neighbour of mum's, who has something to do with a local radio station, to ask if they could help with some kind of group for younger people with Alzheimer's. To my surprise, she contacted the station for me and we are going to meet at some point to see how the station can help.

21 July. Social worker phoned to say that Derek's paperwork for extra care money is going through and has been approved.

23 July. We all went to Center Parcs for a well-earned rest. This was a very expensive break of three days, costing as much as a holiday abroad, but it's the best I can do as Derek knows the environment and I feel more at ease taking him there. We were not so stressed; the only difficulty was swimming and the changing rooms. We went down water slides, played crazy golf, and went on bike rides through the forest and on one evening saw deer running ahead of us through the trees. Derek got very excited in a kind of childish way about the rabbit and squirrel outside our lodge. But all in all we had a great time.

28 July. Louise and I went to Brighton for a couple of days. I felt I needed to take her away for some one-to-one time. We visited the Sea Life Centre and had a meal out, followed by a stay at the Travelodge. When I booked this it didn't enter my head about the height of the building, i.e. how many floors it had. We were given the seventh floor. I must say I didn't sleep that night. I felt an alarming sense of responsibility for Louise and I think that every worst scenario went through my head about being on the seventh floor, together with the street noise that went on till 3am and the endless noise of the seagulls. I will just have to put this one down to experience.

***

On the train journey home my mobile rang. It was the social worker to say the money had been granted for the extra care for Derek and that I now needed to set up a bank account in his name for a direct payment.

29 July. Went into Emsworth to set up a bank account for Derek, armed with my legal power of attorney documents. The bank didn't have a staff member available to open an account, so I then drove to Havant to ask them to set up an account. We were taken into a small room and were asked to see the power of attorney papers. They then had to fax them to another branch, to verify that they were in order, only to be told that they were not stamped on both sides of every sheet and that there was no mention of Derek's illness on the paperwork. So therefore I could not open the account. What was the use of paying all that money out for legal papers that don't work? When I got home I phoned the solicitor who is now looking into this for me. Why, oh why, is everything such a problem?

31 July. The start of our so-called holiday to Stratford upon Avon. The weather is good, unlike most of our holidays which end up a total wash out. Only Louise and Derek came as Donna could not get the time off work.

We found our way to the Travelodge thanks to the satnav. It was too early to book in so we went to visit Anne Hathaway's house, a lovely old Tudor-type building with old cottage gardens.

Booked into the Travelodge and we were on the top floor again. What's with the top floor? Someone upstairs must be having a laugh, knowing I am a little wary of being high up. Anyway, turns out it must have been the hottest floor of the hotel. The window was small and due to health and safety the window was fixed so it couldn't be opened more than about six inches. No matter about our health, the room was so hot we had to purchase a fan and at night we had to run the towels under cold water and lay them over us.

The following day we went into Stratford upon Avon. We visited a Tudor museum called Falstaff Experience, supposed to be the most haunted house in Britain; we then visited another place called the Creaky Cauldron, which held references to Harry Potter, lots of witches, wizards, potions, etc., with narrow stairways and very dark corridors – brilliant.

We then went for a canal boat trip on the Avon. Up until that moment we felt that life was not too bad. Derek seemed to be enjoying himself, although he doesn't show much emotion. We were told to wait a few minutes before boarding the boat as they needed to restock supplies. Derek proceeded to try and get on the boat. I raised my voice to Derek so he could understand not to get on the boat. The owner said to Derek, 'Is she always this bossy?' Derek did not reply, but I shook my head to a yes. When we got on the boat and sat down I noticed Louise had tears running down her face, which then set me off. She said that people don't understand what it's like living with dad. For me, the worst thing is people thinking bad of me, believing that I am a nagging old woman who henpecks her husband. If only they knew. Part of me wanted to scream out 'My husband has Alzheimer's and doesn't understand you!'

The second day we went to Birmingham to Cadburys chocolate factory, followed by Warwick. We were going to visit the castle, but it was going to cost £70 so we decided we didn't want to see the castle that much.

We also went to Cheltenham to travel on a steam train, which I thought Derek would like. But as I said before, Derek doesn't show much emotion.

In three days we had managed to fit in a lot of sites and it wasn't quite as stressful as I thought it would be.

August 2011
4 August. Almost two years ago we were given the diagnosis of Alzheimer's. This makes me very sad.

The social worker came round to tell us that I can open a bank account in my name as I was having trouble with opening one in Derek's name. I had to sign some paperwork for payment to be made for more care for him.

I phoned NatWest to make an appointment to open a bank account, and they offered to open the account via phone which would take approximately four weeks. But this is easier than making an appointment to go into the bank.

Meanwhile I have been sent a credit-type card which has been loaded with £168 for Derek's care. I went to my bank and asked them to verify how much was on the card so I could draw it out. Yes, there was £168, but I can only draw it out of an ATM. That would be OK except they only give out money in units of ten, so eight pounds was left on the card. Apparently I can use it in the shops, but it was meant for Derek's care.

15 August. Today the bank account is up and ready for action. It didn't take four weeks as predicted – good news at last. But that didn't last long. I phoned the social worker to give her the bank details, but apparently I have to have a letter from the bank saying I have opened an account, account numbers sort code, etc. Pissed off is not enough to describe the way I am feeling at the moment.

Delay, delay, delay is all the system knows. Why the hell they need a letter from the bank is beyond me.

***

Today I had a meeting with support services about me having some counselling. I do hope that they can help. I feel a little more positive about things.

19 August. The social worker was supposed to call to collect the letter with the details on from the bank. Got a phone call instead to say she had been delayed, and could I put the letter in the post. Yet another delay.

26 August. Still no word from the social worker to say funds are in the bank for direct payment. This is almost beyond belief.

Came home from work to find a very tense atmosphere. Derek was insisting that it was Saturday, and no one could make him understand that it was Friday. This all due to the TV magazine which he went and purchased today. He is still looking through both magazines to work out Saturday's viewing. Sometimes it's best to let him get on with it!

***

I am finding it ever more difficult to communicate with Derek. I would like to know if other people are also finding this so. Derek often goes to his brother's house who only lives down the road. Sometimes he goes there two/three times a day, but I can't and won't communicate with them after what happened two years ago. They are so unbelievably ignorant, they even sent Donna's birthday card through the post, to avoid physically putting it through the door themselves. Still, at least they acknowledged Donna's birthday with a card, unlike other members of Derek's family.

***

Today I heard that the great singer Glen Campbell has been diagnosed with Alzheimer's. This made me very sad. He is now organising his last farewell tour, the long goodbye. How many more great people are going to be diagnosed with this evil disease before those who can help with more funding for research listen?

30 August. I phoned the social worker today as I have still had no word from direct payment and money is running out. Yet again she said she was going to phone me today as I need to sign some more paperwork. Anyway, she came over to our house within half an hour for me to sign it, so hopefully it will not be much longer.

As if I didn't have enough to deal with, I had almost finished the housework, went to put some rubbish in the dustbin, looked up at the ceiling to see a brown wet patch over the front door. The upstairs loo was leaking. I phoned my brother who gave me the name of a plumber, who kindly came and had a look. Because the loo is fixed onto a false wall, tiles had to be taken off the wall and a section of wall taken down. This has now become an insurance claim. Why do these things keep happening? This caused Derek to be unsettled and edgy as he didn't understand what was happening.

September 2011

Derek's auntie died. Her daughter phoned me to tell me the sad news. I didn't think Derek would want to go to the funeral, but when I told Derek of the death the first thing he mentioned was going to the funeral. In all fairness, his cousin is the closest member of Derek's family, she is like a sister to Derek. They grew up together, and for many years when the girls were young we holidayed in their caravan.

I am not sure if Derek's brother and sister will be attending the funeral. According to Derek's cousin they have not told Derek's mum that her sister has died. And to my horror they have also not told her of the death of her other sister and brother. What kind of a family are they? And why do they insist on keeping Derek's mum wrapped in bubble wrap? She also has Alzheimer's, but that does not make her stupid. And surely she has a right to know what's going on around her. I do believe that Derek's family have also withheld the fact that Derek has Alzheimer's, but who am I to comment on their behaviour? As far as I am concerned they are no longer related to me.

5 September. Today Derek went to the Isle of Wight with his carer. They went by hovercraft. Derek was a little edgy first thing, but I think it was because he was going somewhere different.

The trip was an extra £30 on top of the normal day care cost. This meant that I had to put in £10 of my money because the one-off payment has all been used up and there was still no sign of the direct payments. I also informed the carer that Derek would not be wanting day care next week because of the funeral. She said that I would have to still pay £10.

6 September. Still no word from direct payments. I tried to phone the social worker, but she was not in her office; I left a message for her to call me back, no reply; so I have now sent the social worker a text message saying, 'Tried to contact you today. Still no word from direct payments. No more funding left for me to pay so I will leave it until end of week and if I hear nothing I will stop Derek's care. It's not fair to expect me to pay and I think the fact I have been waiting five months for this to be sorted is past a joke.' Now waiting for a reply.

7 September. The social worker contacted me to say that direct payments will be in the bank on Friday. Hurray! And true to her word, on Saturday I got a letter from direct payments to say they have credited the account, at long last.

10 September. I have decided to reorganise the garden a little bit to make gardening easier, but yet again as I start to work Derek takes over and then when I go back indoors he stops. I am finding this very frustrating, as when I try to explain what needs doing Derek seems to not understand me. I think his hearing ability is very damaged; this must be the area of the brain that has the disease.

12 September. Derek's auntie's funeral. I am not feeling comfortable with having to attend a funeral so close to my mum's, but for Derek's sake we are going. I am concerned about meeting Derek's side of the family.

We left home just after 9am as the funeral was in Worthing. We passed Derek's brother travelling in the opposite direction so I knew that they wouldn't be going. Two less to confront.

I had to rely on the satnav to get there as I had no idea. I felt a sigh of relief when I saw Derek's cousin, as I then knew I was at the correct venue. As we got out of our car there was a small gathering of people – Derek's sister and brother-in-law included. They ignored me but then I didn't expect anything less from them.

Derek's sister brought along with her a flower arrangement, making a point that it was from her mum even though she doesn't know her sister died.

Derek's auntie came over to me and said about the bad atmosphere which I thought only I could feel. The rest of Derek's family were kind and chatty. Derek was very quiet and I am not sure if his lack of empathy swallowed his emotions.

Derek also found conversation difficult due to him not hearing, or the brain not comprehending words, and too many people talking at once. After the service Derek's sister introduced Derek's family from up north to other members of the family and even though I was standing right next to Derek she purposely did not introduce me which I thought was extremely rude.

We went to the wake which was held in a pub. We sat down with Derek's cousins, and had a good chat.

Then Derek's sister tried to interfere with getting some food for Derek as if I wasn't capable of doing this task. She was trying to offer Derek egg sandwiches, which I said Derek didn't like, and I said we would go and get something to eat later.

Derek's sisters voice seemed to be ultra loud at the funeral, and she was broadcasting how Derek's mum had Alzheimer's, but she was very well and very happy. Good for her.

Towards the end of the wake, Derek's cousin asked me how I was. I felt tears welling up in my eyes and had trouble answering him. I felt so stupid for being so emotional.

A good piece of news that day was local radio had forwarded my name onto the Alzheimer's group in Cosham and they contacted me and told me about group meetings and outings. They are going to send out some details for me.

***

As well as dealing with Derek's Alzheimer's and other issues associated with this illness, I am a mother who has in all respects become a single parent. This became more apparent when my eldest daughter decided to go night clubbing. Nothing unusual in that, but it was to a club she hadn't been to before, and she was meeting a friend in town, which meant that she was going to catch a train by herself at 10.30 at night. I waited at the last minute hoping she would change her mind, but as she approached the front door I offered her a lift into town. I wouldn't be able to sleep anyway knowing she was out. Derek was fast asleep at this point and unaware of what was taking place. Louise decided to come along to keep me company.

As I started driving, what I hadn't anticipated was thick fog. I don't think I have ever driven in such thick conditions. Because I hadn't had the car that long I had no idea where the fog lights were. Louise got out the car manual and while I was driving she was looking up 'fog lights'. It was like something out of a comedy sketch.

We eventually arrived in town and Donna met up with her friend. We arranged to pick Donna up at 1am by the bus station.

The fog was so bad I didn't want to drive home and then back again to pick Donna up, so Louise and I went Tesco shopping. Good job it was 24-hour shopping! After that we sat in the car park chatting as it felt safer sitting in a floodlit car park. Louise said she was a little scared, but I told her there was nothing to be scared of. It made it even more apparent how the girls rely on me and me alone to protect them.

I was also concerned that we had left Derek at home on his own, should he wake to an empty house. But my fears were not founded, because I believe if Derek had woken he would most probably be unaware that we were not home. As it turned out we didn't get home from that outing until about 2.30am, but at least Donna was safe. I could feel my mum looking down on me and saying why?

The next morning I started to tell Derek of our expedition, but he lost interest.

***

Louise is in her last year of school and is hoping to go to college to do performing arts. At the moment she is very stressed, she puts a lot of pressure on herself, as in her mind it's 100% or nothing. As well as exams, Louise is in rehearsals at school till 5pm, for the school production of *The Little Shop of Horrors*, then at 5.30 she has to be in Havant for rehearsals for *Les Miserables*. On top of that she has a dance show in January and I think it's all too much. I contacted the school today to speak to her drama teacher, and asked that she keep an eye on Louise, as the situation at home is also not helping and I am worried about her.

Donna is hoping to go to Camp America next year. For her sake I think it will do her good, but yesterday it hit me that it will leave just me and Louise to deal with things. And my thoughts continued to think about when Louise goes to college and how she will be more independent, leaving just me. At the moment, having to rally around for everyone is what keeps me going. When things die down what will happen to me?

19 September. Did lots of running around today. Derek went to day care at Waterlooville, then I picked up dad to take him to Goodwood to scatter his sister's ashes. Previous to this, Louise's bedroom was looking a little babyish, and as Donna had recently redecorated her bedroom with the help of my brother, I wanted to help Louise with hers. But I felt I couldn't ask my brother again to help so I did the next best thing and decided to revamp it. So previous to going to Goodwood with dad in the car I did a few shop stops on the way, managing to get a new bright duvet cover and some dye to dye the bedroom curtains.

Anyway, back to the Goodwood trip, dad said he had only brought half the ashes as there was too much to scatter at Goodwood. We parked up, but there were a few cars there so as dad eagerly got out of the car I told him not to be in such a hurry. I went to put the ashes in my bag so as not to be so obvious, but unknown to me he had the ashes loose in the carrier bag so we had to carry them as they were. Dad seemed to be in such a hurry to get the job over and done with. I felt this was very sad. He obviously has not got the same sentiment as me.

I dropped dad off home and said we would see him over the weekend. He agreed because he would need some shopping done as my sister was going away again. Both my brother and I were unaware of this. She really has disengaged from the family.

When I got home Ellie our lovely rabbit was sunbathing in the garden. she was lying out flat. I then had to go to Havant to do some banking and then pick Derek up from the carer's. When I got home I noticed Ellie was still lying in the same position. I went into the garden thinking she would jump up and run around in the skittish way she always does, but she just lay there. I phoned the vet realising she was ill. They said to bring her in straight away. We had to cut the wire to get her out as she was lying at the furthest end of the run, and we took her to the vets. Unfortunately she had to be put to sleep. There was nothing she could do to save her. I was crying my eyes out. Ellie was only 21 months old. This has made me realise that we cannot have any more pets. I was unaware of signs of Ellie's illness – I was too busy to notice as Derek took care of her most of the time; I thought it would do him good to have a little responsibility. But in all fairness, he probably would not have noticed if she was ill. This was my fault for not being vigilant. I am sorry Ellie if you suffered because of my neglect.

Ellie died 19 September; mum died 19 January.

***

Derek is slowly getting worse. His understanding is very bad. A couple of times last week he asked me if I wanted a cup of tea. I said, 'Yes please, no sugar' as he seems to think I take sugar which I have never done. But on hearing just the 'no' on both occasions I landed up with no cup of tea.

After coming out of the shower one morning I could smell gas, and as I approached the landing it got stronger. I went downstairs and saw that the gas hob was turned on. Only Derek would have done that, but he said he hadn't. I have no other explanation for it.

29 September. Went to Anna's for the evening and got home about 11.30pm. I opened the front door to the sound of water running, went upstairs and found our bathroom tap running full on. Derek was fast asleep.

I now need to find out how I stand with my house insurance as regards to accidental damage.

October 2011

This year is passing far too quickly. Louise has just turned 16, Donna now 20. Derek is getting so confused. His mum's birthday is on 3 October. Derek wanted to see his mum on her birthday, but he will be with his carer most of the day, then I have to pick Louise up from school to take her to another rehearsal in Havant. I suggested we go and visit his mum the day before her birthday, but we need a key from Derek's brother as Derek's key did not work the last time we visited her. Derek got very confused and could not understand this concept. I know I should have made a phone call to his brother, but I am not ready to speak to them, if ever.

To make things easier, I took Derek to his mum's in the hope that someone would be around to open the door. I am embarrassed to say the door would not open due to holding the key to the camera instead of the key ID. This was the problem last time and there was nothing wrong with Derek's key after all.

At least we have now solved the problem of Derek going to visit his mum. When we entered Derek's mum's flat we were greeted by a nurse who was just leaving. She asked that when we leave we lock the door to the flat as Derek's mum tends to wander. I was shocked to learn that Derek's mum was actually locked in her flat. What if there was a fire? She would have no way of opening the door. To me she was kept like an animal, no windows were open, and it was 25° outside and very hot in the flat. I am appalled at the way she was treated by her own family. It was also noted that on the bedroom door was a small piece of paper approximately 3"x3" with Derek's sister's writing saying 'Don't go to bed, wait until I arrive. The voices you can hear are from the television.' I guess she must be worried about hearing noises, and going to bed without turning off the television.

I know I must not get involved, but I am angry that Derek's mum is left on her own, without company or proper care. The note was written in small handwriting that she had no way of understanding. While Derek was there she was wandering around with her walking frame, looking lost. Derek's family have no way of understanding this illness, for if they did they would not leave a 92-year-old woman locked in her flat.

10 October. After picking Derek up from his carer, we had to do some banking. Both girls were with me. We had about half an hour spare before Louise had drama. We were parked alongside a road waiting for time to pass, and some girls were walking towards us with school uniforms on. Derek says, 'Here comes Louise!' Well at first we laughed as Louise was sitting in the car with us, but my laughter soon turned to tears as it sunk in that Derek was unaware that Louise was with us.

17 October. Had a shit weekend.

Phoned dad up to say I would take him shopping. He replied, 'I will read out the shopping list and you can bring it round to me.' I said, 'But you said you would come over for the day.' His excuse again was he needed to wash, so I said I would pick him up at 11.30am giving him time to wash and change.

Picked dad up, did the shopping at the local Co-op, went back to our house, made lunch of soup and crusty bread. Because there were four of us I heated dad's and Louise's soup up first. They started on theirs while I was warming up Derek's and mine. Just as I sat down to mine dad went to get up from the table and go sit in the lounge. I asked him if he wanted a pudding. His reply was 'What have you got? Something good?' He was in a hurry, so I got up from just starting my soup to get his pudding. I was very angry that he just expects to be waited on hand and foot. He did realise I was upset and apologised.

I threw my lunch away. I am worried that my temper is getting out of control. I want to talk to someone about it, but yet again there is no one.

***

I love my dad very much but he needs to want to get better. It must be hard losing your wife after 50 years of marriage, but he's lucky that he had 50 years, something I will never have.

This happened on the Saturday; Sunday was worse. Donna had an interview in London at 5.30pm. She went to work as normal. I decided to do some housework, a task I find very tiring and thankless. I always seem to get in a bad mood when doing this. I think it is down to the fact it's another job I have to do, when others living in the house could help. In my temper, I hit our bedroom door so hard against the wall it has made a hole. I am not proud of this, more ashamed that yet again my temper has got the better of me.

At approximately 4.20pm Louise received a text message from Donna saying that the sinks at work were blocked and she had to stay behind to help. I was fuming as I was driving Donna to London and we were pushed for time. We were hoping to leave home at 4.30pm to give us plenty of time to get to London. I messaged Donna back saying, 'Forget it, I won't drive and break my neck to get you to your interview you obviously had no intention of keeping to. Traffic will be bad because of the weather, no chance getting there now. We needed to leave at 4.30 at latest, you will have to keep working in a shithole.'

I would just like to say I have gone out of my way, arranging with work not once but twice, to leave early so I can drive Donna to London for this interview, and twice it had been cancelled. So I didn't want her to not turn up or be late for this one. When Donna got home I was so very angry, she said she had cancelled the interview. I was livid. We had such a big row which left all three of us girls in tears.

We eventually headed off to London in silence, we arrived at 6.40pm. As usual it was all my fault. Donna said I was a bad mother, plus other words. I replied, 'At least you have a mum.' To end it all Donna not once said thank you for taking her to London. If you ever read this, Donna, that hurts big time.

A friend has loaned me a book written by John Suchet whose wife has Alzheimer's. I am finding the book quite heart-wrenching and a little too close to home. In the book, John Suchet says he has a lot to thank Admiral Nursing for. This is the equivalent to a Macmillan nurse for cancer patients. I looked up Admiral Nursing on the internet and guess what, not available in my area. What a surprise.

John Suchet writes his book with such compassion. I feel so very guilty that all I feel is anger and loneliness. I wish my mum was still here. Or the very least that my sister gave a damn.

Derek fell up the stairs at home. He also tripped on the carer's stairs when I picked him up. Hope this is just a one off. I will have to keep note of this.

**

Half term and as a last-minute decision I arranged to drive to Devon to see Derek's cousin who owns a caravan on a farm. We travelled Saturday morning, stayed with his cousin and her husband for the day, then stayed at a Travelodge for the night. On the Sunday we stopped off at Lyme Regis and Burley. It made a nice break but I was very tired after driving such a long way.

Monday, I started dad at the centre where I work. This I hope will help him on his road to recovery. He didn't want to go, but I said to him what would mum want? That seemed to do the trick!

On the Tuesday Louise went to London to see *Les Misérables* with the youth theatre. Pick-up time was 12.30am but they were running late so pick-up was 1.30am. As usual I picked Louise up, but yet again it hit home how everyone depends on me. I sometimes get an overwhelming fear of how much people depend on me; part of me longs for someone to help carry this big load on my shoulders.

31 October. Halloween, my favourite time of the year, but today I have a lot of sadness in my heart. We usually have a party this time of year, but not this year. It seems my family has been severely reduced over the past year. I have felt so sad and alone.

I had decorated the passageway leading to the front door. It was lovely to hear the comments from the children – 'Awesome!' 'The scariest house!' It boosted my faith in life, if only for a couple of hours.

**

I phoned my sister as I was concerned about dad's health. He was complaining about dizziness and that he could not walk as his legs had seized up. I wanted to check with her that it wasn't just part of his breakdown that was causing this to happen. While we were talking, I asked if dad had said anything to her about the day centre. My sister asked why was I running dad to and from the centre? She said it wasn't fair on me and if for some reason I couldn't do this, she didn't want me to expect them to do the running around because she has other things to do on a Monday. Part of me cannot help wondering which part of that conversation was about me.

Went to visit dad on Sunday, the door was unlocked and I found him asleep in an unusual position as though he had just keeled over. I was worried that something was wrong, but he was OK. He said he was cold, so I put the heating on. I did get angry with dad as he was moaning about going to the centre tomorrow, and saying he wasn't well and he couldn't have a shower because it was too cold etc. I asked him if he wanted to get better? He said yes, he did. I replied that he had to have some input in it. At least he has the opportunity to get better. He replied that I didn't know what was going on in his head.

I feel so very sad when I see my dad like this. He was such a strong man and now he has become very dependent on others.

Today when taking dad and Derek to their clubs, Derek had another of his turns. He became very hot, with beads of sweat and looked pale. When he went to get out of the car he was giddy. He lay down in the back of the car while I took dad into his club. By this time I was in tears. I feel hopeless, alone and just want to run away. I hate feeling like this. I have forgotten what normal life is like, and all I see around me is illness. There comes a point when I am not sure anymore if my life will ever be happy again.

November 2011
Today I took Derek to the doctors about his episode yesterday. We saw a doctor who was brilliant. He explained that this was because of a drop in blood pressure which in turn is part of the Alzheimer's, so the diagnosis is the same as before.

As much as I was determined to not break down, my attempt was downright pathetic. I am ashamed to say I broke down when the word 'vascular' was mentioned. The doctor then turned to me and was concerned about my health. Guilt was what I felt for taking up Derek's appointment time. The doctor asked if I wanted an appointment to see him alone. I declined. As I am writing this I am in floods of tears.

2 November. Today I went to an Alzheimer's workshop in Bognor. Donna was supposed to go with me, but she couldn't get the time off work. Luckily I have a friend who owns a shop in Bognor who directed me to the correct building as I am not that familiar with the area.

I was one of the first to arrive, but as others started to turn up it became obvious that I was the youngest there. I felt dread and the sense that I didn't want to be there, and hoped that I didn't make an idiot of myself and start crying.
The workshop was kind of interesting, but at the end of the day it left me feeling like a rubbish carer. Yet again it highlighted the lack of compassion I feel towards Derek, and the absolute fear of letting down the brick wall I have built around me to protect me from my feelings.

3 November. Today at 8am dad phoned to say he wasn't going to the club anymore. I asked him why and he said because his nerves can't stand it and he didn't want to sit around for seven hours. I didn't argue with him, as I am starting to lose the will to help him. It seems whatever we do, it backfires on us. If Derek wasn't ill I would probably had a bit more patience with him, but I am starting to lose control of my feelings and I can feel myself slipping into a black hole with no escape.

***

I am not convinced that Derek's strange turns are anything to do with Alzheimer's, so when I was at the meeting yesterday I asked the Alzheimer's advocate if he had heard of this happening. He said that I should contact the CPN about it, so when I returned home I phoned Derek's nurse. She also was not familiar with this problem so she asked the psychiatric hospital to give me a call.

Just as I thought, they said it didn't seem to be anything to do with the Alzheimer's, and although they were at a loss as to what it could be, and as the doctors have done blood tests and an ECG, the best they could offer is to reduce the drug Citalopram from 20mg to 10mg and see if that makes a difference. It might be that the brain is getting too much serotonin.

***

It's my first day back at work after a week's holiday and I am feeling that it is time to change my job. I need to be with people who are not sick. I do not know how nurses cope working with the sick. It seems everywhere I look, everyone has a mental health problem. I can't clear my head, and think that life is like that for everyone.

21 November. After a lot of soul searching I have decided it is time to give up work. I just need the courage to do this. I know deep down it is the right thing to do but my head keeps trying to stop me. After deciding this on Friday evening I must admit I had the best weekend in a long time, as if a weight had been lifted off my shoulders. I want to spend more time finding myself. I am at my happiest when doing my psychic work and I think I need to spend more time doing this, and thanks to my auntie leaving me some money in her will I am able to do this financially. I have however checked with all the allowances we get to make sure that I am not jeopardising these by not working, but they all assure me that things will stay the same.

Giving up work means not only allowing time to find myself, but to also give more time to Derek. And we hopefully can visit people we never get to see, go for long walks and bike rides, spending more time with dad to help him on his recovery.

22 November. Today is not a good day. I am having second thoughts about giving up work after spending just one day at home with Derek. I am racking my brains as to what other job I could do, but I keep coming up with nothing.

Today Derek has left the downstairs tap running. Luckily I noticed it just before we left the house for Derek's dentist appointment. Derek was supposed to have two repairs done, but when the dentist asked him to bite down on the repaired tooth he bit down too hard and broke the repair. The dentist decided to file the tooth instead saying that his bite was too strong which made the repair undoable.

My first counselling session was a bit weird, the councillor was nothing how I expected her to be. She just sat opposite me and waited for me to speak. Of course straight away I started to cry, telling her my sad story and generally feeling sorry for myself. Not sure what good that was. Not feeling any benefit today, if anything I am feeling less positive about life in general. I just wish someone would wave a magic wand and all would be good again.

December 2011

I still haven't handed in my notice. I am still unsure as to what to do. I was so positive to start with, but now I worry that if I had no job to go to it would destroy me.

On Saturday Derek lost his glasses. He spent most of the day looking for them. This carried on until the Sunday, it was as though he had tunnel vision on finding his glasses. It became an obsession with him, resulting in Derek kicking a radiator and hitting a wall in his frustration. Sunday evening he found his glasses in a drawer he looked in many times over the weekend.

On Saturday I went out for an Indian meal with Anna and Jane, but I didn't feel comfortable as I had cystitis again. I just wanted to get back home. I am going back to my homeopath on Tuesday. Hopefully she can sort me out.

4 December. Tomorrow is my birthday. Derek was a little bit sad because he hadn't got me a present, but I said not to worry, he could buy me a Christmas present. That made him happy. He did offer to buy me some flowers, but I already had two lots of flowers in the house, so I said not to worry. Writing this makes me feel sad that I turned down the flowers, but deep down I think that maybe I didn't want anything from Derek because I wanted to feel punished for the way I feel about him and his illness. I don't feel I deserve anything from him.

My sister called round to see me and the first thing she said to me was, 'Just a flying visit, can't stay, just bought you some flowers for your birthday.' I hadn't seen my sister for a while and she still can't spare any time for me. My sister asked if I had received a card from dad, which I hadn't. She said she had asked dad to post it. Well I don't think that's going to happen as dad won't even walk to the shop to buy milk when he runs out. I ask myself, why didn't she just post it, as I did when it was her birthday? Probably didn't have time!

My sister's comment was, 'Well, if he didn't post it you're taking him to the dentist Tuesday, he will give you the card then.' That comment hurt more then she will ever understand. To top it all, when my sister left I looked out of the window and was surprised to see that my sister's husband was in the car and couldn't be bothered to come in to see me.

This evening was the light a candle service at Chichester Cathedral in aid of St Wilfrid's Hospice, which me and the girls were going to. But as the day progressed I realised that I could not go to the service because I knew it would be too upsetting. I seemed to have been so emotional, maybe as it gets closer to Christmas and mum's birthday this is what happens in the first year of them passing.

BIRTHDAY FROM HELL

At 8.30am dad phoned me to wish me many happy returns of the day. In the next breath he said he had fallen out of bed, broken his nose and there was blood everywhere. I told him I would come over as soon as possible, but I had to take Derek to his carer first. I then phoned my sister who said she had clients over. I was angry that she couldn't go and I hung up on her. She then rang back to say not to get angry with her. I said to her she always says she's busy. She started to have a go at me so I hung up.

I took Derek to his carer, then drove straight to dad's, let myself in, went upstairs. Dad was lying on the bed with blood over his face, bedsheet, carpet, door frame and with a bloody hankie. He tried to get out of bed but started to fall again. I put him back to bed. I didn't know whether to phone the doctor or dial 999. I went downstairs and Donna pointed out that there was water coming through the kitchen ceiling, by the lights. I then phoned my brother who said he would be straight over. I then phoned the doctor and explained what happened. They told me to call an ambulance.

The ambulance turned up and were very thorough with dad, checking all possible reasons for dad's fall. His nose was not broken, but cut and very red with carpet burns. It was noted that dad had been missing taking his pills, not drinking enough and possibly not eating enough. They asked for a doctor to come out and check a urine sample, to make sure that the cause was not an infection. At about 11am my sister turned up while the ambulance was still there. She was angry but stayed out of the way till the ambulance left. She asked me to come into the kitchen to sort out our grievances.

That's when all hell broke out. I can't remember what order things were said in, but I said about my sister never having time for family, that friends came before family, and she admitted that her friends were more important, that dad was her family, and she had to keep her distance from me and my problems. She wanted nothing to do with them. She talked about how hard it was for her to deal with dad at the mental hospital, and mum's illness, about how I shared my problems with mum who then shared them with her which burdened her. How she felt put upon, just because she had no family. But I replied, it's not just because she has no children, I have a sick husband. Her reply was 'And don't we all know it?' What's that supposed to mean? Does she think I use that excuse as a sympathy vote, because if I do it's not my intention, sympathy is not what I am looking for.

What I told my sister I regret, but I said how mum was hurt that she didn't have time for her, that she was always in a hurry. I guess it had to be said, but I don't feel good telling her this. But I was angry and hurt by her comments. I also asked my sister what would happen if anything happened to her husband and she was left alone, she would need her family then. Her reply was, it would be no different than being an only child.

My sister then went on to say that she is happy on her own, she wanted to be left on her own, how she felt lonely as a child as she didn't fit in and would rather play on her own. This I found hard to accept as I remember a different childhood. I am now quite worried about my sister; I just don't understand her thought or reason. She has made it so clear that she does not do family life, end of. Another comment she made was that she felt uncomfortable at family gatherings and didn't enjoy them.

I am going to leave this subject here, for I think I have said enough. My head is throbbing with what has gone on today; it's almost as though I was whisked away to another planet for the day, it's the only way I can describe it. After all this, I had a counselling session, then a doctor's appointment to confirm that I had yet again got a urine infection, so back on the old antibiotics.

Did I have a nice birthday? Well I still have presents and cards to open, but it's now 12.09 on 6 December.

No birthday card from dad or Derek.

***

We now have to sort out some sort of care package for dad, as he is not looking after himself.

Decided to write a letter to my sister.

I just feel I needed to write to you. I am very concerned about how you feel about family life, and how you feel the need to distance yourself from myself and our brother.

I feel that this is probably part of your grieving process. I understand how hard it was to see dad in his mental health state, and to watch mum battle her illness, knowing how close you two were. But we all felt that pain too. I am truly sorry that mum burdened you with my problems, but being part of a family is sharing problems, especially with your mum. When my girls have a problem they turn to me, that's just the way life is. I am truly sorry that this caused pain to you.

If I am totally wrong and you truly don't want anything to do with me then I will just have to accept that.

I have never asked for yours or anyone else's help with Derek and I sure as hell am not asking for any sympathy. Life is what it is and we just have to deal with it the best way we can, and I am sorry you were involved.

In an ideal world, family support is what gets us through the bad times, but I guess you do not believe this. Just know I will always be your sister, that is how it's supposed to be, and I will be here for you whatever.

20 December. WELL LAST WEEK I HANDED IN MY NOTICE AT WORK. I had been thinking about it for some time, and without thinking I asked to meet with the two owners and just blurted it out. It seemed the right thing to do at the time. I hope I don't regret it.

Part of me is excited, wondering what my new adventure will be. I have not told Derek or my dad yet. I wanted to spend more time with dad, but I am not sure if that will happen, as when I am with him he brings my mood down. It's as if he has no incentive to get better, he continually says the heating does not work and he is not washing or taking his medication. It's almost as if he has given up; I just don't know how to help him. Even Christmas has not lifted his mood, I am glad he is going to my sister's for Christmas, as we as a family need some cheer. Dad has not given us a Christmas card as yet. I believe he will not do cards for the family and no presents, which I think is hard on the grandchildren, not because of no present but that he can't be bothered. I am cross that dad has become so self-absorbed that the outside just doesn't exists.

Derek is no better, in fact I think there is a slight decline. He is in his own world. He shows no emotion, his manners are rude in as much as he burps out loud with no pardon and eats like he is starving. A good example of this is last night I opened a packet of my favourite honey-roasted cashew nuts. Derek was sitting in the next chair. I asked him if he wanted some, hoping he would put out his hand for me to tip some into it; but no, he took the packet and eat the lot, putting them into his mouth as quick as possible!

22 December. Derek was out with his carer. I was finishing off the housework when there was a knock on the door. When I went to open the door I was surprised to see Derek's sister and her husband. She asked if Derek was home, I said no. She said what a shame. What I should have said was that there were 364 other days in the year that he is home. She handed me two envelopes and said they were from mum for the girls, then walked away.

Derek seems to be constantly on edge. He goes out for walks many times in a day; if he's not out, he is sitting with his eyes closed.

We had my brother and his family over for Christmas Eve. We played some games, but Derek found them too difficult, especially with all the noise going on.

25 December. Christmas turned out to be better than expected. It was quiet and enjoyable. Dad went to my sister's mid-morning after spending Christmas Eve with us. Derek didn't show much emotion when given presents, and needed to be prompted by the girls to give me my present, which by the way I got from Amazon and paid extra for it to be gift wrapped. Derek gave me a Christmas card, but forgot to write in it.

***

Derek's behaviour has become quite bizzare, continuously charging his phone while hiding it under the chair in the conservatory, having pieces of paper in his pocket with numbers on, and he had some £20 notes in his pocket which I do not know where they came from. When I asked him he said he didn't know. Derek has become very secretive.

26 December. We all went to Southampton to see *Peter Pan*. Donna sat next to Derek. Afterwards Donna said she didn't know why dad came as he sat through most of the performance folding and unfolding his jacket, paying no attention to the play.

2012

January 2012

A new year and I wish a new start.

Derek has, I believe, taken the next step in his Alzheimer's deterioration. Since Christmas he has become more unsettled, continually going upstairs looking through drawers, wandering about the house, constantly going out for walks, losing his glasses and getting confused as to which glasses he should be wearing. I can feel his decline slowly pulling me down, I am getting so angry with him, even though I know he can't help it. I wanted 2012 to hold new hope for us, but if l am honest it will be the same old same old.

Matters are not helped by the fact that dad just doesn't get any better. I don't even know how to help him anymore. Anything I suggest to him he doesn't want to do. I called round on Sunday and now he is saying that some premium bonds have been stolen. It's just never-ending.

One good thing has happened. Louise has got into Southdown's College to study performing arts. Both Louise and I cried when we found out.

6 January. I left work. The day was OK up till the last five minutes when a lovely crystal butterfly was presented to me. I could not stop the tears and some of the staff were tearful too. I stand by my decision to leave, I just hope I have done the right thing.

26 January. How time flies. It's been almost three weeks since I left work. So far I am enjoying being at home. I don't know how I found the time to work! Progress is going well in clearing out the loft. I have also cleared out the large shed of unwanted rubbish, but I can only do this on a Friday when Derek is with his carer. When I told Derek his face was like thunder and I was frightened as to what he would do, but when he went down in the shed he was pleased with what I had done and he had tears in his eyes and apologised for being angry. Already made three trips to the tip, plus charity shop, the rest we will boot sale and eBay.

***

Towards the end of last week Derek lost his house keys. After much searching I phoned my brother to find out the cost of replacing the lock. This was quite an expensive job so I said I would leave it for a while, hoping the keys would turn up. While searching Derek's drawers and pockets not only did I find t-shirts and jumpers put away dirty, but a small piece of paper with a phone number on it.

Yet again I was suspicious of this phone number. I dialled it and a female answered, I didn't recognise the voice, then hung up. I told the girls about it and Louise said she would phone it. She phoned on the pretence of getting a wrong number. When she asked who she was calling the person on the other end said 'Sara'. Alarm bells started ringing as I know Derek's ex-girlfriend had two children, now adults, and I think the girl was called Sara. Anyway, not able to leave it at that, I asked Derek about his ex-girlfriend Jen and the two children she had and their names, but he couldn't remember, or maybe he pretended to not know. I am sorry, but they say that people with Alzheimer's can remember in the past so excuse me if I find that Derek not remembering a part of his past prior to me a bit strange. I asked him outright about the phone number in his pocket. His reply was that she gave him the number. I asked him when did he see her. Derek then became confused and didn't understand what I was saying.

This is when the disease messes up my head. Is Derek lying or does he really not remember, and if he's that bad why is he contacting an ex-girlfriend? I don't believe that the handwriting on the piece of paper is Derek's, so whose is it? Derek only visits his brother so I can't understand who gave him the number, unless it was his brother. So many questions and yet no answers.

I got very angry with Derek, and said if he wanted to go back to his ex-girlfriend he could. I would divorce him. He said he was sorry and wouldn't do it again, but he said that last time.

I feel that my marriage has become a mockery, with Derek wanting to contact his ex-girlfriend, and I feel so very sad for the girls who have to live with the fact that their dad feels it's OK to carry on like this.

Derek eventually found his keys in his dressing gown pocket.

***

Went round to dad's on Friday after receiving a phone call from my cousin to say that her mum, my dads' sister, was in hospital with a severe case of pneumonia. I didn't want to relay the message via the phone to dad so I called in to see him. He didn't seem overly concerned, when I told him the news.

One piece of news that did concern me was that dad said he was going for a brain scan to see if he has any form of dementia. This not only shocked me but upset me that the medical profession would even think that dad had dementia.

31 January. Already we are almost into February. I am getting more stressed and my tolerance of Derek is getting weaker. Not only does he not understand the simplest of words, he hovers about the house doing less and less. His obsessions about having the same cup to drink out of, to have the orange towel to dry with, to have the TV magazine within eye distance, the remote to be within reach of him etc., it's all doing my head in. And still I try to hold a conversation with him, but to no avail. I am so fed up with my life, there seems to be no let up, no escape, no help.

I have been racking my brains to decide what I can do as a celebration for Donna's 21st and my 50th, but in reality I am just going to concentrate on Donna's birthday. There is no way I can go away as I have no one to keep an eye on Derek. And at the end of the day Donna's 21st is more important. This makes me sad that I can't even celebrate my birthday with Derek. In fact at the moment everything makes me sad.

February 2012
7 February. Well at long last, with help from my brother, we have emptied the loft. Mind you, we cannot move in the lounge now as all the loft contents are scattered, filling it. It's a nice feeling knowing you have achieved something.

10 February. It's been quite a stressful week. I have not left the house, as it's taken all week to sort out the loft contents, boxing up boot sale items, items to keep, labelling, and in the end I had to have a skip delivered as there were lots of items no longer wanted. I found our wedding cards and acceptance-to-the-wedding letters, but in the end I binned them. I am also selling my wedding dress as I feel I no longer need these items. Derek will not know either way, so it's best I don't hang on to the past.

***

Whilst sorting out the loft contents, I came across a box belonging to Derek, with lots of cards, valentines, loving gifts, and a few photos of the woman whom Derek has been trying to make contact with. Also there were letters from her kids asking Derek to visit them. These were from before I knew Derek, but I am puzzled to know why he has kept them for so many years. My mind starts to question my marriage. Did Derek only marry me because I was young enough to have children? My head is so confused. I think back to our first years together, and I see no reason to doubt Derek's love for me, but I can't reason why this woman has a hold over Derek, and why he has so much proof in this box from the loft of their love together. And the sad thing is, I can't even ask him about it. I also found in amongst our wedding cards an embroidered wedding card from her.

A couple of things I have come to notice about Derek's illness. He has been muttering behind my back and using swear words, he has also been putting on two vests with a t-shirt and wondering why it's uncomfortable. When questioned about the swear words he denies it of course. We have also noticed that Derek has put on lots of weight around his middle. This could be due to the amount of biscuits he consumes during the day.

14 February. Valentine's Day, not that it makes any difference to me, just another day. Yesterday, for the first time, Derek frightened me. I was tidying up the kitchen and there was a paper folded up on the kitchen stool, one of those free mags with offers in. I picked it up and tore it in half to put out for the recycling. Derek, quick as lightning, strode across the kitchen with his fist raised ready to hit me, because he thought I picked up his TV mag. I was quite shaken up because I wasn't expecting that reaction. I am finding that Derek has more anger in him. I don't know if this is due to the emptying of the loft or the progression of the disease.

Today Derek has gone to his carer for an extra day, I have decided to go into the shed, as since we have put all the boxes from the loft into the shed, Derek has decided to spend some time in there. I found Derek had moved boxes around, and had emptied the shed loft of more books, so I had to rearrange the boxes again and tidy it yet again. I also whitewashed the window to the shed to protect the boxes from getting sun-damaged in the summer. I just don't know how I am going to stop Derek from moving things around in the shed. Repeatedly Derek keeps telling us that it's his shed and his house. This hurts both myself and the girls.

15 February. Today Derek got angry at us again accusing me of hiding his shed keys, which I didn't do. He obviously has mislaid them again, the same as he mislaid his house keys a few weeks ago. My brother's daughter, who was staying with us, wanted to go home as she wasn't feeling too well so I arranged to meet my brother halfway. When we got back home I couldn't open the front door with my key. Derek had locked us out. Donna had put on a wash before we left and the dial was turned off when we got back, plus she had put some items on the landing to take downstairs later and they had been spread over the landing. I find this quite worrying how Derek's behaviour is changing. When questioned he denied it all. The following morning Derek did apologise, saying he had found his keys in his coat pocket.

Derek is getting more confused about the days. Today he bought a new TV mag in the middle of the week. It seems that he looks through the TV mag and then decides what day it is. No matter who tells him it's the wrong day, he still insists on keeping the magazine open on that day.

Another thing is becoming apparent, Derek is constantly looking for and changing over his glasses. He obviously finds it very difficult to distinguish between reading and distance glasses.

I am sitting in the dining room now and I can hear Derek talking to himself and constantly turning over the pages of the TV magazine.

***

Yesterday I went to visit an ex-work colleague. On the way I stopped at the local greengrocer to buy some flowers. As I got out of the car I came face to face with Derek's niece. You know when you're about to say hello but something stops you? Well that happened to me. We just looked at each other and carried on as if we hadn't seen each other. That was a very awkward moment, but I do believe she had no intention of acknowledging me. I was glad that I had not said hello, as I am almost sure she had no intention of speaking to me.

Over the last couple of days I have not been feeling too great, not ill but just not right. I have been feeling giddy and today I have had a headache all day. This could be to do with stress or maybe my age. I wish I could talk to mum about the symptoms of the menopause, there is no one I can talk to. Yet again I feel so alone. It's very hard to explain how I feel, but I guess the best way to describe it is part of me feels like I am living a parallel life in another world, and the other part of me is here in this nightmare of a life, having to deal with the two males in my life with mental health issues. I don't know if the way I feel is a protective coping mechanism.

25 February. Today yet again Derek got very confused about the TV mag. For some unknown reason he had purchased the end of week magazine on Wednesday which means he had two mags. He asked me what today was and I said it was Saturday. He replied that he needed to get a new TV mag. I explained that he had already got this week's, so I took the old TV mag away, gave him the new one, but then he started looking at Thursday's page. I got angry then upset. Derek also started crying, and hitting his head with his fists. I felt so helpless, part of me wanted to put my arms around him and say it's OK, but I couldn't do this. Why, I don't know. I feel so ashamed at not being able to show my emotion. I am just rubbish at showing any compassion. It's yet again the fear of losing control of everything. In the end I opened the page to Saturday and paper-clipped the pages open.

***

At long last we have a meeting with the doctor at my request. I want to have Derek reassessed to see how far into the Alzheimer's he is, but I am not holding my breath as I have learnt over the years not to expect too much from the doctors.

March 2012
Met up with Susan at the garden centre. We had coffee and chatted for a while. I got very emotional. Even after all this time I still get upset when talking about Derek, and only Susan truly knows how I feel as she is going through the same nightmare. Anyway, we decided to have lunch which Susan treated me to, which was a lovely gift.

The next day I had a carers' meeting at the psychiatric hospital. I was the first to arrive and at first thought I would be the only one, but thankfully three other ladies arrived. We had a good meeting, it helps to know that there are others out there dealing with this evil disease.

Lesley who organised the meeting was Derek's original nurse. I asked her how I could help the girls to understand their dad's illness when I am having problems myself. She asked me why I was beating myself up about this, and that I was doing the best I can and the girls were a credit to me. This made me feel more positive, but at the end of the day I will never stop beating myself up, as I always feel I could do better.

I asked Derek to clean the car out for me and to wash it as I hadn't had time to do it and it would give him something to do. Well, other than putting the car mats back in upside down and missing large parts of the car when washing, I guess he did an OK job. But even that's an indicator of how the illness has progressed.

9 March. Went shopping with Donna in Portsmouth, but became unwell. I couldn't wait to get home. I think it was a kind of panic attack, but I phoned the doctor and I am having blood tests and an ECG to check

***

Two days on and still I don't feel 100%. Headaches and dizziness and very tired. Also I feel a tightness around my chest. I can't pretend I am not worried. I am. For if I am not well who will look after the girls? And everything else?

My sister's birthday was on 8 March. I sent her a card and present, as I couldn't face her after what she said, but today is 11 March and I have not received a thank you as yet.

11 March. Last night for tea I made a pasta bake with garlic bread. Only Derek and Louise had some. There were four slices of garlic bread left on the table, ready to put out for the birds in the morning. After we had all had breakfast, Derek was pointing to where the bread was on the table and was mumbling. I thought that he had given the bread to the birds, but no. Turns out he had eaten it. How bizarre, he had eaten breakfast and then garlic bread which had been left out all night. The girls laughed and said we had better watch out what we leave lying around now.

13 March. Had a review from Crossroads Care to update records. I was surprised, how much had changed in a year, i.e. records showed we had a rabbit, hamster and fish. Now we just have fish. Also my sister was listed as a stand-in carer. If I were to become ill, that obviously had to be changed. For some reason, Derek's date of birth was not correct either.

14 March. At 6.25am I was woken up by Derek's constant movement in bed and his mutterings and his bloody mobile kept beeping because the battery was low. No wonder I feel so stressed. I also feel resentment at having been woken up and my stress level has risen already. I can't continue to carry on this way, yet I know it will get worse, it always does with this evil disease.

Today we also received a wedding invitation from Derek's sister to her daughter's wedding. I personally do not want to go and the girls have said the same. I was going to ask if Derek's carer wanted to take him, but to be honest I don't think it's a good idea for Derek to go as it would probably confuse him too much, what with all the people, half of which he wouldn't know, plus the noise at the reception would be too much.

15 March. Today I had a doctor's appointment to find out the results of the ECG and blood test. All was OK, but I broke down and cried when I got in to the room. I feel I am losing control of everything. Last night after picking up the girls from dancing I sat outside the house and cried, I didn't want to go indoors. When I did go inside I went upstairs and I could hear Louise in the shower crying her eyes out.

***

I feel completely useless and stupid for losing control. I should be setting a good example to the girls not breaking down. When I got back from the doctors I phoned our social worker to say I couldn't cope. She said that because Derek was over 65 now she would pass our case on to the older persons' department, who in turn phoned me and made an appointment to meet us next Thursday .

When the carer came today he thought I was unwell. I broke down again. I think he was very worried about me and offered to come and stay for a weekend to look after Derek. I thought that was very kind of him and I may well take him up on his offer.

Out of complete desperation, and worried for my own mental health, I contacted Derek's cousin to ask her if she could help with having Derek stay with her for a while. Talk about bad timing. She had had a fall and fractured her right elbow, and two weeks before got rid of her spare bed. She was very sympathetic. I apologised for having to ask, but she replied that she would do her best to see what she could offer us in the way of some care.

That evening I went to my meditation course, but I found it very difficult to empty the problems out of my head. My tutor gave me some spiritual healing, and I really did feel a lot better after this. It really is amazing how spiritual healing works, I would recommend it to anyone. It feels like the piece of me that went missing last week has returned.

17 March. Louise and I went to the pictures, just to give us a break. When we got home, Donna was back from work. She said when she got home Derek was crying. I asked Derek what was wrong. He said that his head was getting worse. I asked him if he knew what was wrong with him and he said yes, Alzheimer's. We were both very tearful. I wanted to wrap my arms around him and say it's all going to be OK, but it's not, is it? Just for a fraction of a second I got a glimpse of my Derek, but then it was gone again.

18 March. Mothers' Day. Today dad was going to come over for tea, but I woke up this morning to the sound of Derek retching and when I got up he said he had been sick three times. We did have a Chinese last night but I think we would all be sick if it was that, so I am not sure how today is going to go.

Spent the day doing housework. Had to cancel dad coming over as I didn't want him to become sick. Had some lovely gifts from the girls, and watched a film in the evening. We couldn't visit Derek's mum for the same reason dad didn't visit. ·

19 March. Had to buy some more flowers for Derek's mum as the ones I purchased a couple of days ago didn't look too good. I put them in a reusable vase with a bow to make them look good. We went to Bosham where Derek's mum lives, just Derek and myself. As we walked into her room I was shocked at how she had deteriorated, but also because not only was the TV on but the CD player as well. The combination of the two was too much, it reminded me of a caged animal. In fact, I don't think you would keep a caged animal in these conditions, so why would you leave a 93-year-old woman with Alzheimer's in a room on her own with both TV and CD player on quite loud? It doesn't make sense to me; it also upset me.

Now I have never got on with Derek's mum but to see her being left like this I think is inhumane. I could see she had deteriorated since the last time we saw her. She was confused as to who Derek was. We didn't stay long, I didn't want Derek there too long. Derek's mum started to cry. I didn't know what to do. I went downstairs to see if anyone was on duty, but there was no one around except the cleaner, who I spoke to about how upset Derek's mum was. She said she would make a note of it and said that she was usually OK. Maybe it upset her to see Derek, who knows? I do believe that I won't take Derek down there again, it's too traumatic.

***

For me to see Derek's mum and how she has deteriorated, it shows me what I have coming my way. Derek in his state of mind would not see the situation his mum is in, but I know in my heart if he was not ill himself he would not let this happen to his mum. I know I shouldn't be too eager to judge Derek's family, but I do have more insight into this disease as I am living with it.

20 March. Today Derek was very tearful. He just sat at the kitchen table crying, I asked what was wrong but other than saying his head, there was no other reason. I thought maybe listening to music might help so I gave him an MP3 player with his music on, but sadly that just made him cry more.

21 March. I was just about to go out to buy myself a new pillow as Derek had decided to take mine (not sure how that came about) when my neighbour, who is moving tomorrow, called out for a chat. He asked how Derek was and said that a man came to his house that morning to help clear his garden and Derek was talking to him. The man then asked my neighbour about Derek, saying he seemed unwell. My neighbour said if a stranger noticed how Derek was he must be getting worse. He also mentioned that he had talked to Derek about the football and Derek didn't seem to understand what he was saying. I said that Derek had become worse since Christmas. My neighbour then said he didn't know how I coped. I told him that last week I couldn't and I felt very low. He gave me his mobile number and said to ring him anytime for a chat and a bottle of wine. I thought this was very sweet of him to offer.

22 March. Today our new social worker is coming to hopefully help sort out some kind of care package. The appointment is for 9am at our house. As I am writing this it's 9.40 and guess what, no social worker. I can feel my anger building up. Not even a phone call to say she is running late! But hey we're not important, just a number to sort as and when we have time. Shit I have to stop being so cynical.

I am starting to feel edgy now, what to do? I have no contact number for the social worker so I will have to contact the nurse to get it, but I am so annoyed. I feel like just leaving it and forgetting social services, but I need a break and Louise needs a break. She is getting tired with the stress of her GCSEs and home life.

9.48 the doorbell rings and the social worker arrives with the excuse of her car breaking down. I must admit I was a bit off with her because of her lateness. The social worker agrees that we need respite and more care. She is setting out a plan for more funding and to look at us having a holiday, us being me and the girls.

April 2012
The months are flying by. As of today (the 2 April) I have heard nothing from the social worker, not even a phone call to pass on the information on the care plan we are supposed to be looking at. I don't think that the social worker fully understood just how much we need respite care. I get so angry at Derek for not understanding what I am asking him, it's driving me crazy. I fully understand he cannot help it, it's part of his illness, so why do I get so angry? HELP.

3 April. Donna came home from work saying my sister had texted her saying that she was there for her. This I found bizarre, when she had made it quite obvious that she wanted nothing to do with us as a family. It was like rubbing salt into my wounds. Plus Louise said what about her? Why is she only there for Donna?

Part of me wants to phone her up and ask what she is playing at, but I know that by doing this I will lose my temper and say things I might later regret.

It's been two weeks since the social worker came round and I have heard nothing since, so I am not holding on to any ideas of us having respite anytime soon.

It's half term but Louise has had to go into school to revise for her GCSEs, so it's made going out for days a little difficult. Derek is going to his carer a couple more days this week to give us a kind of break, but it's not enough.

***

The social worker said that they have agreed to increase Derek's direct payment and they will fund respite, which can be taken now. The nurse holding the meeting said that I should have phoned every day and made a nuisance of myself to get them to listen to my cry for help.

This has now taken Derek's illness to another level in my head. If I felt scared and alone before, this has now been doubled. I feel sick with worry as to how Derek will feel being put into care for a week.

On my way home I visited a dementia home, but I knew almost straight away that it wasn't the place for Derek. To start with the clients were over 80, plus the staff were foreign and I had trouble understanding them so Derek would have no chance.

5 April. I visited a nursing home recommended by the social worker; it was in Selsey. The building was listed and very old-world looking, with lots of character. One of the members of staff was at the same secondary school as me.

This home was for dementia patients and they said they had clients aged 50 plus – not that I saw anyone there of that age. There was a day centre attached which ideally was where Derek would go to do activities and then transfer at teatime to the care home. Louise came with me to look around. We could choose which room we wanted Derek to stay in. I told the member of staff who showed us around that I would let her know. I really wanted to sleep on it.

I understand that I will never find the ideal home for Derek, but several things about this home are playing on my mind. One, that I didn't see anyone of Derek's age at the home; two, the activity room had no tables to work at so I am not sure what activities, if any, were organised; three, when walking around the building I noticed some double doors wide open which clients could have walked out of; and lastly, while we were there, a client was calling out to be helped and the lady showing us around said she would attend to him in a while. She then carried on showing us around and I am not sure if the client did get help. This worries me.

8 April. Easter Day. I receive a text from my friend Jane saying to give her mum-in-law a call, as she is worried about Louise. Turns out that we can ask for special allowances when Louise takes her exams and the examiners must be told of her problems at home. If I get no joy from the school I must let Jane's mum-in-law know, and they know someone who can help. I now have to wait until half term ends to make an appointment with the school without Louise knowing.

9 April. Donna is unwell and finding it hard to breathe. I am taking her to St Richard's Hospital for an out-of-hours doctor's appointment. The doctor thinks it's her asthma playing up and she is put on a nebuliser. I think it's to do with stress.

***

I had a busy day with an appointment at the psychiatric hospital with Derek, followed by looking around care homes. The doctor spent, as promised, an hour with us talking to Derek and I. She could see Derek had deteriorated from the last appointment about a year ago, and when I asked she said his illness was out of the early stage and now moderate+.

In total I have looked around six care homes. Not sure what I am looking for really as there is no place like home. I have narrowed my choice down to two – one on Hayling Island, Hampshire, the other in Bognor, West Sussex – so hopefully one of these will be acceptable to social services. I really don't feel good about doing this, but I guess the time has come to seek more help, and as I will not get it from family the next best thing has to be a care home.

There was a lot of toing and froing with social services to fund a home in Hampshire. At first they wanted me to top up £10 each week, which I agreed to, then they said it could be as much as £100 each week. I said I would not pay that amount and would just have to carry on looking after Derek without the break. The social worker said to leave it with her and she would see what she could do. Later that same day she phoned me back to say an emergency fund had been set up and they would pay the full amount. Result or what?

***

The date has been set for Derek to go into a dementia-only care home for two weeks from 18 April. I have decided not to tell him until the day before so as not to cause any agro. I am not proud of having to do this. I feel I have failed not only myself but Derek too. I never thought I would be putting him into respite this early into his illness, but friends I have spoken to say I am doing the right thing.

***

The doctor from the psychiatric hospital said at a meeting when they discussed Derek's case that at this moment in time they didn't think it necessary for Derek to have another scan. Well no surprises there; I didn't think for one moment the outcome would be any different.

***

I have been going through Derek's clothes, washing and labelling them, and packing them into a case which is kept in Donna's room, so as to not alert Derek to what's going on. I am dreading telling him, just the look on his face will break my heart.

Telling Derek about his break away went better then anticipated. I know he didn't understand a lot about how I explained I needed a break, but maybe that was better than listening to me twittering on.

18 April. Derek was quite angry at the prospect of going away from home, hitting doors and banging walls, but he got into the car no problem. I drove him down to Hayling, parked in the car park and although Derek's face showed anger I had no problems getting him into the building. The staff were very friendly and chatted and joked with Derek. It was as if he was a changed person. We went to look at his room, but I was concerned that it smelt of wee, so the home asked the maintenance person to shampoo the carpet for us.

When I went to leave, Derek said that he liked it there, which was a great relief to me. I phoned later that evening and all was OK with him. On the same day me and the girls went to Southampton to buy a kitten. We are calling her Skye. She's a beautiful black and white fluffy female, very cute. We have two weeks to settle her in before Derek comes home. It was nice to hear the girls laughing and having fun last night with the kitten.

***

It's amazing how such a small animal can make a big difference to everyone. Louise is much less stressed, and both girls are working together to look after Skye. I have to admit I never really appreciated just how much a small kitten needs looking after – at the moment she is into everything.

***

The first two days of Derek being in respite took its toll on me, with very little sleep and being sick and having an upset tummy. I think this was paired with the fact of having a kitten, and hoping I had made the right decision in letting the girls have one.

I have been phoning the care home each day and all seems OK. I was going to go and visit Derek at the weekend, but when I phoned on Friday they said he was wanting to come home so I decided to wait until he was a little more settled.

23 April. Went for my counselling today and for the very first time I did not shed a tear. I talked about how relaxed the girls were having a new kitten, and how our life has got a more normal feel to it and how much more positive I felt towards life.

That evening Donna and I went to visit Derek.

He came down the stairs in jeans and vest. He was crying his eyes out and asked if I had come to take him home. I was shocked at how disoriented he was, confused more than normal and very tearful. He showed us to his room. He said he liked his room and the staff, but he said that everybody was talking about him. He was a little paranoid. He had packed some blankets into his suitcase – not sure why – and wanted to know when he could come home. I wanted to pack his case and bring him home there and then, but I knew I needed the full two-week break.

I am not sure how long we were at the home. Not that long but it was Derek who told us to go. So we settled him on the bed watching *Coronation Street* with a large bar of chocolate. I promised that the next time he saw me I would be bringing him home. On the way home Donna had a cry; she said she thought Derek was going to be much worse.

We came home to a kitten who had pooed and then walked it into every surface in the bathroom, including over her feet, tummy and head. We had to wash down the bathroom and then bathe the kitten in the sink. The only good thing to come out of that was Louise didn't ask how dad was.

***

I have decided not to visit Derek again until I pick him up on 2 May. The nurse came yesterday to see how I was. I told her how shocked I was to see Derek in a bit of a state. She said that it was possible that when he comes home he may still be unsettled and it could take a few days for him to return to his previous mental state. The nurse asked how I was going to be when Derek returns. I asked her what she meant and she said about me self-harming! I was shocked to think she thought I was self-harming. I replied that I had not self-harmed, yes when I get annoyed or angry I hit my hands against the wall, but is that self-harming?

28 April. Wednesday, when I pick Derek up from the home, is fast approaching. I have mixed emotions about this. It's been nice not having the tension in the house, it's made me realise that a normal life still exists out there; I also feel this last week has dragged a bit. I think that's because I feel sad that Derek has had to spend time away from us, but I hope in time he will want to go into respite and life will be a little easier for us. I must admit I am a little worried about how Derek will react once back home.

***

A couple of changes I have made whilst Derek has been away, namely the front door has been repainted and I have bought a new mattress, not that I expect Derek to notice this change.

30 April. In two days I will be picking Derek up from the home and I have still not received payment to pay for his stay. I am worried that the money will not come through by Wednesday. I have yet again chased this up. I have been feeling a little unsettled the last couple of days, not sure if this is due to Derek's return or my conscience about leaving Derek for so long.

I wondered if Derek's brother might phone to ask if Derek was OK, as he hadn't seen him for a couple of weeks, but there has been no call. I have enjoyed the time at home with the girls, the house has been relaxing, no shouting, bad tempers, banging doors, bad language, and that's just from me.

I guess that what I am about to admit can only make sense to those who have lived this nightmare, but I am not looking forward to Derek coming home. The feeling of dread has overcome me. I like not having his presence at home, hard as that might be to openly admit. I have had enough of tears, bad tempers and no communication with him. I want

92

some kind of life back. I am surprised at how well I have coped on my own with the girls. I have felt most relaxed, enjoying both girls' company, and we have attended two events at the school (one at which Louise gained four awards), gone out for a meal, and friends of the girls have visited. And most importantly laughter.

***

I picked Derek up from the home on my own. I was full of mixed emotions, because I wasn't sure how he would be, but I needn't have worried. It was almost as if he was drugged. He didn't say much, in fact that was yesterday and since he's been home he has just slept.

Our first meal together was fraught and in the end I moved Louise into the lounge to eat. The girls stayed out of Derek's way which left me in charge of the kitten, as she is still confined to the kitchen. All I could smell was the home on Derek and his clothes, so I washed all of his clothes. I must have a very sensitive nose. I found a missing t-shirt and facecloth, found someone else's t-shirt and Derek's reading glasses are missing. Oh well, these things are meant to try us I suppose.

Going back to picking up Derek, I apologised to the home as I couldn't make the payment for Derek's stay because I had still not received the money to do this. Twice in the last week of Derek's stay I chased up the social worker to say I hadn't received payment for his stay. They say I should receive it in the next couple of weeks. I feel this is disgraceful and I should never have been put in that embarrassing position.

May 2012
12 May. Today I received the long-awaited cheque to pay for Derek's respite care. I had chased it up again during the week. I just don't think it's good enough that we had to wait this long for the payment. I now have to pay this into the bank which will take a further five days to clear.

***

Since Derek has come back from respite he has been extremely sleepy. He has also been talking a lot in his sleep, sometimes going to bed as early as 7pm and sometimes waking at 5am. I find his behaviour very odd; maybe this is another step in his deterioration?

13 May. Went out for a meal to celebrate dad's birthday. Can you believe that Derek fell asleep at the table?

18 May. Went and paid the long overdue payment for Derek's stay. His shirt and lost glasses were waiting for me. I was a little annoyed that the home had not phoned to tell me they had found Derek's glasses, as tomorrow we pick up his new ones at a cost of £50.

Have booked an appointment for Derek to see a doctor on Monday just to check that he hasn't got a water infection, which could be why he is so sleepy.

21 May. Derek had a doctor's appointment to see if they could shed any light on Derek being so sleepy. The doctor said it was probably to do with taking the Mirtazapine at morning time as he knows of no one who takes this medication in the morning. It is sometimes given to patients who can't sleep because of its sleeping capabilities and the doctor questioned why they were given in the morning. I couldn't remember, so I went over my notes because the doctor had no medical notes as to why this was so. Luckily, my notes revealed that Derek was having upset stomachs from this drug and the nurse had told us to change to morning.

24 May. Yesterday I had yet another skip delivered, as the rubbish seems to accumulate. The little shed was in need of a sort out, my aim being it would make a good shelter for Skye if we went out for the day. Louise and I creosoted the outside of the shed and emptied the rubbish. Even the old rabbit hutch was there, dismantled and placed in this shed. For what reason, I do not know!

***

The last two days I have worked very hard, sorting out things we no longer need; but yesterday yet again it was thrown in my face that it's Derek's house, shed, garden. My anger yet again is welling up inside of me. If I could, I would find somewhere else to live. I am almost certain that if it wasn't for the illness Derek would not be saying this to me, and I wouldn't feel the need to get the house and garden in some manageable order.

Whilst writing this Derek has just walked in with a baby blue tit in his hands. I thought at first it may have fallen out of its nest, but when I went down the garden another one came out of the box to take their first flight. Derek obviously didn't understand this and thought it was OK to handle the baby.

31 May. This week has been stressful with Derek losing his shed keys and yet again accusing me of hiding them. He is becoming angry and has no understanding of what's being said to him. Yesterday he also lost the two padlocks to the sheds and the padlock which opens the side gate. How on earth you can lose that number of items in a week I do not understand. This morning I thought I would use my pendulum to find some of the missing items, so I got my spare set of shed keys to open the large shed, only to find that something had been broken off in the lock. So there is no way anybody can get into the shed now. I called my brother to see if he could help. I feel awful having to bother him again, but I am hoping he can fix it without too much expense.

***

Susan came over during the week to see Skye. I made us a coffee then Derek came and sat with us the whole time, so it was difficult to talk. She did however say that they were closing down the ward where her husband is, so her poor husband will have to be moved to another care facility. I am so angry that this is allowed to happen.

***

Yesterday I phoned the care home that Derek stayed in to see if I could book Derek in for a couple of weeks, so I could book some holiday away. But I was told that I could only book two weeks in advance, which makes it difficult to arrange going away. I am not happy with this as I need to plan what we would do, so it doesn't look too promising for a holiday.

***

My brother came and fixed the shed lock. Derek was acting very cagey. When he got inside the shed Derek was holding a blue hankie. I asked him what he had in his hands. Turned out it was his shed keys. We have also lost three padlocks, two for the sheds and one for locking the side gate which leads to the garden. I know Derek has lost them, but when I ask him he doesn't understand.

I have gone and bought two new locks, one for the large shed and a combination lock for the side gate. At least we will feel safe knowing the side gate is locked. I did eventually find two of the missing padlocks, one was in the kitchen bench seat, the other was hidden inside the dart board cupboard inside the large shed.

Derek is getting very possessive and angry over his shed, and repeatedly telling me it's his house, shed, garden. On Friday he was so angry he put his hands around my neck while I was out the front of the house watching Louise wash the car. I told him to never do that again, but he passed it off as some kind of joke. I don't know how I am to feel any compassion towards him when at times I feel hate; I so want to walk away from this situation, but there is always some part of me that cannot leave him to fend for himself.

June 2012
2 June. Another bizarre day of Derek asking a neighbour for a screwdriver. Derek was going to chisel out the putty of the large shed window so he could get into the shed. He had already wiped all the whitewash I had painted on the glass to protect the plastic boxes in the shed from sun damage. This extreme action would be understandable if there were no keys, but Derek had the shed keys in his pocket.

I was so angry that every time I moved forward in regards to tidying the shed or garden Derek makes the time I have spent to do this wasted.

I was so very angry with Derek for asking a neighbour to borrow a screwdriver, so he could remove the glass from the shed that myself and Louise left the house for the afternoon to put some normality back into our lives.

It seems to me that Derek is going downhill, he has become so possessive of 'his house' I don't want to be here anymore. Derek is all so happy to sit and watch me clean the house from top to bottom, I hear no mention of it being his house while I clean it.

9 June. Today I attended a unique crafters market to try and sell the felt cushions I had made. It was the first time I had done a market like this and it was nice to see other like-minded people making handmade items.

I was surprised when my sister and her husband came to look round, although it was a bit strange seeing her for the first time since Christmas Day. Not much conversation passed between us, from the outside world you would never have known we were sisters, but then she would like it that way I guess.

10 June. Both new padlocks are now missing from the shed door. This is driving me crazy. I just can't make Derek understand that the shed needs to be locked. When I ask him where the padlocks are he seems unable to understand what I am asking him.

11 June. What a day! After a month's worth of rain falling in 24 hours, the south coast was under water. I have never seen so much water. The roads were completely flooded. I had my last counselling meet so felt I must attend. I dropped Louise off at school for her maths exam, and started to make my way into Chichester via the back roads, but had to turn around when I reached Woodmancote as the road was like a river. So I made my way to the main road only to be in nose to tail traffic. The main motorway into Chichester was closed so all traffic was using the A27. This means big juggernauts as well. The roads in some parts – Southbourne, Bosham, Fishbourne – were under water. It took me over an hour to get into Chichester.

I had some shopping to get for dad, so after my counselling session myself and Donna went to Tesco then had lunch before the long drive home. We called into dad's with his shopping and found the back door was unlocked. So we went in, but couldn't see dad. He was asleep upstairs on the bed. The house was cold and dad didn't look too good. He hadn't had a shave and just looked unkempt. We told him to put the heating on which he did, and told him yet again not to leave the back door unlocked. It took us almost two hours to get home!

12 June. At 9pm dad phoned to say he'd had a fall, but not to worry. Now I don't mind dad calling me, of course I don't, but why is it he feels the need to call me when something is wrong, and at 9 at night. Of course I am going to worry. Dad said he fell over at the end of his road whilst posting a letter. He hurt his shoulder, but said otherwise he was OK. He asked me to phone him in the morning to see if he was OK, but I will go around there to check for myself.

The most annoying thing is I know that my sister was round at dad's yesterday, and the letter he was posting was a birthday card. Why couldn't my sister have posted it for dad? Now I know she would have got dad to post it to make sure he went for a walk, so I can see both sides of this situation.

***

I think dad needs a kind of alarm system, as this is the second time he has fallen over. Each time he has called me. One of my worries is that while at the moment I can still leave Derek at home on his own, there will come a time when I can't and therefore can't be there for dad, and I don't want to be put in that situation.

***

Dad had indeed fractured his shoulder and is now wearing a sling. When I called round to take him to the hospital he was very scruffy, unshaven and unwashed, but I had no time to sort him out as I had to be back home for another appointment. After the hospital I took dad back home, made him a cup of tea and said he needed a carer of some kind. He can no longer shave and he's not washing himself. I said to him what would mum say if she saw him in this state? I think he looked a little tearful, and eventually agreed to getting some help. I am going to ask Derek's carer if he could look after dad.

13 June. My friend came over to visit today. I used to work for her. She wanted to see how Derek was. Derek was chatty and laughing and my friend got more out of him in one hour then I can in a week. This illness is shit; it yet again makes me feel useless. How can Derek have a conversation with an outsider but not with me?

Last night was very bizarre. Derek went to bed early as usual, but when I went up to bed Derek got up and started to get dressed. That has become the norm for a while now. Several times I told him it was bedtime and proceeded to get into bed myself, but I couldn't get him to understand. He said he would lie on top of the bed with his clothes on. I said he needed to get undressed. So to avoid any more confrontation I left him. Derek went downstairs fully dressed. I thought maybe once downstairs he would realise it was dark and bedtime and would come back upstairs to bed. I was so tired I went straight to sleep. Next thing I know it's morning and Derek is not in bed. He stayed up all night. He slept, I think, in the armchair if the position of the cushions are anything to go by. I also believe he had two breakfasts that morning. Still, Derek doesn't seem any the worse off for this.

15 June. Donna and Louise did a sponsored ten-mile moonlight walk around Chichester in aid of St Wilfrid's Hospice. I went to my psychic development course as usual in Portsmouth, then came home to pick the girls up to take them to Chichester. I did think about walking with them, but to be honest I didn't think I could have walked that distance. Derek was in bed when we left, so I hoped he would sleep through the night no problem.

The walk started at midnight. I decided to follow the route as best as possible to ensure the safety of the girls. That's not so say I thought they were in any danger, because the event was run very well. But I will admit I am an over-protective mother at the best of times, and over the past few years this has increased tenfold due to the fact I am their only protector now.

After the event, to which I must say I was very proud of both of them for walking the whole ten miles, we arrived back home at 4.15am. Some of the lights were on in the house, but then I thought that maybe I had left them on. I opened the front door to find Derek was up, fully dressed, wandering around the house. He then proceeded to make himself breakfast. We tried to explain it was bedtime, but yet again he didn't understand, so we left him downstairs.

The next day we were all shattered. Derek started getting ready for bed at 7pm and was asleep by 8pm. At about 10pm Derek came downstairs fully dressed again, and went into the kitchen to have breakfast. After this he came into the lounge and fell asleep in the chair. We went up to bed and left him asleep. At 3am Derek was walking around the house in and out of the bedrooms, eventually waking the girls and then myself. At this point Louise was very distressed at Derek walking in and out of her bedroom. I managed to calm her down, but if this continues to happen I am not sure what to do to prevent it. I did manage to get Derek back to bed, but he did keep moving around a lot. Having said this, he is also wandering around the house a lot as though he is lost. The nurse is due a visit next week so hopefully she will have some answers.

20 June. So much for the nurse having the answer. First of all she arrived 15 minute late, which normally would be OK except today was a busy day. Louise needed to be taken to a homeopath appointment at 1pm and the nurse was to arrive at 12.30pm to take Derek out for coffee. The first thing the nurse said when she arrived was that she was short of time and wouldn't take Derek out today. I said I needed to ask her a quick question as I had another appointment. I told her about Derek's strange sleep pattern and about him waking the girls during the night. She asked me what I wanted to do about it. I replied, maybe sleeping tablets. She asked if I was asking for sleeping tablets, because they're not a good idea. She suggested that maybe the girls could have locks put on their doors so they could lock themselves in! Oh that's a much better idea, then if there's a fire they won't be able to get out or I won't be able to get in to save them. Brilliant idea, so humane. I think the nurse was a bit annoyed that I couldn't stay for her visit, but at the end of the day she made the changes to the appointment, and as well as taking Louise to her appointment I then had to take dad to his hospital appointment which lasted two hours.

The last comment the nurse made to me was, 'I guess I will have to phone you for the next visit if you have to rush off.' I think maybe she was not pleased with me today!

I have phoned the care home to see if I can book Derek in for a stay in two weeks' time, only to be told I need to phone nearer the time, and at the moment there are no spaces. I was hoping to book some places to visit with the girls, which I cannot do now. It's so frustrating; yet again I feel trapped at not being able to move forward. The system needs to be changed to enable carers with young families to pre-book respite that fits in with school holidays.

21 June. Derek was not in a good mood with his carer today. The carer said Derek was moaning about me hiding his keys, which of course I didn't do. I have no reason to. Derek as usual went up to bed early, but he was continually opening and closing the drawers in the bedroom. I was sitting in the lounge underneath our bedroom and, without any exaggeration, I guess he must have opened drawers at least 50 times. When I eventually went to bed at about 11pm Derek got out of bed and by the time I had come out of the bathroom, he was fully dressed. I told him it was bedtime and he needed to get undressed for bed. I proceeded to get into bed, while Derek was opening and closing drawers again, including the drawers under the bed. This made it impossible for me to sleep. So I decided to go downstairs and sleep in the dining room. Unfortunately it took me ages to finally get to sleep.

***

3am the next morning Derek came downstairs to have breakfast, so I sneaked back upstairs for some more sleep. Unfortunately the next day I felt shattered. I took Derek to his carer at Waterlooville, with the intention of going back to bed, but whilst driving back home I thought of the idea of gluing the drawers under the bed shut to help stop some of the opening and shutting. This meant sorting out Derek's drawers, but that job needed doing anyway, and to sort out clean from dirty clothes as Derek cannot distinguish between either.

I found a few items of dirty clothes, but more importantly I found one of the missing padlocks, plus wrapped up in two separate handkerchiefs were the missing shed and house keys. I organised Derek's drawers so it was easier for him to find things, and glue-gunned the drawers under the bed closed.

When Derek came home, first thing he did was go upstairs. He was angry because he thought I had thrown his things away, and because he couldn't get the drawers under the bed open. I told him that I had thrown nothing away, only tidied the drawers up. His anger, my lack of sleep – not a good combination. I was so upset that regretfully I told him if he wasn't sick I would divorce him. I think the only person I hurt here was myself. To think I would stoop so low to say that to him, when he only behaves like that because of the illness. I came so very close to hitting him. Thank god I didn't, but I have heard of others who have. I can totally relate to this. I am not saying it's right, but this illness turns the carer into a person they no longer recognise themselves. To make matters worse, Derek turned round and said to me 'What can I do to help? I would do anything for you, just ask.' For one fraction of a second the real Derek came back.

23 June. Derek said he was going for a walk around the village, as he usually does, only he locked the front door with Louise and myself still in the house. No problem, I thought, I will open the door with my key, except Derek had taken the front door key off my set of keys, so I went upstairs to Louise's bedroom to ask for her keys, but they were also missing! Luckily, Derek wasn't gone for long, but he had everybody's house keys in his pocket.

July 2012

5 July. It's 3.04am as I write this. My head is full of too much information and I can no longer sleep, so I hope by writing down what's on my mind I might be able to get a couple more hours' sleep.

Over the last couple of weeks, I have been looking at care homes again. This is because the last home Derek had respite in no longer has any appropriate rooms until who knows when. I am starting to feel like I did before the last respite, no energy, loss of appetite, no positive feelings left for the future. In fact, I met up with my friend Susan yesterday and I was very tearful. At least she knows what I am going through.

My mood is so low that I fear my future without Derek, and I feel completely lost and alone and overwhelmed at what I will have to face with regards to my future without him. The fear of a life without Derek and very little family behind me is just too scary. How did my life get to this point? I wish my mum was still here so I could talk to her about it, I just have to get a grip of myself and try a bit harder to have a more positive outlook.

***

I found one home in Bedhampton which had the wow factor. Not only was the building built like a castle, but the grounds were beautiful, with views to sit and stare at a pond and aviary. The rooms were like hotel rooms, but as well as having 50 members of staff, a library and a whole memorabilia room and a pet dog, a lady was playing a piano. The first entertainment I have actually seen in progress in any of the homes I have visited so far. The only downside was the residents were in their eighties, but I felt happy with the feel of the home and it did not smell of wee. Always a good sign. The cost of this however was £800 a week, minimum stay two weeks, but I have the direct payments which luckily have so far mounted to £2,000. But I phoned the social worker to check about paying that amount for respite. Her answer was if you have the money in the direct payment account use it.

So later today we are having an assessment and all being well our respite will be in place.

10 July. Derek has gone into respite. Yet again he was very angry and while on the journey pretended to open the passenger car door while I was driving. The home is more like a hotel, with great views and gardens, and the rooms are lovely with their own bathrooms. And it doesn't smell, a very important bonus.

We unpacked Derek's case and were given a cup of tea and biscuits, we went to set up the portable TV we'd brought with us, only to find I hadn't brought the power lead. Derek was quite agitated about some money he said was left at home on the top of what I couldn't quite get out of him. He clearly thought I was going to take his money. When I left I said I would return later with the power lead. I left Derek eating his favourite meal of gammon.

***

When I got home I hunted high and low for the power cable. I found two possibilities and put them in a bag to take to the home. I decided to go the following day as I was tired. Whilst looking for the power cable I found Derek's bum bag hidden underneath his bedside drawer. When I looked inside I found £120. I have no idea where this came from, unless his brother gave it to him. I am angry and concerned that if that was the case they clearly have not one brain cell between them to realise that you do not give someone with Alzheimer's large amounts of money, as they have no monetary skills and could quite easily lose it. I have to stop myself from making that phone call, for I know that if I start I won't be able to stop pouring out my feelings towards this family.

Next day I visit the home again with a selection of power leads, but unfortunately neither are correct. The only thing I think could have happened is Derek has hidden the lead somewhere to stop anyone else using the TV, only it has now backfired. Not that he would understand the result of his actions, the same as when he hides his shed and house keys.

On taking the power lead to the home, Derek asked to come home. It breaks my heart to hear him ask, but I know I have to be strong. I so need this break, I am officially mentally exhausted, hence why I have been feeling so low and tired. The blood tests I had were all good, so as the doctor says it's mental exhaustion as well as the grieving process I am going through.

13 July. Today I phoned the care home to check how Derek was. They said he was doing OK.

Lunch time I get a call from the home to say Derek wanted to speak to me. He was handed the phone and he said, 'Oh, have they told you what's happened? Can you come and pick me up?' He then passed the phone back to the carer. I asked what was going on and she said Derek wanted to talk to me, and everything was OK. We then hung up, but 20 minutes later I phoned the home back for I was worried about Derek and was very surprised that he had phoned me. The reason I was not going to visit him was because last time I visited him in respite he was so upset. The last thing I expected was a phone call.

The home looked into this matter for me and then phoned me back to say Derek was fine, sitting colouring, and not to worry. I am well aware that it's not the ideal situation Derek being in a care home, but for my own sanity I need this respite.

14 July. This second time of Derek going into respite has felt different from the first time. I feel a sense of loss; it's almost a feeling of disloyalty towards him and yet I know I needed this break. My emotions are all over the place, from calmness to panic at the reality of this situation. It's almost as though I am in limbo. I also feel a sense that something is brewing and heading my way with regards Derek's family. I have decided to start looking at care homes for him in the future, as it's unfair to keep changing him to different homes. One thing I am certain of is people with this disease need continuity in their life and in my ideal world that means staying in the same care home for respite, getting to know the staff and them getting to know Derek as a person not a patient. I will do my utmost to make sure this happens, even if I have to travel further afield.

15 July. Spent seven hours weeding the garden and getting it to look more like it used to. I can't believe it took me so long to weed. I couldn't manage to cut the hedge as the hedge cutter is too heavy for me to use and my height, or lack of, makes it a difficult task. Due to the huge amount of rainfall in June and July I was unable to cut the grass as it was more like a bog than anything else. I was pleased of the seven hours spent in the garden. I had made a huge difference, although to be honest it killed my back. Oh well, Louise and I are to go to Glastonbury on Tuesday so looking forward to a break away. I have booked two nights at the Travelodge, but maybe we will stay for three nights, as this is the best I can do for a summer holiday.

17 July. Louise and I set off on our journey. Donna is staying at home as she has work, and is quite happy to have the house to herself.

We head to Clarks Village in Street for some retail therapy, then on to the local supermarket for some tea to take back to the Travelodge. I must admit we were both tired from the travelling and shopping, so we chilled out watching TV and playing cards. At about 9.30pm I get a phone call from Donna to say the care home phoned. Derek had escaped and they had to get the police, and please could I phone the care home. My hands were trembling whilst dialling the number. Apparently Derek had escaped twice that day, opening the fire doors. On the second time he was quite aggressive and that's when they called the police. The home wanted me to talk to Derek over the phone, but I knew that would make him worse. They said he was calmer now so I thought it best not to talk to him. My gut instinct was to drive back home and pick him up, but I was so tired I decided to wait till morning then phone the home to see how he was, with the understanding that if he got worse or tried to escape again the home would phone me.

Of course, I got no sleep, or should I say very little sleep, maximum of an hour. I kept playing over in my mind how they had to call the police. At 9am the next morning I decided to phone Derek's nurse to ask for her help. I hoped she would offer to go visit

Derek, but she had a heavy schedule and was unable to visit. She offered to phone the home, but I felt that would not make much difference. I felt very let down by the so-called system. After hanging up, the nurse phoned back to say she could try contacting the dementia team to see if they could help, but I had visions of Derek being taken to another home which would cause more problems.

The nurse also asked why I didn't go away the first few days of Derek's stay in the home. They just don't get it, do they? I had a doctor's appointment, Louise had an appointment and I had to take dad to his hospital appointment. I just can't drop everything and go away. Also have you tried booking a break away at very short notice? She just did not need to ask why. I then phoned the home and asked how the night had been. They said OK. I asked how distressed Derek was and they replied on a scale of one to ten he was seven. I then asked to speak to Derek. When he heard my voice he was crying and saying about the police and thought he was going to be killed. At that point I made the decision to come home. We picked Derek up on the way home.

I asked what exactly happened, and the home said that Derek had got out of the fire door with his suitcase packed, walked out the drive, turned right then turned round and started walking in the opposite direction towards the flyover. At that point they called the police because they thought he might throw his suitcase over the flyover and cause an accident. I asked about a refund, as Derek was only there for one week and a day. They said I needed to phone up tomorrow to ask, and also to get the whole story.

When Derek saw me he was so pleased to see me and gave me a hug. I must admit I was angry with him, call me selfish but I needed that little break away. To make matters worse Derek kept asking us if we had a nice time away. I tried to explain that we didn't because we had to come home because he tried to escape from the home. But the sad thing is he just didn't understand what I was saying.

20 July. I went to the home to rewrite the payment cheque for Derek's stay as they agreed to refund for the days he came home. The story is still unclear, but the home said they were now fitting locks on all fire doors due to Derek's escape, so I guess you could say one good thing came out of this situation.

Also on this day the social worker came out to visit us to have a chat. She said that I should never had come away from our break, and that I should have phoned her or the nurse who would have stepped in. But no one tells you this until it's too late.

***

I feel rage building inside of me because I couldn't even have a few days' holiday. I am angry at Derek, but equally angry at myself for not being able to cope with my feelings. I feel I should be more tolerant of Derek and be able to show sympathy for his illness, for he didn't ask to be like this. I feel torn inside. I feel like I am going mad. I see two sides of this illness but still I feel angry at Derek and his behaviour. I just want to scream and shout and hit out at the situation. I want to be stronger than this. Always I feel alone in this situation, it's taking control of my life. I feel that even the girls are worried about my mental state, my memory has gone and left me, I can't think straight, I need help!

**

The social worker has suggested I start looking for residential care. She suggested that maybe Derek would be better off in full-time care. It would take away all the tension and we could visit Derek and take him out for days and even have him home a few days, so it would be the reverse of what happens now. While the social worker was saying this I felt a huge sense of nausea at the idea. I never expected to hear that suggestion so early on in this disease. I should be stronger and stop acting like a spoilt child, a part of me is saying I should get a grip on myself, act like an adult, pull myself together, we're married for better or worse. Just because the water is a bit choppy, don't give up. I told the social worker that I should be stronger and be able to cope, but she replied that I also had to think about the girls and how would I feel if they left home because of the situation and I was left on my own. I hate being put in this situation and my gut feeling is not to put him in a home, but I also need some space to think and with Derek at home I find that difficult.

The social worker also asked if we were on high DLA payments and if so we should be on mobility income which means we would be entitled to a car and free car tax. But alas when I phoned the DLA we were on moderate rate and the higher rate should have been applied prior to Derek being 65, which means that his DLA payments will never be increased ever, even though they know his illness is degenerative. I think this system is so very wrong, but hey that is never going to change hence no help with a car.

22 July. Since Derek has been home he has just sat in front of the TV, but not watching it. It's sad that even on a hot day like today he hasn't even attempted to go out in the garden. He hasn't noticed that I had done all the weeding or moved some plants around, he has just lost interest. Last night we got the old videos out of when the girls were babies. Derek looked at some of it but was more interested in what the cat was doing. Deep down I still think Derek has some of the old Derek inside and that's why the decision of a home is so very, very hard. I have no one to ask what they think I should do. When I ask the girls they either say they don't know or when.

22 July. Sunday evening, Derek was in and out of bed, waking up Louise by turning her bedroom light on and trying to have a conversation with her. He then came back into our bedroom and was tugging at the duvet calling my name. I remember him looking out of the window, saying 'Oh I am home, I can find my way home from here.' All this happened on the evening before my long two-hour drive to Tunbridge Wells for a recording session which I bought for Louise for Christmas last year. We had waited this long to book it for two reasons: one the weather and two for when Derek was in respite.

As it turned out Derek was back home, so there lies another problem, which we overcame by Donna being at home to keep an eye on things.

I had little sleep before the drive but I seemed to be able to survive.

***

On our return home we played Derek the CD that Louise had recorded, telling Derek that it was her singing, but yet again he was more interested in what the cat was up to. I felt a trail of tears fall, for it's so sad that Louise receives no praise or acknowledgement for what she has achieved from her dad.

24 July. Yet again a disturbed night with little sleep. It started off with Derek having a shower before bed, then getting dressed again with shoes on. I asked why he had dressed when it was bedtime. I think he was waiting to be taken to his carer which was the following day. I lost count how many times he went up and down the stairs with different tops on and then with no top on. He got quite angry because he didn't understand the concept of going to the carer the next morning.

When I went up to bed, Derek was asleep sitting up in bed. I tried to get him to lie down, but even that was a challenge. Eventually he lay across the bed, which meant another night of sleeping downstairs for me. 4am the next morning Derek was up and dressed and yet again in Louise's bedroom waking her up. He then came downstairs, turning on all lights and waking me. I took him back to bed, turned off all the lights. At 6am Derek was back downstairs, all lights ablaze. I went upstairs at about 7am to have a shower to find the hot tap running in the bathroom. A couple of nights ago I found the shower running as well.

In the last couple of weeks I think Derek has got worse. I am hoping it's just a blip and the consequences of Derek being in the home, and the upset of the police being involved, and that it will all settle down. But to be truthful I am probably just not facing the reality that Derek's condition is in decline. I know I can't put off any longer the fact I have to start looking at long-term care, not for today or tomorrow, but for the day I can no longer cope.

25 July. Donna passed her driving test. It hasn't been an easy task, and she was overjoyed at passing. She wasn't going to tell Derek, but I said she should try. Yet again there was no real emotion from Derek at the good news.

26 July. Today the nurse came to visit. She had a quiet word with me first of all. She also said that I should be looking towards full-time residential care for Derek, and that he is no longer happy in the home environment as he picks up on the upset and maybe the resentment from us. She said that possibly Derek would also benefit from being away from home. I was yet again very tearful, in fact the last week I can't seem to stop crying. I feel such sadness that it's making me feel sick. I just want to wake up from this nightmare, to realise it's been a mistake and Derek is well.

After the nurse had spoken to Derek I asked her how Derek seemed. She said that Derek said I hated him. Things have got to the point where my own husband thinks I hate him, and that makes me very sad. I said I would look round another home in Bognor the next day that caters for people with mental health problems, but I am not ready to put him into a home yet. It seems so final, and it makes me feel that not only have I failed in looking after him, but I feel like I am discarding him like a toy that no longer works and you throw it out.

27 July. Derek went to his carer for the day. Louise was going to come with me, as we were going to my brother's. Louise was extremely tired and I had difficulty waking her. It turns out that she was awake most of the night trying to get Derek back to bed. He kept getting up and walking around. I was unaware of this as for the past week I have been sleeping downstairs.

Louise and I went to look around the home in Bognor, but I am not convinced it's the right place for Derek.

A new tactic to try and get Derek to sleep through the night. I made him a hot milk with sugar, and put his favourite music on. I am keeping my fingers crossed that it does the trick. I am trying to stay awake, so that Louise doesn't have to get up in the night. I just don't know what else to do.

While sorting Derek out getting him to bed, Donna walked down the road to post a letter. After about half an hour, maybe longer, it was getting dark. I phoned Donna on her mobile to see if she was OK. Each time it rang it went to answerphone. A couple of times it sounded like she was trying to answer it. Well my mind started to panic, thinking the worst. By this time Louise was getting in a bit of a state. She then got a text saying she was on her way home. Finally I got through to her, she was in Prinsted. By this time it was dark. I asked her if she wanted me to come and pick her up. She said no, but I wasn't happy her walking alone in the dark, so I drove down to Prinsted and there were blue flashing lights. My heart stopped, I was shaking, obviously thinking the worst. I saw someone I knew and stopped her to ask what was happening. She said someone had collapsed at a party. I broke down at that point. She kindly walked down the road with me, and there was Donna strolling down the road, walking with a friend. I just wanted to give her a big hug. Clearly I had embarrassed her and she was not too pleased with me. We went back home and Louise was really upset as well. It has made me realise just how fragile we all are at the moment and to be honest I am scared.

For a couple of days the new plan seemed to work, although to be truthful I am not sure he's sleeping, but he doesn't walk around upstairs. I am not sleeping too well on the couch downstairs, so I decide to sleep upstairs in our bed. The first night Derek was in bed wearing his PJ shorts and pants underneath, but throughout the night he was getting undressed under the covers, getting out of bed, putting his night clothes back on. This was interrupting my sleep so much I landed up sleeping downstairs again.

The following night I decided to try sleeping in our bed again. All through the night Derek was constantly moving about, in and out of bed, rearranging the pillows and duvet. At 5am he decided to walk around the house letting out the cat, waking both girls as well as myself. This no sleep is becoming a major ordeal for us. In the morning I feel shattered and the girls are feeling the same.

August 2012

1 August. Went to a carers' meeting at the psychiatric hospital. After explaining my respite ordeal and no sleep I was told of a new unit for younger people with dementia just down the road from our house. So on the way home I stopped by. The lady who opened the door was the most unwelcoming person I have come across so far. She said that there were no younger people staying there, which contradicts what the nurse at the hospital had said. She said that they don't have people who wander or who are aggressive, or who will try to escape. I replied that I thought they offered dementia care. She said they were rethinking that because they had an incident there that day which resulted in a resident putting a jam jar in a microwave and it exploded. She then went on to show me the small bruises on her arm. I was shocked to see that a home which was supposed to offer dementia care was anti-dementia and not aware of what the disease does to the person! She also said that they had to be careful as they had fragile elderly residents.

2 August. After a chat with the nurse at the psychiatric hospital and then with Derek's GP it was agreed that we would try him on a sleeping tablet called Zimovane. I must admit I was a little worried about any side effects this might have on Derek, but we all need to sleep. So last night I gave him the pill. He did seem less agitated and when I went up to bed he was fast asleep, mouth wide open, snoring. His breathing seemed a little erratic, but I guessed it was what happens when you take these pills. I went to sleep in Louise's room until I was woken up at 12.30am by Derek fully dressed heading downstairs, After much persuasion he went back to bed, but at 2.50am he was up and dressed again. This time I decided to let him go downstairs and have breakfast, hence I have now got up as well to keep an eye on him. So much for sleeping pills.

3 August. I went to see yet another home, this time in Southsea, but the owner was not keen on Derek staying there as he does not sleep well and I said I could not guarantee he wouldn't try and get into other people's rooms. The owner said we could try Derek in his care home for a couple of days, but if he was agitated then he would ask me to come and take him home. I just can't believe that in just two short weeks Derek's condition has become worse, and as a result has lessened my options for care homes.

Today I also collected Donna's secondhand car. I placed all paperwork and keys on the worktop in the kitchen. I then had to go out. Derek came home from the carer before I got home. The car keys and my satnav were missing. After an endless search and many tears we found both items in a basket in the office. Before that point I truly thought I was losing my mind. I thought I had put the items away and forgotten.

***

Tonight, yet again no sleep, but the situation has got worse. Derek refuses to go to bed. He is very agitated, accusing me of hitting him around the face, saying I am horrible. Up and down the stairs continuously. Louise is very upset. I am trying my best to try and get her to get some sleep.

I am now at the end of my tether. I don't know which way to turn. I phone my friend Susan to see if she can advise me. She says to phone the 24/7 mental health line, who advise several options – to phone the psychiatric hospital, the out-of-hours doctor or take Derek to A&E which is not an option. I am now waiting a call back from out-of-hours. It's 1.19am and Derek is walking around the house eating biscuits. A couple of times he has opened the cutlery draw and on the second time he got out the large knife. I am not sure what's going on in his mind. I just can't tell anyone about this for fear he might be taken away. I know there is no way I will sleep again tonight, but I just can't keep going on with no sleep.

2.30am a doctor arrives, takes Derek's temperature, blood pressure, oxygen levels, and all good. The doctor prescribes Temazepam, 10mg on a prescription. I have to wait till the chemist opens to get this prescription. Meanwhile Derek is still wandering around. The doctor came out and said that Derek's condition was in its advanced stage, which made me very upset. I am now at the point of complete exhaustion, I feel sick and lost and just want someone to come and take this pain and heartache away.

At 8.45am I take Donna and Louise to work. Donna is too tired to drive. I am pleased she has acknowledged that fact. On the way back I call into the chemist for Derek's prescription, but alas they cannot give me the drug because it's a controlled drug and the doctor had not written down the amount of tablets to give. I then had to phone the out-of-hours doctors again and another doctor came out and prescribed Derek with another drug called Haloperidol, 5mg. This is an antipsychotic tranquiliser, very scary stuff. I was very reluctant to give Derek this drug as after seeing what he was like after the first sleeping pill, I was scared. I phoned my friend Jane who came over to our house as I was in a bad state. I couldn't think straight due to no sleep and I felt so drained, and due to this I myself am confused as to what happened next. Derek was very paranoid and was telling Jane how I kept hitting him around the face, which I will add I didn't do.

Social services were involved and then the mental health crisis team, who came to visit at teatime. The crisis team were very good. They suggested I give Derek half the tablet and then again at bedtime. This should be enough for a good sleep for all of us.

By bedtime Derek was still sleepy so I decided to not give the other half, but at 12.30am he was out of bed and wandering again so I gave him the second half and he went back to sleep. We all had a good sleep last night. This morning the crisis team came back to check on us. They were pleased that Derek had calmed down and that we had got some sleep. They said that if he was still in the same state as yesterday they were going to section him. They also said that the doctor who came out to the house was extremely worried about me as well.

5 August. Three years today Derek was told he had Alzheimer's. The day went OK. The crisis team came out to check on him. They said they would probably stay with us for a week to give support. Last night was a different story. Talk about déja vu. I gave Derek half a pill at lunch, then again at 8pm when he went to bed. When I went up to bed at about 10pm, Derek was not asleep. Strange, as I expected him to be asleep. He was talking about smashing someone's head in. I tried to get some sleep but alas Derek was yet again in and out of bed, trying to make the bed, up and down the stairs. By 2am I had enough so I gave Derek another half a pill. He settled for maybe half an hour then he was up and about. I think because I was so tired I fell asleep, or it felt like passed out. I woke at 6am and Derek was still up and about. I just can't see any way out of this situation, it's so sad.

6 August. A psychiatrist came to visit today with a suggestion Derek be put on a drug called Risperidone. This is an antipsychotic which comes, like all drugs, with side effects, including death – a small risk but still a risk. My biggest worry is that this drug is licensed for the short-term treatment (up to 6 weeks) of psychosis and other mental disorders. Unfortunately, Derek's psychosis is due to Alzheimer's and therefore this is not going to go away, so either Derek stays on the drug beyond the time stated or he takes it for a little while, but if he stops there is a high risk of the psychosis returning. I just don't know what to do for the best. I phoned Derek's cousin to inform her what was going on. She has offered to come over tomorrow to meet with the crisis team.

Also, today one of the doctors from our surgery called to ask how we were, then later on in the day phoned again to say they will send out a nurse to take bloods and a urine sample. He said he was sorry we were having a bad time. Today Derek put the gas hob on without lighting it, for no reason. I am now worried he will do it again.

Yet another disturbed sleep, first when Derek went up to bed I could hear him talking. I thought he was talking to the cat, but then realised she was downstairs. Derek then came downstairs saying there was a man upstairs. He was adamant so I went back upstairs with him to look. Of course, there was no one, but then Derek said he must be downstairs, so we went back downstairs to look. Derek was frightened, you could tell by the expression on his face, plus he was close to tears.

Derek's condition has got worse over a very short period and to be truthful I never thought this would happen so early after his diagnosis. I am left with such major decisions I feel unable to make.

My days are now blurring into one due to the lack of sleep. I don't ever remember feeling so tired. Every so often I feel like I am going to faint, and also I am getting headaches.

8 August. I went to look at two more homes, this time in Bognor, one of which was a purpose-built Alzheimer's home. The reason for not looking at this one before was the size of it, but I was surprised how lovely it was. All the residents were well dressed and clean, they also didn't look old. I had a chat with the deputy and explained our situation. I also told her about the drug they were thinking of introducing Derek to. She knew all about this drug and some of the side effects. She also told us about sundown syndrome, when the person with Alzheimer's becomes worse at night. I am now wondering if this is what Derek has.

***

We had no sleep again last night, Derek was calmer but constantly talking, making the bed and saying he couldn't believe the house was his. This is driving me crazy. I phoned the mental health line but I am confused as the person who answered said that this line was not open but I thought it was 24 hour. I just don't know who to turn to. I have had enough, I need sleep.

9 August. The crisis team are visiting today. I cannot go another night without sleep. I am going to have to insist Derek go into some kind of respite. When the crisis team came they said a decision had been made, if I was in agreement, to put Derek in to the psychiatric hospital to be assessed. I agreed as I could see no other way. The crisis team asked Derek if he was prepared to be taken into the hospital. He said no, he wasn't going anywhere. I then asked him if he would go if I took him. Again he said he wouldn't go. This then meant Derek had to be sectioned under the Mental Health Act section 2. Therefore they had to arrange for a doctor from the psychiatric hospital and from our surgery and a social worker to come into the house to all agree that this was the right thing to do.

I felt so very sorry for Derek as he had no idea what was about to happen. An ambulance was arranged to transport Derek to hospital. Getting Derek into the ambulance was quite a challenge. The ambulance people were going to call the police for assistance, but I didn't want that to happen as it would cause more confusion. In the end I lied to Derek saying he was going for tests and would be home again that night. I went in the ambulance with him. He was very angry and threatened to kill me, but I know deep down he didn't know what he was talking about. When we got to the hospital the ambulance person asked if she had heard right that he was going to kill me. She then asked if he had ever hit me. I said no, I don't think she realised how ill he was from the Alzheimer's.

Later that night I went to the hospital with a suitcase of clothes and a wash bag for Derek. He greeted me with a big hug and asked if he was coming home. I said not yet.

10 August. After a good night's sleep I phoned the hospital to see how Derek was. They said he had had a bad night with no sleep. He was walking the ward and trying to get into other rooms. He was quite aggressive when trying to get him back to his room. In a way I was glad that the hospital had seen for themselves how bad he has become.

11 August. I phoned the hospital today. They said he didn't have a very good night again, although he did sleep from 1am to 6am which is an improvement. That was with medication. They have had to take out all furniture from his room as he was climbing all over it. With each deterioration of Derek's illness I have managed to cope to some degree, but this time I am finding it difficult. I feel lost, sick and alone. I have booked in for some spiritual healing, well needed.

***

After some thought I decided to let Derek's family know about him being admitted into hospital. I did this by text message as I did not want to face any backlash from them. Now my conscience is clear that I have informed them.

Later that day I got a phone call from Derek's sister saying she had a garbled message on her answerphone from her brother to say Derek was in hospital. She said she was sorry to hear that, but not surprised, as her brother had told her that Derek had become worse. She then went on to say she was sorry she hadn't stayed in touch, but they were in rented accommodation because they were having a bungalow built, and her husband was busy, and it's quite a trek to get anywhere, and if she had Derek over there was nothing they could do, blah, blah, blah. She did acknowledge how hard it must have been for us and it sounded as though she was ready to write Derek off, assuming he was going into a home. I told her I had hoped Derek would be coming back home once his medication had been sorted out. She said that I had to look after myself and the girls.

Also today I phoned my friend to say Derek was in hospital. She was, as ever, very supportive. She has offered to come to visit Derek in hospital with me tomorrow.

12 August. THE VISIT. Went well with Derek. He was fast asleep when we got there and took some coaxing to wake. I guess this was due to the drugs. He didn't at first recognise me which upset me because I thought he had forgotten me in a few days, but yet again I think this was due to drugs. Derek was wearing tracksuit bottoms, not his, and had a small pile of clothes in his room, also not his. Also I noticed his watch was missing. When I questioned this the staff said leave that for them to deal with.

Derek said he liked it there, which I found strange, seeing that when he was in respite he was trying to escape from what was a nice place. The ward was very short-staffed and we had to ask for a cup of tea, and wait for about 20 minutes. It was served up in thick mugs and looked like dishwater, hence we didn't drink it.

I phone up the ward every day to check on Derek and every time they say he hasn't slept and they say he's looking shattered. Each time I comment on how many nights he's not slept, and they say at some time he will sleep and probably for a long time.

14 August. Derek's sister phones again to see how Derek is. If that's not a guilty conscience, I don't know what is. She says that Derek's mum is in hospital and that when she's feeling better she is going into respite.

19 August. Every day I phone the hospital, still Derek hasn't slept. Yesterday I went to visit and I found it quite upsetting, as Derek was very tearful. He kept whispering as though he was frightened to speak too loud. I didn't understand what he was saying, but I think he's just frightened, understandably as the hospital is not that nice an environment. I so want to bring him home, but I know that's not possible as we would be in the same situation again with no one getting any sleep. It's been a strange summer as we haven't achieved a lot, just one night away, no holiday. I feel sorry for the girls as we haven't had a holiday in four years. The best I could offer was to take them to the Warner Bros Studio – The Making of Harry Potter on Friday. It was great fun and for one whole day it felt normal.

20 August. The social worker phoned to say that I needed an assessment of my finances as I am or will be classed as a single parent if Derek goes into full-time care. I have already been told that my carers' allowance will stop on the 30 August. I am not sure how I am expected to pay bills with no money coming in, and at the moment I don't think I am in the right frame of mind to work, plus I don't know if Derek will be coming home again. If he does I can't work, I will need to stay home and look after him. I am very annoyed that I am classed as a single parent. It's as though they have disregarded the fact that my husband is still alive, and written him off.

***

The home that social services were looking into as a possibility may not take Derek if his sleep pattern is not corrected, plus if his mobility is not good this could be another factor for not being accepted. This would not have been a problem, but the antipsychotic drug they gave him has caused problems with his back. At this point in time I am not sure if they are still giving him that drug. I will never understand why a purpose-built Alzheimer's care home can be built and still be selective as to which patients to accept. Surely, if built for Alzheimer's care why does it matter about the conditions of the disease? This country has got it all wrong, why does no one understand or care about this illness?

21 August. I phoned the hospital to see how Derek was. As usual the same reply, he didn't have a good night, they had given him the maximum dose of sleeping tablets that night but still it hadn't worked. They are hoping that a couple more nights on that dose will do the trick. If not I don't know what will happen. My very worst fear is that Derek will be so drugged up that he will be like a zombie.

Today was also eventful as Donna's car had to go in for repair. I drove it to Portsmouth and caught a bus and then a train to get back home, which for me is quite an adventure as I was driving from the age of 17 and therefore public transport is a bit alien to me. Later that day a friend offered to drive me to Portsmouth to pick up the car which I gratefully accepted. After she had dropped me off, the garage said that the car still needed some adjustment, so I said they may just as well keep it until completely finished which left me with a dilemma – how to get back home. This time I caught a bus to Havant, then a train home. Now to some it may be that there is nothing unusual about this, but for me it was a mini challenge, which I overcame on my own, and as sad as it may seem I am proud of the fact I did this on my own.

24 August. This morning, as I do every morning, I phoned the hospital to see how Derek is. Every time the reply is that he didn't have a good night, but this time he was also climbing furniture and had hurt his head. I replied he didn't have any furniture in his room to climb, but apparently he was climbing in the lounge. They were waiting for the doctor to see if he needed stitches. I phoned up again later and they said they had decided that stitches were not needed.

25 August. Donna's 's 21st birthday. A high point in our lives, the party went great with no hitches. The only sad time was when I did a little speech for her and was thinking 21 years ago life was very different, and how sad Derek wasn't present at the event.

***

The following day myself and the girls went to visit Derek with some birthday cake. This was the first time the girls had visited. As we walked into the lounge Derek was bent over a cup of hot tea asleep. I managed to prise the cup out of his hands, and with great effort woke him up. He was confused and didn't acknowledge the girls at all. This was the worst I had seen him, he looked drugged up. The girls were very upset and had to leave the building. They went and sat in the car. I went back in to see him, but he was complaining of pain in his back and sides. I don't know if that's a side effect of the drugs.

I put some photos of the girls, myself and the cat up on his wall. He knew who Louise was but didn't recognise Donna. Whilst sitting in the lounge with Derek another of the patients was saying Derek had been with one of the other woman. I didn't need to hear this. I know it's not true, but it planted a seed in my head, as I had heard of such stories happening in that environment.

27 August. Phoned the hospital, yet again no sleep. Derek was now complaining of pain in his legs. The duty doctor was off sick so they were trying to find another doctor to see what was wrong. Alas no doctor available, but the hospital gave Derek some painkillers and said the situation could wait till tomorrow.

***

113

I am starting to feel ill at ease with the situation at the hospital. I don't think Derek will improve in this environment and I wonder about the care they are given. The fact that Derek was fast asleep holding a hot cup of tea; he was unshaven, hair needed cutting; his sweatshirt was dirty, in fact the new cardigan I bought him I haven't seen since; 70% of the clothes in his room are not his; the fact that during the day he looks drugged up; he is bent over when walking, because of the pain in his back.

Through Derek being in hospital another dilemma has occurred – tomorrow all our benefits will be stopped. No carers' allowance, no disability living allowance. This means a drop of £500, but still the household bills will come in and because I gave up work to look after Derek I have no money coming in.

28 August. Just phoned the hospital again to see if the doctor has been to see Derek. The decision has been made to take him off all medication except Memantine and Heminevrin. That means the Mirtazapine has been stopped. Not sure how that's going to work, as when it was stopped before he became very down. I just trust they know what they are doing. At 8pm I get a phone call from the hospital to say Derek had escaped, but had now been found, and they were waiting for a doctor to call to check him over. I asked if I could come and see him and they said yes. On arrival, I noticed Derek still had the same dirty sweatshirt on. He was sitting in the lounge unaware of what he had done. I took him into his room, sorted out his clothes (more than half were not his) and got him ready for bed. I managed to get him to lie down, but you could tell his body was rigid with no relaxed muscles. I noticed that his ankles and feet were very swollen, and he also had a rash around his ankles. I started to do some healing on him, and he did stay lying in bed. When I left he was still lying down with his eyes shut.

29 August. Phoned the hospital. Derek had slept for two hours, but was still lying in bed when the changeover of staff took place. They said that the new meds must have started working. I would like to think my healing helped. Derek's nurse phoned. I told her I was not happy with the situation at the hospital. I have a meeting at the hospital on Friday with the doctors.

30 August. The meeting with the doctor was not as intimidating as I thought. They are still trying medication to get Derek to sleep at night, but they will not use too strong a medication because this will result in him being too drugged during the day as well. The Mirtazapine withdrawal had the results I expected, as Derek was very tearful when I saw him, so they are going to start him back on these. The most upsetting result of this meeting was to be told that with the sleeping meds the best results they could hope for would be Derek sleeping for four hours. I truly thought that they were aiming for the normal eight hours' sleep. This has turned everything in my head upside down because this means that Derek will never come home. We as a family cannot cope with four hours' sleep. It's not as though he would go to bed at say 10pm and wake up at 2am. It could be he would sleep from 2am to 6am. This would be unacceptable to us. This also means that I have no money coming into the house, and will have to use my savings to

live on. I am trying to rack my brains to come up with a solution to this problem.
I have sorted out some clothes from home, labelled them and taken them to the hospital, bringing back the clothes I could find and the suitcase. I have made a list of Derek's clothes, but some of his original clothes are missing, hopefully in the wash, but his distance glasses and his wash bag are now missing.

September 2012

3 September. Derek slept a whole night, the first in over four weeks. So much for the doctor saying that this could not be achieved.

4 September. Went to visit Derek, he was very tearful. He was wearing four layers of clothing and the weather was hot. I am starting to wonder if he is wearing all his tops at once because his clothes go missing. I guess I will never know the answer to that. Derek had slept for almost four hours last night so that looks more positive.

5 September. Derek's sister phoned to ask how he was. She asked about visiting him. I said she needed to phone the ward first. After I put the phone down I phoned the ward to say she might visit, but I'm not sure how Derek would react as he hasn't seen her for a year. They said they would keep an eye on the situation.

7 September. Last night the hospital said Derek didn't sleep well, but he was less agitated. There still seems to be inconsistencies in his sleep and behaviour at night-time.

***

I don't know how much longer Derek will be in hospital or if he will come back home, but all our disability living allowance and carers' allowance has now been stopped so me and the girls are on our own, with Derek's state pension and private pension which amounts to £559 a month. Oh well, I will have to get a job of some kind.

7 September. One of the nurses from the hospital phoned to ask if it was OK for me to speak to Derek on the phone. Derek had been asking for me, wondering where I was. He didn't have much to say, I think he just needed to hear my voice.

9 September. Went to visit Derek and to do a changeover of his clothes. He was wearing two t-shirts on yet another hot day, but he said he was cold. When I questioned this with the nurse, she said it could be because he was tired, which makes sense I guess.

On checking Derek's clothes – I make a list of all the clothes I take to the hospital and check them again when I bring them home – I find three pairs of socks missing (and the socks he's wearing do not match), 1 pair of pants, a dressing gown, and still his distance glasses missing. Toilet bag, colouring book and pencils all missing. This is really annoying me that there is so little care of personal items being made.

Derek was very tearful again. I felt he wanted to be close to me for reassurance. I asked him why he was so upset. He said he wanted us to be all together. Part of me just wanted to pack his bag and bring him home, but I can't due to his behaviour at night. I decided to do some healing on him, so I closed the curtains, got him to lay on the bed and closed his eyes. After I had finished he remained asleep for 25 minutes. I hope he sleeps well tonight.

***

My head is so mixed up I fear the time is approaching that the doctors will want a meeting to discuss Derek's future, and I am not ready to make that decision. I guess I don't want to lose Derek completely, which I feel I will if he goes into a home.

13 September. My head is not in a good place today. After two nights of restless sleep, worrying about Derek and Louise starting college. I dropped Louise off at college. It was like her starting school for the first time over again. When I got back home I was very tearful. I think that reality is starting to kick in. I had yet another discussion with benefits to see if I could claim anything. The same answer came up – no. I am worried about that.

***

Yesterday I went to visit a home in Portsmouth, designed and built for Alzheimer's patients. It was recommended to me by a friend.

The outside was very similar to the place in Bognor, but its staff and atmosphere were warmer. I was very impressed with this home, so much so that I contacted the social worker as soon as I got home. The social worker was also trying to contact me about Derek's discharge and to say that this home was not able to offer Derek a place because he is awake at night and would try getting into other residents' rooms. I just cannot get my head around this, as it is an Alzheimer's home, and not sleeping is part of the disease. The social worker also said that the first respite care home would only accept Derek if I paid £38 per week top-up. How do I manage that with no income? The criteria for getting into this new home is that you live in Portsmouth, but as I told the social worker there is no alternative, it's there or home. I am hoping that this will make the authorities listen. I will not let them put Derek in an old peoples' home.

The reality is starting to set in. With no financial help, a home to run, no job and no husband, and taking care of two teenage daughters, I try to think of the positives in this situation, but sometimes I can't see the wood for the trees.

14 September. Probably one of the worst days so far. I felt so low that I sobbed uncontrollably. I don't even know why I felt so extremely low, it was as though the end of the world had begun. I went to see Derek in the evening, but that just made me worse.

He too was upset, crying and telling me how much he loved me, and he was sorry. He asked to see the girls, but I don't know if I can get them to the hospital, it's too painful for them.

I keep asking myself why has this happened to us, what did we ever do to deserve this pain and torture? It seems to be never-ending, it's so cruel to watch someone you love deteriorate in front of your eyes. I find myself now thinking of what he will be like at the end of life and can I cope with this on my own. I feel so lonely. And scared.

15 September. I made myself do a boot sale today, I need to offload the shed of items, in case we do need to move. We have so much unwanted stuff that the money will also come in handy.

Donna went out last night – one of her late-night events. I just wish she would stay in contact with me when she's out. It got to 2.30am when I started to panic. When I did get hold of her she was waiting for a taxi to come home on her own from a night club. Because I can't get to the night club by car I told her to only go to the train station in town and I would come and pick her up. Why do these young girls not see the danger of catching a taxi on their own in the early hours?

19 September. Today I attended a meeting with the doctor from Derek's ward and his nurse and social worker. There was supposed to be a ward nurse attending who knew Derek's case, but they were short-staffed. We discussed Derek's sleepless nights and the fact I should be looking for a suitable home for him, as it's most likely he will not be coming home. Again I got very upset to the point I couldn't even speak. I hate the fact I am left to sort this out on my own, and the anger I feel towards Derek's family, I just can't believe that his brother hasn't even phoned to ask how he is, and his sister who says she will visit hasn't done so far. How can a family wash their hands of a family member when they become ill?

The doctor said that Derek was not so aggressive now, and they, with my permission, want to try one more drug, an antihistamine which sometimes works. As they said, in their words, they are scraping the bottom of the barrel now as they have tried all drugs. I agreed to the drug as at the end of the day it has to be the least aggressive one they have tried so far.

I asked if Derek was allowed out during the day maybe I could take him out for a coffee. The doctor agreed to this, so next Tuesday the plan is to take Derek out of the hospital for a couple of hours. It will be interesting to see how he reacts outside of the hospital.

21 September. Today I had a visit from the benefits. A lady came and asked various questions about our income. She then pointed out that they would take Derek's two pensions leaving him £23 per week pocket money. Basically that's what me and the girls will live on. Great, not only do I have the upset of losing my husband and finding a home for him, but also having very little money to live on. I asked what would happen if I sold the house. She replied that after I had purchased another one half of any money gained would be taken for Derek's care. So I can't even sell the house without the government getting the money. I don't see how this can be fair.

That afternoon I got a phone call from the first respite care home to say a room had become available if I was interested, but it was sharing with another gentleman. I turned it down. I can't have Derek sharing a room. When me and the girls go to visit we don't want to be in the room with someone else there, it's just not right.

22 September. Our wedding anniversary. My brother sent us a card, but I couldn't put it up, I just wanted the day to pass. Twenty-two years ago, who would have thought that our lives would be like this? Derek and I used to talk about celebrating our special wedding anniversaries and that because of our age difference we would probably only celebrate our 25th. How wrong we were. We didn't even manage that.

I phoned the hospital, they said Derek was OK, but the day before he was very aggressive and had to be restrained with drugs. I find this very upsetting. I just don't know what's going on at the hospital.

Instead of celebrating our wedding anniversary I went to look at yet another care home. This one was 19 miles away, in lovely surrounding countryside. It is now my top choice. The home was amazing, with farm animals, a pond, cats walking around inside the building, the residents' ages start from 40, the rooms large, and the residents can walk around the large building inside and out and are safe. I was totally blown away with the whole concept of this home. All dementia homes should be like this. The possible downside is the fees, but I have left a couple of messages with my social worker to call me tomorrow, so fingers crossed.

The possible downside has become the downside. No way will social services pay for this lovely home. Again, I have come up against a brick wall. Why can't my husband spend his last few years in a nice home?

25 September. I went to see Derek. When I arrived, I was surprised to see Derek's nurse open the door. She has taken over the ward for a couple of weeks due to illness on the ward. This gave me a sense of relief as she has been in contact with us since the beginning.

Derek had been moved to a new room, bigger and with furniture including drawers and wardrobe. We were just walking down the corridor to his new room when I saw Derek's sister. Of all the days to visit I thought, she turns up on a day I am here. After seeing Derek's room I took him out on a visit for the first time. His sister was nowhere in sight. I thought that because I was there she had gone home. Derek's feet were still swollen, so getting shoes on was impossible. He had to wear his slippers. We went to a drive-through

McDonald's and ordered ice cream and coffees. I then drove to Goodwood and parked up and we admired the views.

Derek was quite chatty, but I noticed that he was now stuttering a lot. This is something new. He also said that he hadn't been to Goodwood before. This was quite a shock as he had been there many a time, so I guess his memory has got worse. I asked him if he knew who I was. He said, 'Angela.' I replied, 'Yes, but who am I?' He said I had a good job. I really believe he doesn't recognise me as his wife. We had a few laughs. I told him about the cat and the small gifts she brings in for us. I said it was Louise's birthday soon, and he thought she was getting married. This further confirms that his illness is taking a downturn. On the upside he was not tearful.

I was told that the antihistamine had been stopped after one dose. I guess he had a reaction to it.

When I took Derek back to the hospital we were both desperate to go to the loo. I asked if it was OK to use the ladies loo. If I hadn't been so desperate to use the loo believe you me I wouldn't have, for in the wash basin was a pad with faeces on and all over the toilet, the floor, toilet seat, faeces. When I got home I stripped and put all my clothes in the wash and detoxed my shoes.

26 September. Derek's sister phoned to say she saw me at the hospital and that she wasn't there to see Derek, she was dropping off a wheelchair. I felt disbelief that she was in the hospital, standing just the other side of the door and didn't come in and see Derek. Unbelievable, again every excuse was given why she hadn't been to see him. I just let her speak her excuses. At the end of the day, she didn't see Derek, end of. She did however ask if he would still recognise her. How the hell would I know?

27 September. Over the last couple of days Louise has been very tearful. I don't know if it's because she's tired due to college or if she feels down. I worry about her because she does tend to have low periods, which understandably she will have, but her low moods tend to have an effect on me. After dropping her off at college I phoned the college to speak to her support worker, to make her aware of her low mood. I was surprised that Louise had told her about not being able to find a home for Derek and how some homes didn't want him. It made me realise that I have been too reliant on her and perhaps spoken too much to her about the situation and made her worry unnecessarily. The problem is I have no one else to offload to, and my major mistake is to offload to Louise. I have made a conscious decision to now look at homes on my own and to give just a little detail to Louise about what's going on. The support worker also kindly gave me the name of a home to look at in Lovedean which I will look at on Monday when Louise is at college.

29 September. I went to visit Derek, thinking that maybe we could go out for a drive. He was fast asleep or maybe drugged. No matter how many times I gently shook him and called his name he mumbled but never once opened his eyes. In the end the nurse said you may as well go home.

I think today for the first time I can see Derek has Alzheimer's. This may sound strange, but he was slumped in the chair dribbling, totally not with it. My heart is broken all over again.

30 September. Phoned the hospital to ask how Derek was. They said he was asleep. I said still? They are going to give the drugs at a different time of day to see if he will sleep at night.

October 2012

2 October. Louise's birthday. Yet another birthday Derek has missed. I wanted to make it up to her that her dad was not at home, so I arranged to meet my brother and his family in town to celebrate.

3 October. I have had enough. I don't see why I should keep looking for homes when I don't know what I am looking for, and then to find out that the funding is not there. I contacted West Sussex County Council to ask for a meeting with my MP. Someone has to get the point across about care for Alzheimer's patients. It might as well be me. Getting the appointment was not easy. They wanted me to write a letter, something I had already done two years ago. I explained I had already done this with no effect, and this time I wanted to speak face to face, and if this wasn't possible my next step was to go to the papers. They must have been the magic words because I now have an appointment to see my MP in three weeks.

4 October. Had a carers' meeting to attend at the hospital, but went up early to see Derek. Yet again he was slumped in a chair fast asleep, with no hope of waking him up. His clothes were dirty and he was dribbling. I went to his room to sort out his washing, yet again a large portion of the clothes were not his. The pile seems to get bigger each time I visit, and his good grey jogging pants were missing, and one of his t-shirts was in his drawer wet. I gathered the clothes not belonging to Derek and took them to the nearest nurse, saying that some of Derek's clothes were missing and that I do his washing, so his clothes should not be taken out of his room. She asked if I visited every day, implying that I needed to in order to do his washing. She said she would go and look for his missing clothes, but I didn't see her again. Maybe she went missing as well! His slippers were also missing so he was walking around in socks, also not his.

After sorting out Derek's washing I went back to the room he was asleep in and sat in a chair watching him, wondering how we had got to this state. Derek then got up with his eyes closed and tried to walk. I took his hand to guide him to his room. He raised his hand in mine and kissed it. My heart just broke into pieces.

When back in his room I undressed him to put clean clothes on. When lifting off his t-shirt I noticed bruising on his upper arms. I was horrified. I asked to see the member of staff in charge, to find out why Derek had bruises on his arms. They said that he was very aggressive at night and force had to be used. I replied that if he was at home and had received these bruises I would have been reported for abuse so how come it's OK for the hospital to do this. No comment.

Derek's feet and ankles have been swollen for some time since being in hospital, but today I noticed that the swelling is now going up his legs. This worries me, but when I mention it to the staff they say it's because of lack of sleep and not having his feet elevated.

6 October. Phoned the hospital to see how Derek was. He had been up all night and was aggressive and tore down a noticeboard from the wall. It's very hard to believe, let alone understand, how a kind gentle man could turn into this monster they describe at night.

7 October. I went to visit Derek with my friend Anna. Today was a good day. Derek was up walking about and trying to talk, a vast improvement from the last two visits. His feet, ankles and legs are very swollen. When I asked the nurse they said he had oedema and were giving him tablets for it. The nurse also said that Derek was awake all night, moving furniture and undressing and redressing, going in and out of other patients' rooms and biting whatever he could. I just don't know what to do. The nurse I spoke to implied that he was uncontrollable and in his words just wanting to come home.

9 October. Went to visit Derek today and had a meeting with his doctor. Derek was unaware that I was there. He was slumped in a chair again, drugged/asleep. I could not wake him. I now have a list of the drugs that Derek is currently on. They consist of Risperidone, Valproate, Memantine, lorazepam and his normal antidepressant. I asked the doctor why he wasn't re-sectioned as his behaviour was aggressive. I explained how difficult it was to find a care home who would accept him, and he asked for Derek to be put forward for continual nursing for which I have to go back to the hospital tomorrow to fill in forms. I believe this to be a good thing as it may get Derek into the home we like best.

23 October. Not much has happened. Derek is still not sleeping at night. The hospital phoned to say they were trying yet another drug, this one they give to children. Who knows, it may help. Tomorrow I am taking Derek to see a home at Bishops Waltham to see what his reaction is. If it's good then I know I need to fight to get him there. I am a bit worried because the hospital asked if I was taking him on my own, and did I have child locks on the doors. This has made me a bit unsettled as I didn't think this would be a problem.

***

For the past couple of weeks I have not been feeling too good, probably stress, but my mood gets quite low, and I feel helpless. I can see no end to this everlasting sadness. I question the meaning of life.

24 October. Arrived at the hospital just after 10am only to find Derek slumped in a chair, head on the table. I guess he had been there since breakfast. I could not wake him, so I went along to the office to see what was going on. The nurse said there was a meeting at 11am to discuss Derek's case, but they had forgotten to tell me about it. I was adamant that I was going to take Derek to see the home in Bishops Waltham, but the nurse in charge was very concerned that I was taking Derek on my own since the previous night Derek was very aggressive. He went to punch a member of staff, was biting and trying to dismantle furniture, climbing the windows and hallucinating, thinking he was eating food but sucking on his fingers, shuffling on his bottom along the floor. The person they were describing was not my Derek, to me it sounded like a caged animal.

The aggression had carried on in the morning and the staff were saying that Derek is being aggressive during the day as well. I didn't think I could feel more destitute, but I was wrong. I think I hit bottom. I could see no way out and I actually said to the nurse that it would be kinder if he were to pass in his sleep. I know for a fact the person they were describing was not my Derek; this evil disease was taking over his mind and body.

I phoned the home to cancel the appointment and attended the meeting, to which there was a room full of people consisting of two occupational therapists, two social workers, two doctors, Derek's CPN and the staff nurse and a trainee. I was asked if I had any questions. My reply was I wasn't told about the meeting so I had no list prepared. A lot of talking was done. They decided to reduce some of the medication to see if that made a difference. The subject of a scan was brought up. To which I told them I had asked many times for a scan, but it was never granted. I then asked the doctor in charge of Derek's case why he didn't just admit that he didn't know what to do with Derek. He agreed that they were scraping the barrel to find a drug to help him sleep. The doctor assured me that this phase of Derek's illness will pass, but of that I am not sure. The outcome of the meeting was to reduce some of the drugs, ask for a scan, and also to re-section him.

25 October. Phoned the hospital to be told Derek had a bad night, and they had to get reinforcements from another ward to help. Derek was also sectioned under the Mental Health Act section 3. This could be looked at as a positive because my understanding is that Derek's care will be taken care of financially without taking his pensions, so it's lifted a weight off my shoulders.

27 October. I phoned the hospital to be told that again Derek had not slept and he was still aggressive. I asked if there was any news on Derek having a scan. He is booked in on Monday at 10.10am. Good of them to let me know! The nurse asked why he hadn't had a scan for such a long time, my reply was it wasn't for want of asking. How many times have I asked the doctors, his CPN and psychiatrist for this with the same old reply – why put him through a scan when we know he has Alzheimer's? The nurse's question has made me feel like I hadn't bothered, but as usual the system does not work and too many people in Derek's case just didn't listen.

I have also received a letter from my MP asking if I would like my letter to be passed on to the Chief Executive of West Sussex County Council.

29 October. Arrived at the hospital at 9.30am, prepared to wait a couple of hours. No sooner had I sat down than Derek was wheeled into the CT scanner room. I am amazed at how quickly they had organised the scan and how Derek was put through the scanner ahead of the waiting queue. At no point did Derek show any recognition of me, but in all fairness he was quite sleepy. I was told that the results should only take a few days. I eagerly await the results. I guess that in my mind's eye I am hoping that maybe, just maybe, they were not right on the first scan and in fact Derek has a brain tumour which they can remove and he will get better. But I guess that happy endings only happen in fairy tales.

My mind is working overtime and I am thinking what if that was the case, how could I get my head around the fact that they had made a mistake? And how would it affect my life? For I believe I have become a different person since Derek's illness.

My mind is planning a big holiday to celebrate Derek's return to us, maybe America. Why am I letting my brain get carried away? Deep down I know Derek has Alzheimer's.

November 2012

2 November. Today I had a meeting with my MP. To be quite honest, it was a 20-minute appointment, but I was in the meeting no longer then ten. My impression was I was wasting his time. He asked if I had brought the matter up with West Sussex County Council. I explained that he was my first port of call. He said he would set up a meeting with WSCC and to write to him again so he can pass it on to the prime minister, but not to get my hopes up as we were in a financial struggle.

Copy of letter sent to MP.

This letter is to show my concerns at the total lack of help in care for the under 65s diagnosed with Alzheimer's. My husband was diagnosed with Alzheimer's four years ago at the age of 62. Four years down the line he has spent the last three months in hospital due to the fact he no longer sleeps at night and is quite aggressive, this all being part of the Alzheimer's disease. Purpose-built homes all being very few for Alzheimer's patients will not accept my husband because he does not sleep at night. My argument being why are there no facilities to look after younger people with Alzheimer's? We hear all the time about Alzheimer's becoming an epidemic, yet still there are not the facilities to care for them. We have a young family and going to visit their dad in an old peoples' home is NOT an option. I understand this country is in financial crisis, but you cannot surely ignore the problem of Alzheimer's? If any of the people in government had any idea just how hard it is to watch someone you love die a slow death, maybe you would stop and listen to all the people out there crying out for help. If my husband had cancer, then the Macmillan nurses would get involved; with Alzheimer's there are Admiral Nurses. But our nearest is Southampton, not our postcode so we are left to our own devices. Yet another downfall. I am asking all in government to LISTEN. Take note that this problem is NOT going away, and neither am I.

***

Also today I went to visit another care home at a forensic science hospital in Surrey suggested to me by our social worker. The house was very impressive and set in beautiful grounds. The only downside was it's 30 miles from home and the route is not the best with regards to lit up roads. I would be a bit concerned about driving back alone at night, not least of all because we got lost today coming home as the satnav also got confused. Also there is a risk of not being able to access the home in severe weather, i.e. snow. Being the other side of the Downs they are more prone to snow. I am going to visit the other home again so I can decide between the two. I need to revisit to get things clear in my head. I think that the forensic science hospital comes a close second to the other home.

***

I have another carers' meeting tomorrow at the psychiatric hospital so I will visit Derek. I have not seen him since Monday. I am hoping that now he is off some of the drugs he will not be so sleepy and be able to acknowledge me.

3 November. Went to a carers' meeting run by Derek's previous nurse. She told me that Derek had slept for five hours the previous night, so sounds like things are looking up. She also implied that it's possible Derek could come home, also that I can bring Derek home for a couple of hours to see the cat and have a cup of tea. I would need to notify the hospital because paperwork has to be signed for this to happen. She said to ask Derek's doctor at the meeting on Thursday.

8 November. Another meeting at the psychiatric hospital with a social worker, an occupational therapist, a couple of doctors, Derek's CPN and a ward nurse. Derek had been sleeping approximately five hours, although not consistently throughout the night. He seems to not be as aggressive, and some concern was raised about the swelling on his legs and that he may have an infection, so they have put him on antibiotics as a precaution.

I spent a while with Derek and stayed while he had his lunch, but although the doctors say his aggression is no longer there I am afraid they are wrong for as I was standing in the corridor with Derek he was getting agitated that all his t-shirts are missing and that someone is coming into his room to take them. This is most probably to wash them, even though I have made three posters, laminated them and put them in his room to say I will wash his clothes. Anyway, Derek then said he was going to knife the person. I could see the anger in his face. I said to the occupational therapist who also witnessed this, I thought there was no aggression?

At the meeting it was discussed that it was not a good idea for Derek to visit home, because it might make matters worse and he may not want to go back to the hospital. Now I am in such a quandary as I am getting different stories from different members of staff at the hospital. The outcome of the meeting was that Derek would move from the hospital to a care home when ready.

9 November. Myself and the girls went to visit the care home at Bishops Waltham. Both girls agreed that this was the right place for Derek to be. We even picked out a room which overlooked the animals.

11 November. Received a phone call from the hospital this morning to say Derek had a bump on his head and that they had no idea how this happened. He was awake all night again, and the duty doctor been to look at Derek and all was OK.

12 November. Went to hospital to see Derek. He seemed to be OK – awake but his speech is very difficult to understand. I gave him a haircut and changed his clothes. I was annoyed that he was wearing someone else's pants, but I have given up on that now, it's like banging your head against a brick wall.

Whilst I was in the hospital sitting in Derek's room, he wanted to go to the toilet. I told him he knows where it is and waited in his room. I then thought I would watch him. He wandered for a few minutes, went in the toilet, then came out, tried to talk to the other residents, then went into the lounge, clearly forgetting that I was there. Yet another sign of the deterioration in him.

Today I also phoned the social worker to put into motion Derek being placed in the home in Bishops Waltham. I just have to face the fact that he will not be coming home.

15 November. Today Derek, myself and two social workers went to visit the care home in Bishops Waltham. Derek seemed to be quite taken with the animals there. We had a good look round and we were shown the pink room. I asked about the green room the girls and myself had looked at a few days before, but an assessment was supposed to be done that day for that room, but it fell through. It must have been a sign, as we were then shown the green room and it was definitely the best room for Derek – the feel and the outlook was much better.

The home gave Derek a cooked meal of spaghetti bolognaise with salad and a side dish of vegetables followed by a large dish of strawberry ice cream and cream which he ate all of.

I did feel a little bit of uneasiness from Derek as if he didn't want to be put in a home, but that might be me misinterpreting his thoughts or it's my own thoughts telling me I shouldn't have to be doing this. But there is no other way. Derek is still not sleeping at night.

***

When we went back to the hospital Derek was happy to go back there, with no hesitation on his part. The decision is now with people higher up as to whether they accept Derek at this home, so I am keeping my fingers crossed as I do not have a second choice. In my heart, I know it's the right place for him. I do believe that Derek will improve at this home. There are lots of things for him to do and he will be with others with the same illness.

***

Had my counselling session today and I feel this may be third time lucky. Although my last counsellor was good, I feel that maybe it was not the right type of counselling.

When I got home the answer machine was flashing. I pushed the button and there was a message from the ward asking me to phone back ASAP. I felt sick and my hands were trembling at the thought that something had happened to Derek. I tried phoning the ward, but no one was picking up. In desperation, I phoned our social worker to ask if she knew what was wrong. She kindly said she would go and find out and ring me back.

Turns out Derek's sister, brother and sister-in-law turned up at the hospital to take Derek out. After three-and-a-half months without any warning they expect to just visit and take Derek out, but of course Derek had been re-sectioned and without my permission he was not allowed to leave the hospital. That was why the ward phoned. I can't even begin to describe how angry I was that Derek's family thought it was OK to just turn up to take him out. It was done in such an underhand way, and after three-and-a-half months of no contact with his brother and he hadn't seen his sister for over a year.

I tried to phone both of them, but neither were home. I left a message with his sister's husband to phone me back, to which she did later that day. She said she had been to see Derek and he was excited to see them, waving through the window at them and then saying 'Oh my family's here!' She said that they were having a nice chat with him, but the way in which she said these things were like a red rag to a bull. The 'my family' bit was like a knife. Shame they didn't think about family three-and-a-half months ago when Derek went into hospital. I questioned this with her and her reply was they didn't think Derek was well enough for visitors. Well I am sorry, but that's absolute rubbish. Weeks ago I said it was OK to visit. I explained that Derek had been re-sectioned and that's why permission was needed for Derek to come out of hospital. She then said in her abrupt way, why was I phoning her? I explained that it was because they had visited Derek thinking they could take him out and to explain why it wasn't possible. But she is so domineering in her attitude one thing led to another and the outcome was me having a go at her about how the family have treated me since Derek's illness, and that I want nothing else to do with any of them ever again, and that Derek is my family and me and the girls will carry on looking after him as we have been.

At the end of the conversation I was shaking but it felt good to release the pent-up anger I felt for Derek's family.

17 November. I went to visit Derek and took the Connect game which Derek played with his carer before he went into hospital. I was shocked to realise that Derek didn't know how to play and in the end we were putting the coloured counters in any old way.

19 November. A feeling of sickness and dread when Donna came downstairs and said, 'You will never guess what I have just heard on the radio!' Three woman were being questioned on suspicion of wilful neglect and conspiracy to make false reports, from a care home on Hayling Island. The name of the care home was Derek's first respite care home. Is my judgement of care homes completely wrong? If so I am worried.

21 November. Another meeting at the hospital, hopefully with good news on Derek going to the care home. I should have realised that nothing was going to be easy. Apparently, the person who can say if Derek can be placed in a home was concerned as to whether the home could cater for Derek's needs at night. As they were talking of funding of just over £1,000 a week they would expect Derek to have one-to-one nursing. Although it's not a definite no I have been asked to start looking at homes again. This makes me very sad as I can see Derek doing well at this home and at the end of the day I feel he would be at home there too. So our plans for Christmas are on hold, as we had decided to spend Christmas Day at the care home with Derek. But if he is still at the hospital I know the girls will not visit.

***

The results of Derek's brain scan were that there was deterioration of the brain.

24 November. Today I took Derek out for he was in desperate need of shoes due to his feet swelling up. He had been wearing someone else's slippers, but as the hospital staff are now taking Derek for walks around the hospital grounds, slippers are no longer an option.

I picked Derek up at about 11am, and drove to Havant Sports Direct as one of the doctors had suggested that croc shoes may be a good option. I parked the car and we went into the shop. It was quite busy. We walked to the back of the shop, found Derek a seat and he sat down. I turned my back for a few minutes to look at shoes and then saw Derek was no longer sitting where I'd left him. I felt a wave of panic, realising how vulnerable he was and how quickly he could go missing. Thankfully he hadn't wandered far. I admit it was a nightmare taking him out on my own. I also bought him some more tracksuit bottoms, as the hospital are forever shrinking the others. Derek and I then went through the KFC drive-through to get lunch and ate it on Portsdown Hill. There was not a lot of conversation on our trip out. I can see a lot of change in Derek, it's almost like he's lost a part of himself, the part that says 'I am Derek Hogarth'.

Yet again Derek was accepting of going back to hospital as though it were his home.

28 November. Someone from the care home went to visit Derek at the psychiatric hospital to do another assessment. Fingers crossed all will be OK.

My hope is Derek will be placed with them before Christmas and that all three of us can spend Christmas Day with him there.

December 2012
4 December. Our social worker phoned to say that Derek has not been accepted at the care home due to concerns over his unpredictability at night, and they are not classed as a nursing home. Gutted is an understatement. I was so sure that it was the right place for him. It looks as though I will have to start looking again.

5 December. Today is my birthday, but not just any birthday – it's my 50th, a time of great celebration, or should be. But alas I do not feel the need to celebrate this year. I would rather it pass me by as just another day. I have a carers' meeting at the hospital this afternoon so I will also visit Derek.

When I arrived at the hospital it was very warm, but Derek had on two t-shirts and a fleece sweatshirt. We went to his room to change as his clothes were yet again very dirty. We then sat on his bed and I tried to have a conversation with him, but it was very difficult. I mentioned that it would soon be Christmas, but there was not a reaction. I then asked him if he liked staying there, but again no reaction. I am finding this very difficult and frustrating. I just want to hold a conversation with him. I ask myself, can he understand anything I say to him or is it that he can't find the words to answer?

***

They have had a new patient admitted who is very verbal and screams a lot. I hope it's not because he's mentally tortured. I find it very unnerving and I would have expected Derek to also find it upsetting, but he just laughed and said he does that all night. I know for a fact that when Derek was first admitted into hospital he would have certainly found this behaviour frightening, which I guess is an indication of how much Derek has deteriorated. I was tempted for a fraction of a second to say to Derek it was my birthday, but I was also afraid that it would upset him that he hadn't bought me a card, so I didn't say a word.

At this time of year, Derek would have been busy doing several shopping trips to buy birthday and Christmas presents. He always moaned that my birthday was so close to Christmas, but it made me laugh that he had to make so many shopping trips because he only had to buy for me. The girls were going to treat me to dinner out, but by the time I got home from the hospital and then picked Louise up from college the weather was -2°, so we decided to order a takeaway. So my birthday turned out very low key, just how I needed it to be. I received no cards from Derek's family so I hope they finally got the message.

7 December. I returned home mid-afternoon. Donna and Louise told me they had arranged a surprise party for me that evening. To be quite honest I was not sure if I was pleased or not, which sounds ungrateful I know but I really didn't want a big fuss made of my birthday. But as it was, it turned out to be a great evening, enjoyed by all. The girls had decorated the lounge with balloons and photos of myself and had laid on food and a cake.

***

With Christmas approaching I feel that the girls and myself are more agitated. Two main reasons for that: one is that Derek will not be home for Christmas, and as Louise said to me, I have been fighting to get Derek into a good home, but I am not prepared to fight for him to come home at Christmas. These words hurt, but maybe she is right, maybe I should try and get Derek home for Christmas. I feel very much in the middle of all this. I am trying to please everybody without much success.

The second problem is my dad. My brother is going to his in-laws for Christmas and my sister is going to friends. This leaves me. Now I would never let my dad spend Christmas on his own and I promised my mum that I would look after my dad, but my conscience feels pressured to have him on Christmas Day, even though I am not sure what's happening with Derek. And it would be nice to have Christmas with the girls without feeling pressured to cook a Christmas meal and waiting on everyone. I feel angry at both my brother and sister for not realising how this is affecting me and the girls.

We started to put the Christmas tree up, but neither girls are willing to help. I have almost had it with Christmas. Part of me wants to just pack it all away again. I know how hard Christmas is going to be, but I can only do my best.

11 December. Today another home to look at, this time a 45-minute drive away. The place was like a luxury hotel, with marble floor in the entrance, but alas it was not the right place for Derek. There was no access to the outside as it was on a second floor, the art and craft room was in pristine condition, the few residents that were there were elderly, three of them in wheelchairs; the whole feel of the place was not homely at all.

From there I went to visit another home built for Alzheimer's by BUPA. The fences were not very high, even though there was access to the outside, but when I was asked about Derek's medication I mentioned Risperidone and that on a couple of occasions Derek had to be injected for sedation. The person showing me around said that they could not accept Derek because he was on this medication, so now I am looking for a home that:

1. is for younger people
2. has activities
3. has access to the outside
4. takes someone who does not sleep at night
5. has 24-hour nursing
6. is homely
7. can manage Derek's unpredictable behaviour

Basically a home that does not exist.

Today I also spoke to a gentlemen who sorts out funding for care, who said that maybe we are looking for a hospital-type home for Derek, and mentioned a unit at a forensic science hospital. I just don't know what to do. I feel useless at not being able to find the right home.

12 December. Went to visit Derek. Took some clean clothes and a large bar of chocolate. He was dozing in a chair when I first arrived, but was easily woken. I gave him a Christmas card which he proceeded to open, but was shocked to realise he couldn't read it. I pinned it up in his room, but I don't hold out much hope that it will still be there on my next visit.

The hospital asked if I could remove Derek's rings as his finger were swollen. Luckily, with the help of washing-up liquid, I managed to get off all three rings. Yet another part of him missing.

Giving Derek the chocolate, I almost had to force feed him, breaking off pieces for him to eat; and when he had finished one mouthful he hovered as a child would, wanting more but not sure if it was OK to help themselves.

On my way home from the hospital I visited dad. It was about 3 30pm and he was still dressed in his night clothes. I asked him what was wrong. His reply was that he was cold. He had yet again turned off the heating. I am afraid I got quite annoyed with him as there is no reason to not have the heating on. I just don't understand why my dad has given up; no amount of help from anyone is getting through to him.

That evening my sister phoned to find out the arrangements for Christmas for dad. She said she was angry that our brother hadn't invited dad, which means it's between my sister and myself. I explained that I was not sure what was happening with Derek so couldn't make plans yet. Again I am in the middle. I asked the hospital if Derek could come home Christmas Day. They are going to discuss the matter. At least it wasn't a no.

15 December. I went to visit the home in Southampton. This is the 24th home I have now looked at. This home is EMI (elderly mentally infirm) with nursing and takes patients with unpredictable behaviour. The lady I met was lovely. We talked for what must have been almost an hour. She then showed me to a room on the top third floor. It was a dark room that felt very oppressive. I must admit it wasn't one of the better rooms I had seen, but that aside the problem was a lot of the residents eat in their rooms, there was a set time for meals and Derek would be the youngest. Also a major problem was at night there were only two nurses to cover three floors.

I am starting to lose all faith in the care system. I just cannot find a home for Derek.

17 December. I phoned the social worker to say I don't know what else to do. If all homes only have two working staff at night then I might just as well stop looking NOW. The social worker said that they were going to ask the unit at the forensic science hospital to do an assessment on Derek to see if he qualifies for the home or the hospital. I said to the social worker that I didn't want Derek to go there, but apparently they are only assessing

Derek. The social worker also gave me the name of another care home in Bognor which I looked up on the internet and it's described as a care home for 'aids/HIV, Alzheimer's, anorexia, autism, bipolar, cancer' and many more. I just don 't understand why they would put all those mixes of illness together.

I also got a phone call from my sister early evening to say dad had fallen down the stairs early Sunday morning. She got upset and said that maybe we need to look for dad to go to some kind of sheltered housing, as he is not looking after himself and it's the fourth fall he's had since mum's death.

18 December. Went to visit Derek today. When I arrived he was fast asleep in the lounge chair. I couldn't wake him. As fate would have it his nurse was back working on the ward so we had a long chat about how difficult I was finding it looking for a home for him. She advised me to stop looking as with my permission they would like to try another drug to help Derek's mood, because maybe if it worked we would have more choice of homes. I agreed.

When Derek woke he wandered past me on the way to dinner. I called after him as he wandered around but with no recognition of me. I was so upset. He has deteriorated so much in four months, so very sad to see. I have been given hope that I can bring Derek home for a couple of hours maybe Friday. The nurse said she would phone me tomorrow with an answer.

19 December. I got a phone call this morning from dad to say he's ill, he's wet the bed and the heating has broken. He didn't know what the time was or what day it was. I know that I shouldn't be angry, and I wasn't at him, but just angry at the situation I am in. As if things were not bad enough with Derek, I have dad to worry about as well. I went round to see dad and the heating was turned right down, and he had wet the bed. This is the second time this week. I just don't understand what's going on with him. I made the decision there and then to transfer his bedroom downstairs so he's right next door to the downstairs bathroom. It was no easy task as all cupboards were full of items which I had to find new places for. I managed to move the bookcase into the garage, but got stuck moving the sideboard and of course I couldn't bring the bed downstairs on my own. So I phoned my sister and she's going to help this evening. I do believe that dad has given up on life. So very sad to see at any time, but at a time when I am also losing Derek, I just don 't understand why all this is happening.

21 December. Today Derek is coming home for a cup of tea. Louise and I went to the hospital this afternoon. She stayed in the car while I went into the hospital. I took Derek into his room so he could change out of his slippers. To my surprise, Derek had several Christmas cards arranged on top of his chest of drawers. I hasten to add that the card I had given Derek was still pinned to his noticeboard. On further inspection I looked at the arrangement of cards to see that they were all from Derek's family, all but one written to just Derek. I noticed on one of the cards it had a message of change of address and that it included 'from bump' which I presume means they are pregnant. But do they not see that Derek would not understand the meaning, and why inform him of change of address? Oh, I see it's for when Derek gets better, he can then visit!

Also hanging in Derek's wardrobe was a new blue sweatshirt and some socks. Derek's feet and legs are too swollen for socks, but then I guess they wouldn't know that as they don't visit. I told Derek we were going for a drive. He climbed into the car. I asked him who was sitting behind him. He looked back, but at first couldn't see Louise, then when he did he did recognise her.

As we got nearer to home I asked Derek if he would like a cup of tea. We pulled up outside home, went indoors, but I am not sure if the recognition of home was there. Donna came downstairs and said hello to Derek, but soon went back upstairs. I think it was too painful for her to see Derek, although both girls said that he wasn't as bad as they thought he would be, but in all fairness it was a good day.

Derek had a cup of tea and a couple of chocolate cakes. We gave him a couple of presents, the photo album I made and a box of sweets. He looked through the photos and I found a pair of reading glasses for him to read the notes I had written beside them. I think he liked it. Derek's clothes were not clean and his croc shoes stank, so I got him to change into clean clothes and by cutting the new slippers I had bought managed to get them on his feet. He got confused when he put his sweatshirt on and started to take it off again. I said to him, 'You need to leave the sweatshirt on!' He laughed and as clear as anything asked me if I was drunk! Myself and Louise just burst out laughing at the humorous side to Derek's comment. He took himself off to the toilets no problem, remembering where that was. He then went running upstairs looking for this new jumper he was given. He went into our bedroom, went to open a wardrobe door then said 'Wrong house!' I must admit Derek did go on about the new jumper as though it was a prize possession. After about an hour and a half I felt Derek was getting restless. He was not sitting down for very long and wandering around, so I said let's go for a drive. We got back in the car and took him back to the hospital. He accepted the hospital return as the norm and went back on the ward. Seeing a member of staff, he was pleased to see them. I couldn't have wished for a better outcome. A very good result for Derek's first visit home.

22 December. Today Derek's carer came over for coffee and we had a lovely chat. Before we knew it three-and-a-half hours had passed. She gave me a lovely photo she had taken of Derek and a large poinsettia plant. We share so much of the same views and interests, it's a gift to have her as a friend.

***

Christmas is fast approaching and although our house is not decorated as much as usual, we have a tree and the outside lights. I am determined to make the best I can of a sad situation. One of the hospital staff asked if I would be visiting Derek on Christmas Day.

I said I didn't think so. He replied that I could visit anytime because visiting hours do not apply. I felt bad that I wouldn't be visiting, as I do have dad on Christmas Day. I am now worried what the staff would think if I don't visit. I hate being in this situation, no wonder I sometimes feel like packing a bag and running away.

I am excited about giving the girls their presents, as I have something very special planned for them, two things in fact. One is to see a show in London in April. Instead of just giving them the tickets, I had t-shirts printed with the details of the date and what show. The second present is a big one – to go to Disneyland Paris for four days in August. I just can't wait to see their faces when they open up that one. This will give the girls and myself something to look forward to in the new year.

24 December. Christmas Eve. To make things different from any other Christmas Eve I decided that as Donna was working, Louise and I would go and deliver Christmas presents to friends who we don't usually buy presents for. It was nice to see their faces light up when giving them the surprise gifts. After this we visit Derek with a bag of his favourite sweets and Christmas cards from the girls. I went into the hospital first to see how Derek was before Louise came in. I gave him his sweets and the two cards were on his bed. In the time I went to fetch Louise from the car, the sweets and one of the cards went missing. Louise and I looked everywhere, but could see no sign of the card or the sweets, but then one of the patients walked by Derek's room eating something. I called one of the nurses who confirmed that the gentleman did have a bag of sweets on him which were Derek's. I guess he also had the Christmas card. Derek was quite agitated about people going in and out of his room, which is quite understandable, but in all fairness I think Derek also goes in and out of other patients' rooms too. I think Louise saw a different side of Derek to the one who came home for a visit a few days earlier. His speech was more muddled and he was showing little signs of aggression. What was interesting was that Louise said that if she didn't know her dad she wouldn't feel safe meeting him. Louise was upset when we got back to the car, understandably. This would be the very first Christmas without their dad. I just hope I can make up for their loss.

When we got home I phoned dad to confirm what time I was picking him up tomorrow. Again, he was very confused. He said to pick him up at 1pm, but I said that's a bit late so I would pick him up at about 11am.

Later my sister phoned to ask if l had seen dad, and that she called round to see him and he was confused. I know she is upset and worried about dad, as we all are. At 10.30pm I get a phone call from dad wondering where I am. He doesn't know what day or time it is. I am getting very worried.

25 December. Christmas Day. A feeling of dread. I have had little sleep worrying about dad. Not a good way to start the day. I want to make this day as special as possible, as we have a big void without Derek. I have to stay strong for the girls but also feel anxious about dad, and also angry at being put in this position. I feel it's not fair for me and the girls. I now just want Christmas to be over. The little excitement I had has now gone.

Went round to dad's at about 11.30am, the back door was unlocked. He was fast asleep and fully clothed, lying on his bed. I was there a while before he woke up. Heating turned off, thermostat low.

Brought dad back to ours, but he hadn't had breakfast so I gave him a couple of biscuits till dinner. Dad then fell asleep until dinner time. Dad had a good appetite and ate all the food on his plate. When finished, he got up from the table, went into the lounge and fell asleep. In the afternoon we asked him if he wanted to play a game. He said no, so me and the girls sat in the kitchen and played Frustration – quite an apt game, don't you think?! Dad slept till teatime, ate tea, went back to sleep. I asked him if he wanted some sweets, but he asked if I had any nuts, so I put out a bowl of nuts which he ate all of. At bedtime I prepared the bed in case he had an accident. He said he hoped he didn't wet the bed. I said that if he did it would be an accident and he could just buy me a new mattress as he had enough money. I felt dreadful after making that comment. I don't understand why I feel so angry at him. What if he really can't help himself? I am ashamed at how I feel.

The one highlight of the day was giving the girls their gift of a trip to Disneyland. Both of them were in tears. It was great to see tears of joy instead of sorrow.

At the end of the week we are having a meeting between my brother, sister and myself to pull together to sort dad out.

26 December. Boxing Day. Dad didn't wake up till gone 12 noon, half the day gone. I will cook dinner, then take him back home late afternoon as we have been invited to friends across the road. Ended up taking dad back to his place at about 5.30pm. After dropping him off I felt so upset, not knowing how to help dad, and with the situation with Derek and finding the right home. We didn't go to the neighbour's party in the end, I just wanted to curl up in a chair and watch TV.

27 December. Made an appointment for dad at the doctors to check he doesn't have a water infection, because that would explain the confusion and the sleepiness. On testing dad's water sample there was no infection so the nurse did some other tests and took blood samples, to which we get the results on Friday week.

After taking dad home I then went to the hospital to see Derek. Although he was quite happy in himself, I am finding it very difficult to make conversation with him. I also find myself comparing Derek to my dad and my head is so full of mental health issues I just want to run away from this whole cruel world. Surely at some point there will be a breakthrough in at least one part of either Derek's or dad's situation.

28 December. I am feeling a bit down today. A new year is approaching and I am wondering what this will bring. I know that Derek will be in a care home, and this scares me as it is further confirmation that the illness is taking him further away from me. There is a part of me that just wants to start over, while the other part is screaming out no, hold on to the past and memories, but memories are what's hurting me the most.

31 December. New Year's Eve. Derek's doctor at the hospital phoned to ask how I was getting on with finding a home for him. I explained that I no longer knew what I was looking for as the problem seemed to be with the lack of nurses at night which is when Derek needs more care. I said that I would look at more homes during the week. I was told that Derek is ready to leave and also that our social worker is soon to leave, which means we will have yet another social worker. I asked if Derek was going to be tried on another drug to help his sleep, but the doctor said that he had already been tried on that drug with no results.

The doctor also said that Derek's agitation was now creeping into the daytime which is quite worrying as I think this may pose yet another problem for placing him.

My friend Anna invited myself and the girls to spend New Year's Eve with her and all her family. We had a great time. Her father-in-law is quite a character and had me in stitches most of the evening. I can't remember the last time I laughed that much. I felt like I had taken a magic tonic to lift my spirits, for that I thank you.

***

2013

January 2013

1 January. Another year has passed. I so hope that 2013 holds well for me and the girls. It's quite scary that time is flying by, yet my life seems to be at a standstill. I went to visit Derek. He was tearful and kept telling me how much he loved me. This makes me so sad, a reminder of what I have lost. His nurse was working on the ward. I told her of the conversation I had with Derek's doctor. She says Derek's not ready to leave, so I just don't know where I stand anymore. She said she would have a word with the doctor tomorrow and phone me to let me know what's happening. I truly feel that my life is in two dimensions. It's weird that I try to live a normal life at home with the girls and when I visit Derek reality kicks in and I sink to a low level of hopelessness. I get scared of how I will cope on my own with the girls and how they have only me to support them and sometimes I am overwhelmed with the responsibility.

To end the first day of 2013 I phoned dad to ask how he was. His reply was 'rough', not good apparently. He had fallen out of bed and hurt his arm. My sister was round there tending to him so I am not sure what's going on. Hopefully the blood test results on Friday will reveal more.

***

Went to visit a care home in Bognor. First impressions OK, bit like a hotel. The rooms were nice and the manager was very caring. I am now not sure if this is the right place or I am just giving up looking. I feel a little pressured, as the manager went to visit Derek in hospital the next day. He did ask me if it was OK. He then phoned me the following day to say that he thought the home could meet Derek's needs, but obviously I need to give more thought on this and I need to visit the home again, possibly with the girls. I wanted to visit one more place nearer to home, but unfortunately I have had to cancel two previous appointments to visit due to both Louise and I having a sickness bug. Dad's results have come back all good, which in a way is great but where to go from here, I just don't know. I am starting to feel I need to move on with my life. I am watching TV programmes offering homes abroad and wondering if I am brave enough to make such a move.

Finally made the trip to visit the care home in Waterlooville. I am now in a bit of a dilemma as I have two choices of home for Derek, both contrasting. One is very much like a hotel, the rooms are furnished to a high standard, the corridors I found a little claustrophobic, the manager was very caring, the staff mostly English, nice garden (although small), the activities were not too good and I am not sure if they did outings.

The other is very much like a hospital, rooms are sparse, but the activities are good, they have a gardening club, outings, and entertainers call at the home. I need to take another look at both homes, hopefully with the girls.

15 January. Went to the hospital to see Derek. I hadn't seen him for over a week due to illness. He was fast asleep in the chair, his legs and feet were very swollen and had broken out in scabs. I asked what was wrong and the nurse explained that Derek had cellulitis which they were treating with antibiotics. His face when he woke up was also swollen. I am afraid I became very tearful at how he had deteriorated. He was trying to tell me something and getting frustrated at not being able to get me to understand what he was saying. The only words I did understand were about his brother selling the house. And that he would do anything for me. I wish I knew what he was talking about.

The visit today has made me very sad. Yet again I question what is to become of us. Part of me still wants to move away, or do I mean run away? For the time I was ill and not visiting Derek I felt more positive about my life, but today I am knocked back into reality.

26 January. Two days ago I attended a meeting at the hospital, the night before I began to feel unwell. I believe this was because I had to attend a meeting. On the drive to the hospital I became very tearful, and that didn't improve once I walked onto the ward. Derek was walking along the corridor pushing a chair along as if it was a walking frame. That and the fact he had no shoes and socks on made me so upset. I seem to be finding it harder each time I visit Derek, and always I end up crying.

The meeting as I had expected was to discuss Derek's transfer to a nursing home, even though I have not decided yet which one. All being well, Derek is to be transferred at the beginning of February, just two weeks away. On Monday, myself and the girls are going to look at the two contenders.

***

The weekend has been very sad for me. I think it's because the time for Derek to go into a care home is close, and to me so very final. Even though Derek hasn't been at home now for six months, I guess deep down I still thought he would be coming home.

I have also been sorting out Derek's shed of all his power tools and machinery. There are so many tools. I guess I will have to try and sell them, as they are no good to me. This makes me sad knowing he will never use his prized tools again. I find myself questioning the meaning of live, what is it all about?

28 January. Myself and the girls went to see both homes. They did not like the hospital-like one, but were quite taken with the other, but admittedly they did question again with me as to why he couldn't go to the home in Bishops Waltham. Part of me wants to try and fight for Bishops Waltham, but I am worried if Derek became unwell in the Bishops Waltham home and needed hospital treatment he would have to go somewhere alien to him, whereas in Bognor he would go back to the psychiatric hospital, to a team he recognises. Yet I could argue would he remember anyway? Who knows?

31 January. My brother came over to help sort out some of Derek's tools. We labelled them and priced them, to sell either on eBay or at a boot sale. Some had to be thrown away due to age and rust.

***

I haven't seen Derek for over a week. I am going to visit tomorrow, but I am finding it very hard emotionally to visit. I just end up crying every time. This disease is so very cruel, not only to Derek but to us as a family.

I have just bought Derek a Manchester United duvet cover and pillow case plus a Manchester United blanket for his new room, just so it will feel more personalised.

February 2013
2 February. Had a carers' meeting at the psychiatric hospital, so I went early so I could spend some time with Derek.

Derek seemed pleased to see me. We went to his room. I was shocked to see endless amounts of sweets in his room, including a large box of Hero chocolates, a box of Maltesers, a bag of peanuts and a bag of liquorice allsorts, plus a framed photo of Derek, his brother, sister and mum. No prizes for guessing that Derek had had visitors the day before. I was very annoyed that they had given him so many sweets in one go. I brought some of them back home with me so I could put them into small bags and give them to Derek when I visit. As for the peanuts, I would never bring peanuts into a hospital – that's just stupid. The more I think about it the angrier I get, and the dislike for Derek's family gets more intense.

Derek was speaking a little more clearly, although I didn't catch most of what he was saying. He seemed happy in himself, although he did ask if he was going home.

After the carers' meeting I had become quite tearful and his nurse took me into a side room for a chat. I could hear Derek shuffling backwards and forwards in the corridor. After our little chat, I walked into the reception and came face to face with Derek's sister and brother-in-law. We said hello and I made a hasty retreat. I am now wondering why they have visited Derek two days running, after only visiting twice in six months. I am annoyed at myself that they affect me so much. I truly meant what I said on the phone to them, that I want nothing to do with them and I know they are Derek's relations but where were they in the past four-and-a-half years since Derek was diagnosed?

4 February. I phoned the hospital to find out about Derek's discharge from the hospital and to confirm the care home where I would like Derek to go. The hospital said that Derek was ready to leave at the end of the week. I phoned the care home and they said that the room we chose is now vacant and just needs cleaning, then all systems go.

6 February. We got the suitcase down from the loft and I started laying out Derek's clothes, making sure I had labelled them and that he had everything he needed. I didn't realise just how upsetting this would be. I guess it is yet another confirmation that Derek is not coming home.

As Derek's chest of drawers and wardrobe slowly emptied of clothes, the pain and heartache is almost too much to bear. I shouldn't have to be packing my husband's clothes and sending him to a care home. I am 50 for god's sake, not 80. Just a couple more things to label – his Manchester United hat and scarf in case he goes for a walk with a member of staff. I also bought a sweet jar for Derek, so each time we visit I can add sweets and biscuits.

I hope I can go to the home before Derek arrives so I can make it his own room by putting away his clothes and adding a couple of ornaments, plus put his duvet cover on his bed. I have also bought a nine-picture photo frame to hang on the wall.

7 February. Going to visit Derek at the hospital with his ex-carer. It will be the first time she has seen Derek in six months. I also have a meeting with the staff nurse and the CPN to discuss the kind of care Derek needs.

When we walked onto the ward I could see in his carer's face the shock at how Derek had deteriorated. I guess when you haven't seen someone for a period of time the changes become more evident. The meeting wasn't what I expected. It seems that I have to discuss with the home my expectations of Derek's care, whereas I thought that was what the meeting was about. I was called into the office and told that Derek was on a week's period of leave from the hospital to enable him to settle. I asked why only a week, surely it will take longer for Derek to settle. Their reply was that it can be extended, but there is no guarantee that if Derek didn't settle he would be brought back to the psychiatric hospital. It might be that he could go as far afield as Horsham, which is miles away. I was very upset at this, as one of the reasons for choosing the home in Bognor was that if anything happened Derek would be taken back to the psychiatric hospital, to the people he recognises. It seems goal posts are moved at every opportunity and that is just not fair. The nurse was concerned that there was a shortage of beds and said that they almost put a bed in the office the other night. I asked why they didn't re-open the ward upstairs. It seems absolutely ridiculous that this is happening when we all know this illness is not going to go away. It makes me so angry, no one is listening.

11 February. Myself and the girls went to the care home today to hang up Derek' clothes and put photos up and make the room his. We moved a bit of furniture around and put the new Manchester United duvet cover on the bed. I was pleased with the finished effect. I was handed a form to take home and fill in. It was about what I wanted to happen on Derek's death. How I am supposed to think of that at this moment in time, I do not know, but I guess these questions need to be asked.

I must admit that I am not 100% sure I have made the right choice about the care home Derek is going to. On our visit today the residents were all just sitting around with the TV on. I guess my ideal care home is not this. I feel my hands are tied and that the home I am looking for is not out there. I guess as long as Derek gets the right care all will be fine. I phoned the hospital to ask how Derek was and they said that his mouth was a little swollen and that they were going to increase his water tablets.

12 February. An ambulance will be picking Derek up from the hospital today at 2pm to take him to the care home. I will be waiting there for him. I am feeling very nervous about this. I just don't know how Derek is going to react. If there was any way of this not happening I would do it. There is something niggling me as to why I don't feel right with this. Maybe my doubts are about whether the home can manage him. Also I am remembering yesterday the manager asking if we wanted the mirror taken off the wall in his room, as it can easily be removed. Why are the mirrors not permanently fixed in a dementia home? I guess I have to give the care home the benefit of the doubt, and just trust that it is the right home.

I arrived at the care home half an hour before Derek. I could fill out some of the forms asking questions about his history, likes and dislikes etc. I was very tearful, but I guess that's only natural. It's a sad day when you put your husband in a care home. A part of me is crying out, saying this has to be a mistake, he can't really be this ill; but that's always going to be there, that disbelief that at the age of 50 my husband and the father of two teenage daughters is living in a care home. There is always a part of me that wants to scream and shout at I don't know who and say this is not fair.

Derek arrived a little confused, but clearly happy to see me at the home. I was shocked at how swollen Derek's face was. When I phoned the hospital they said his lips were swollen, but I didn't expect his face to be as well.

Derek was shown to his room and I pointed out the Manchester United cover and the photos on the wall. I don't think for one minute Derek understood what was going on. A tray of tea and biscuits were brought into the room for us, which I thought was a nice touch. Derek drank two cups of tea and ate all the biscuits. I managed to get him changed into some clean clothes with some persuasion.

The hospital had bagged up all of Derek's clothes, including someone else's clothes, so I took them all home to sort. His glasses were missing again so I phoned the hospital who said they would look for them and bring them to the home.

Several of the staff from the home popped in and out of Derek's room to see if we were okay. At 4.40pm the manager said it would soon be supper time and he would get a member of staff to come and collect Derek. Well it got to five-ish and the home seemed quiet so I guess they had all gone to supper, so I walked Derek into the lounge, and a member of staff asked if they could help. I said that someone was supposed to come and collect Derek for supper. She replied that she would send someone to his room to collect him. I replied that he was here, pointing to Derek by my side. Now in all fairness she didn't know who Derek was, but the thought hit me that she didn't expect to see someone as young as Derek in a care home. I was shocked to see that their tea consisted of a sausage roll in a bowl of spaghetti hoops. I do hope that the meals are better than that.

13 February. I phoned the home to see how Derek was. They said he was fine. He didn't sleep, but was content to take pillow cases off the pillows and wander around.

15 February. Both girls and I went to visit Derek today. It's the first time the girls have visited Derek in the home. Derek was very pleased to see us. We were given a tea tray in his room. Derek told the girls that he loved them, which made all of us cry, another glimpse of what we are losing. This is so painful to watch, a man who would do anything for his family is dying in front of our eyes. Why is life so cruel?

Although Derek was dressed he didn't have any pants on under his jogging bottoms, and the sweatshirt wasn't his. He also hadn't had a shave. The home said it was difficult to shave him at the moment and was waiting for him to settle down more before they tried again. The new slippers we bought him still didn't fit even though they were the next size up. I have lost count how many shoes/slippers we have tried now.

One thing we did notice was that Derek's leg was a dark colour with a nasty scab. Looking closer we could see it was full of pus. I went to ask a member of staff who came and looked at it. She asked if Derek was diabetic. I replied no. She then said she would phone the doctors to get some antibiotics, as Derek had cellulitis. I told her that this would be the third time Derek had antibiotics for this condition. She said there must be an underlying problem which is causing this. This has now got me worried.

The rest of our visit was filled with tears and some laughter. Donna had observed that the many pieces of tissue folded up in Derek's pocket were in fact, in his mind, his money. After she had pointed this out it became more apparent that this was the case, as Derek would have folded his money up in this way, and at one point he gave the wad of paper to me asking me to look after it. I then put it in his drawer and Derek said in his way that someone could come into his room and steal it.

Derek's room looks out over the small garden of the home, and one of the residents walked by the window. Derek put his fist in the air and said that he hated that bastard, he had hit him. You could see the hatred in Derek's face. I questioned this with the staff, and they said that this guy was very territorial and did hit out at people, but after his medication he was OK and they were keeping an eye out.

I thought it would be a good idea to get Derek ready for bed, and put his PJs on. After some persuasion I managed to get his pants, shirt and PJs on, but then Derek was saying that he wasn't going to supper in his PJs, so clearly he has some insight as to what's what. I then changed him back into jogging bottoms.

We stayed with Derek till after five and yet again no one had called him for supper. I walked him into the dining room and then went back into his room to collect the girls and make a move home.

Later that evening I phoned the home up and a man answered with a foreign accent. I asked if they had managed to get some antibiotics for Derek. It was quite difficult to understand what he was saying, but basically they hadn't managed to get them because Derek was not yet registered with a doctor. Now I know that Derek only moved to the home on Tuesday, but wouldn't that be the first thing that should have been done? He then said that they would wait till the morning and see if they can get the doctor on duty to help. I am not sure if that's to get Derek seen or to just get the antibiotics.

I am very worried. Something is niggling me, but I am also concerned that maybe I am blowing this all out of proportion in my mind. But shouldn't the staff have noticed Derek's leg? And the fact they couldn't get the antibiotics, is that not a reason to be worried? Why is it that these things always happen on a weekend and I don't know who to phone to ask for help?

The manager of the home is also on leave for a few days so I am well and truly stuffed. The other thing was that the man also said he had worked a couple of nights and noticed Derek didn't sleep. Hello, is anyone listening? That's why Derek is in a home! Why were the staff not told this? No wonder I am having doubts!

I will phone the home this morning to see what's happening.

***

I thought that Derek being in a home would be less stressful, but at this moment I would rather him be back at the psychiatric hospital. I felt less stressed with Derek being there.

I phoned the home and the person who answered said she had looked at Derek's legs. It was reported that when he came to the home his feet and legs were swollen. I said I knew that but what about the cellulitis? She said that there was a small mark on his front right leg, but no worries. I was starting to get annoyed because the bad leg was his left at the back by his calf. After putting the phone down, out of sheer desperation I phoned the psychiatric hospital and luckily his ex nurse was working. I asked her what to do and she said that really it needs to be seen by a doctor because previous experience showed that when Derek got an infection he became more aggressive. I told her about Derek not being registered with the Bognor doctor yet, and she said that would not be a problem. I then phoned up the home to relay the message and they said they would keep an eye on it and if necessary call the doctor. At this point no antibiotics had been issued. I was still not convinced so I drove down to Bognor to see for myself the situation.

When I arrived, the nurse said that the out-of-hours doctor tried to phone me, and that if there was a further problem they would come out, but Derek was not showing any life-threatening symptoms.

It was so very clear that Derek had had little or no sleep – he looked like he was asleep standing up. I walked him into his room, he lay down and fell asleep for about 20 minutes.

While he was asleep I tried looking at his leg, but the nurse had put a covering over it and I didn't want to take it off in case it didn't stick back down again.

When he woke he had lunch. In fact he couldn't eat it fast enough. He then kept asking me what I said, but I hadn't said a word. He then had got it into his head that I didn't like him any more. He said he loved me, but why didn't I like him. I have no idea why he was saying this, but it really upset me. It wasn't as though he just said it the once. Derek also said he had been in a fight, showing me punching actions. I asked a member of staff if this was correct. They said no, but he might have been hit by one of the other residents. I walked Derek over to the window in the lounge to see if we could see the robins. A gentleman resident came close to where we were standing and you could see the pure anger in Derek's face – he was ready to hit out.

Yet again this made me upset, I am turning into an emotional wreck. I just can't stop crying, no amount of counselling is ever going to stop this.

17 February. I phoned the home to see how Derek was. They said he was fine. They had to contact the crisis team because Derek head-butted one of the carers when he had become agitated. Still Derek has not been seen by a doctor.

18 February. Phoned the home and they said Derek had been seen by a doctor and that antibiotics were prescribed. Derek was still agitated. I told them that I had said this would happen if he had an infection and it went untreated. The person I spoke to said she was unaware of this.

I phoned the home again at about 4pm because I wanted to make sure that they didn't inject him to calm him down. They assured me they didn't; they said that they were getting antibiotics for Derek. So at 4pm Derek had still not been treated for his cellulitis.

19 February. I wanted to contact someone about what had happened at the home and ask for advice. I phoned the psychiatric hospital and asked to speak to the ward nurse but she wasn't working. I then phoned his nurse, but there was no answer. Then I tried the CPN nurse, but she doesn't work Tuesdays, so yet again I was left to deal with this on my own.

I went to the home. Yet again it wasn't my intention to visit so often but I feel ill at ease leaving Derek there. I was offered a drink so they made Derek a tea and myself a coffee. When I picked it up from the table it was stone cold. Why would you serve a stone cold coffee to anyone? They offered to make another one but I declined.

I walked Derek into his room and a few minutes later a gentleman from the crisis team came in. Talk about good timing. This was not planned, but I believe these things happen for a reason. The nurse also came into the room, so a discussion was had about how agitated Derek was and how they couldn't do basic hygiene with him as he would not let anyone near him. The crisis man asked if they had not used the window of opportunity with him. Her reply was there had not been a window at all. They discussed giving Derek a drug to make him more amenable. Is that all the medical profession know? DRUGS? Let's face it, no one knows how to deal with Alzheimer's, it makes me want to say hey let's give a lethal injection and solve the problem. I am so very angry. Why is there no one out there who can help Derek without drugging him?

I brought up the discussion about Derek head-butting a member of staff. The nurse said she was unaware of this. Please god help me to sort this situation out. I feel absolutely useless. I also asked the crisis man when the nurse had left the room as to whether I had made the wrong decision bringing him to this home. He asked if I would be happier if Derek was moved back to the psychiatric hospital. I replied that he couldn't stay there indefinitely.

20 February. I go to bed worried about Derek and the first thing I think about when I wake is I hope Derek is OK.

I phoned the care home today to ask how Derek was. The manager said he was OK, not sleeping and wandering around a lot as normal. The manager had been away for a few days. I asked if Derek was still agitated, the manager said why would he be agitated? I told him about the crisis team being involved because Derek had head-butted a member of staff, and how Derek wasn't seen by a doctor when he had an infection. The manager was unaware of any of this, surely that's not right. I thought that he would have been updated on the weekend's news. The manager said he would phone me back. It's now 5.30pm and guess what, no phone call back. I have been home all day so I haven't missed a call.

I also phoned Derek's CPN nurse and made sure she was up to date with what was happening. She then phoned the crisis team who said that they were keeping an eye on the situation and it was decided not to give Derek the drug they discussed yesterday so I am pleased about that. You know, I don't want to kick up too much of a fuss in case this affects Derek's care, but I didn't think I would feel this unsettled with Derek being in a home. But as the CPN said, Derek may be unsettled due to the infection and hopefully once the antibiotic kicks in things should settle down.

23 February. Went to visit the home with my friend Jane. Derek was in a good place mentally, his speech was sometimes clear, but that happens sometimes. We went to Derek's room so I could check his leg. It was still a little inflamed, but clearly not as bad as before. One of the carers came into the room with a piece of cake for Derek. I asked if

Derek's legs were being creamed with the lotion the hospital gave him. His reply was that corners do get cut and it was probably not getting done. No wonder I lack confidence in this home.

On leaving Derek, the care worker handed my friend a piece of rolled-up paper with his mobile number on asking her to text him. At first both my friend and I saw the funny side of it, as he was a lot younger than her and she's married with three teenage kids, but as reality set in I realised that it was unacceptable on every level to do this in a care home. I now worry in case he does the same to my girls. As I said before, I don't want to make too many waves, but I will keep a close watch.

***

In the week that followed I had spoken to the manager asking how Derek was. I think I had asked about his leg, but whatever it was I asked, the manager said he would find out and ring me back which he yet again failed to do.

March 2013
1 March. Louise and I went to visit Derek. He was asleep in a chair when we turned up. We had bought him a McFlurry. We went into his room and he drank the drink in no time. I checked his leg and it was certainly getting better.

Some of the staff were having a fag break, sitting just outside Derek's window. The manager was also there. We could hear the conversation, and from what we could gather there was unrest amongst the staff over some incident. This didn't help my confidence in the home one little bit.

The manager asked if I wanted to speak to him, so we had a meeting in Derek's room. I told the manager I was not satisfied with the communication between staff with regards Derek's cellulitis. The manager pointed out that it was the weekend he was away, and that two residents had died that weekend and he wasn't informed of that either. That also is so very wrong, no wonder my confidence in this home is low. The manager agreed to phone me every Monday to give a report on Derek. Let's see if he can remember to do this. The manager also pointed out that Derek had dismantled a lamp and broken the zips on the cushions in his room. Part of us was crying out yes! Derek has got his revenge! Do they really understand Alzheimer's?

4 March. Was surprised that the manager of the care home did phone as promised. He reported that there was no change in Derek, but pointed out that Derek was becoming friendly with a younger member of staff and that they were keeping an eye on the situation. This upset me because it's almost like saying that Derek can't be chatty and friendly to the staff. It's possible that this member of staff reminds Derek of the girls, and not forgetting Derek is very young compared to the rest of the residents at the home.

Went to visit Derek. He was unshaved and seemed a little agitated. The nurse was explaining that Derek wouldn't let them do any washing or shaving. My reply was that I had come to give him a haircut.

The carer who gave my friend his phone number asked me how she was. Again this made me feel uncomfortable. I am still not sure what to do about this, as I feel I need to stay out of the way of him asking about my friend.

I took Derek back to his room and cut his hair with no problem. Shaving was another matter. I had never shaved anyone before and unfortunately I cut Derek a couple of times. I also got him to strip wash and put on clean clothes.

9 March. I had yet another skip delivered. I just can't believe how much junk Derek had hoarded. Part of me was angry that I was left to sort out all his clutter on my own. I know he didn't know he was going to be ill, nobody did, but why keep so much rubbish? One thing I have learnt from this is that I will not accumulate junk for my girls to sort through.

11 March. The manager of the home phoned today. All OK with Derek, no reported change, but he hasn't had a shave since I was there because he will not let the staff shave him.

***

It is Derek's birthday on Saturday and all being well I hope to bring him home on Friday for a little tea party to celebrate. Unfortunately both girls work Saturday and by the time they finish work it will be too late.

***

On Friday I finished my last counselling session. Because it's NHS I only get 12 weeks, even though my situation is ongoing. This makes me sad as I had found my counsellor the best one so far. Apparently, I can reapply in six months' time. I am wondering what life will have to offer in six months. I must admit that with every month that passes, the girls are getting more grown up, and of course will want to move on with their lives, and that scares me so much. It's not that I don't want them to move on, that's part of life, it's being left on my own that scares me. Up till now it's the running around after the girls that's kept me going, but without that I think Derek's illness will hit me harder than it already has.

14 March. Went to do some retail therapy as I had had a bad day yesterday. It started off fine, I went for a walk with a neighbour and had lunch out, but when I got home I had a strange turn which I can only put down to a panic attack. I have started to become aware that I have these when I visit Derek or if I have been talking about him and his illness. Anyway, I went shopping to put some normality back into my life. Whilst in the changing rooms at about 12.30pm my phone went. It was the care home. There had been an incident at the home last night and they had only just thought to tell me. Derek had hit another resident which resulted in him hitting out at another, knocking out his teeth. I must say I am not surprised that Derek did this. I had warned the home about him being angry at a couple of the residents. I contacted his CPN and the crisis team who will yet again be keeping an eye on him. When I phoned the manager he didn't seem to know what was going on. I asked if Derek had another infection and he said he didn't know. In fact, he didn't even know how the incident happened.

***

Myself and the girls went to visit Derek with birthday cards, presents and a cake – his birthday is tomorrow, but as the girls work Saturdays it was better to go today. Derek seemed very sleepy, apparently they have given him a drug to calm him down. His brother, sister and sister-in-law had also been to visit this morning, bringing gifts and peanuts again. I was so angry that they have no sense bringing peanuts into a care home.

Derek showed very little interest in his presents and even the cake. He didn't show us that he understood that it was for his birthday. Derek was so sleepy that in the end I laid him on his bed and he fell asleep and that was how we left him. Unfortunately, Donna didn't get to give Derek his present, so she brought it home again. So sad that his birthday means more to us than to him.

I brought the peanuts home with me and initially put them in the dustbin. Then I decided to write a note to say not to bring peanuts into the home due to choking and that there may be a resident in the home with a nut allergy. I then Sellotaped the note to the peanuts and Louise put them through Derek's brother's letterbox. It had to be done!

***

I found the care home staff again very disorganised. One didn't know what the other was doing. They couldn't even be sure as to whether it was Derek's nurse who had visited him this morning or a nurse from the medical centre. It's still not clear what happened with the hitting incident, and the manager is so laid back it's scary. No one knew if the crisis team was visiting at the weekend. I just don't understand why this home said they could cope with Derek. I have such mixed feeling about it that I don't know what to do.

20 March. I went to visit Derek. When I walked into the lounge he was leaning up against the wall asleep. It took a few minutes to wake him by tickling him. I could feel his whole body tense up. He didn't realise it was me at first.

We walked back to his room and got the colouring book out that Louise had bought him for his birthday. We sat and coloured for a good hour, but I couldn't help noticing how

Derek was confused by the picture and found it difficult to know what colours to use. Out of the blue he suddenly said about a nasty fat guy and he said he hit him on the back of the head. I tried to question him, but the moment had passed. How strange that he just came out with something that happened almost a week ago.

21 March. I phoned the crisis team to ask how they thought things were with Derek. They said things had calmed down. I mentioned that Derek didn't seem to be involved in many activities, and they said that they were finding it hard to engage him, which was a worry. Also that they are finding it hard due to the fact he is still young. When I questioned if he was in the right home they said that there wasn't any home which catered for younger people with Alzheimer's.

26 March. When I arrived at the care home, Derek was colouring a picture. This is the first time I have seen him do any activities at the home. He was quite intent on colouring as I was standing next to him for a few minutes before he realised I was there.

We walked back to Derek's room, passing the manager and the head nurse who proceeded to tell me that Derek does not sleep at night! And that while the staff were getting the other residents ready for bed, Derek was more or less getting in the way. Although these were not her exact words, the meaning was still the same, and yet again the dismantling of the cushions was brought up. I swear if those cushions are mentioned again I will personally destroy them myself. Hello, my husband has Alzheimer's, don't put fancy cushions in his room if they are not to be touched.

The question of more funding needed for more activities has now progressed to needing another member of staff to supervise Derek at night-time. I contacted the head of finances who in turn said that the manager of the care home needs to put the requirements on paper and forward them to him. I phoned the home to relay the message, but the manager is on leave until after Easter. This makes me feel a little uneasy, as the last time the manager was away there was a problem with Derek.

***

Easter Day, all three of us went to the care home to see Derek. This was one of his better days. Louise sat and coloured with him. Both girls were amazed at how much clearer his speech was when colouring, although there was not much conversation. We gave Derek a chocolate egg which we had to give him piece by piece, otherwise it would probably still be there at Christmas.

When we left I had managed to get Derek lying on the bed with his eyes closed. Maybe he was asleep? This is the best way to exit the home without too much emotional upset.

April 2013
2 April. Phoned the home to check how Derek was. Apparently he was quite anxious

and agitated, so they medicated him which I am not happy about. It makes me so angry that in this day and age there is no alternative to helping people like Derek. Maybe if they occupied him more he wouldn't become so agitated. Drugs are, in my opinion, over used.

8 April. Waited until 3pm, but had not received the usual Monday call from the home, so I phoned them. The manager answered. He said he had been busy – blah, blah, blah. He then said he would put me through to the nurse, and I then heard him tell the nurse to do a follow-up call to me. I waited and waited for the nurse to pick up the receiver at her end. Fed up waiting, I hung up. About half an hour passed then my phone rang. It was the nurse saying the manager had asked her to phone me. I replied that I phoned them and had been waiting on the other end. No comment was made. The nurse said that Derek's left leg was very swollen and that she would contact the doctor tomorrow for him to take a look in the next few days.

9 April. Went to the care home as I was concerned about Derek's leg. I arrived at about 11am. Derek was fast asleep in the chair in the lounge. I couldn't wake him. I went to his room with the few items I had brought him. In his bathroom the floor was flooded, but finding someone to tell was impossible. I went back to the lounge. Derek was still asleep. Residents were calling out for the loo and asking for a drink. They seemed to be short-staffed. The residents that were not calling out were slumped in chairs asleep.

I found this very upsetting; this was exactly the kind of place I didn't want to put Derek in. He's 67 years old and yet most of the residents look like they are waiting for god.

The manager was showing round a new member of staff and telling the residents that there were going to be two new members of staff. Yet when we originally looked around the home the manager said that they keep their staff for years. Make of that what you will. I didn't stay long at the home, in fact I think it was my shortest visit so far. Derek was still asleep, so there was no point me staying. When I got home I phoned the manager of the home to ask if he had sent off the paperwork for extra funding for Derek. His answer, no not yet. I asked why. His reply was that he had had a few days off. He was supposed to do it before he took time off.

13 April. The visit to see Derek was quite a good one, although he did seem to be talking to a third person. I am not sure if this is something that happens or maybe the paranoia is back, I just don't know, and when I mentioned it to the nurse on duty she made no comment at all.

Derek's room was in a bit of disarray, with seat cushions out of seats and his duvet was out of its cover. Derek's clothes were unclean, he was wearing someone else's t-shirt, no pants and his jogging bottoms were on back-to-front, so I guess we can say he must have dressed himself.

While sitting watching Derek trying to make out what colour crayon to use while colouring the picture I got out for him, my mind wandered back to a time when life seemed normal. For the hundredth time I wondered why this had happened to us, and what would Derek think of the girls and how quickly they are growing up. And yet again it hits me how I no longer can share the experience with him on subjects such as the birth of the girls at which Derek was present, or to chat about things we had done in the past before the girls, the experience of going to Jamaica and Florida.

Then there are the things I would like to ask him about the house, for example the pipes are starting to make a strange noise. Derek would know what to do. The house seems to be cold most of the time yet we have insulation, maybe the windows are the problem, I don't know. I feel that I am just the caretaker of the house and feel I should ask Derek about it, but sadly he would not understand.

22 April. The manager of the care home phoned to say that the extra funding has been accepted, and that Derek will have six hours a day one-to-one care. This is good news. Hopefully the home will manage this funding correctly.

26 April. We all went to see Derek. He was a little agitated. He had found his way upstairs and they had to bring him down via the lift. Obviously the gate had not been locked.

I walked Derek to his room where the girls were waiting. He did acknowledge them. He then went to the toilet and weed on his trousers, so I tried to get him to change, but he became quite angry with me. I also noticed he had on three pairs of pants and his PJ top underneath a jumper. Eventually his clothes were changed, but he did get angry with me. I guess I should have let him be, but it's not my Derek being dressed in such a confused way, and it couldn't have been comfortable.

When we were just leaving the nurse said that Derek had been washed and dressed that day. I pointed out that he had his PJ top on still and three pairs of pants, and he clearly had not been shaved. Apparently Derek had been washed, but throughout the day he does tend to add on more clothes and gets redressed. He wouldn't let anyone shave him. The nurse also pointed out that I had reported that Derek didn't have a good appetite. She said that his appetite was good. Just to prove a point the communication is non-existent as I only complained about the type of food given.

May 2013
3 May. This was a very good visit, not something I often say. When I arrived, Derek came running to the door to greet me. We went to his room and I cut his hair and got him to change his t-shirt no problem. I had bought him some grapes and an apple which you could see he was very grateful for. I noticed that he had eaten all of his sweets in his sweet jar too. I showed Derek some old photos I had found when clearing out. He didn't

recognise some of them, but he did recognise a photo that was taken down our road, and also one of the main road from many years ago. He said that the chemist was there now. We also had a laugh, which was happy and sad, because it gave me a glimpse of a time before this evil disease – another reminder of what we are losing. I also managed to cut Derek's toe nails and check his legs. When I left, he was asleep on his bed. If only all visits were as good as today's.

11 May. I did a mind, body and spirit fair in Emsworth. It was a great day, followed by taking Louise to her first college party at Gosport. I admit I was quite worried about her going, but I realise I cannot and would not stop her from going. It is my problem that I worry so much about the girls. Anyway, I dropped Louise off but didn't come back home as it was quite a distance away, so I went shopping and then sat in the car park for a couple of hours with some sandwiches. I started to feel not quite right, but couldn't put my finger on how or what was wrong. I thought maybe it was the energy from the spirit fair or maybe my anxiety about Louise being at the party.

***

This feeling lasted a couple more days. On the Wednesday, a guy from Donna's work came to sort out the garden for me. We needed some large plants moved and one of the flowerbeds needed to be grassed over, so the garden became less maintenance for me. We got talking about various things and he talked a lot about Derek. He asked how things were and how the girls were coping etc.

That night I was really bad. I couldn't stop shaking. I felt sick, had an upset stomach. I couldn't wait to get to bed. I didn't tell the girls because I didn't want to worry them. When in bed I googled 'panic attacks' and realised that was what I was having, triggered by talking about Derek. At the spirit fair the lady on the next stall to me had asked if I had a husband. I hesitated then explained I had, but he lived in a care home. I think that saying that out loud triggered the unwell feeling I had that evening and which stayed with me for a few days. Add the conversations on the Wednesday, it was too much. I have no idea how I am going to get over this.

***

Today I had a phone call from the home to say Derek needed more pants as he has started to rip his. Not sure if that's true or they just couldn't find them, because he does tend to wear three pairs at a time. Also he needs bigger socks as he can no longer get his on because his feet and legs are too swollen.

16 May. The visit to Derek today was not so good. He was fast asleep in the chair with a cup of tea and cake in front of him. It was very difficult to wake him and when I did he was focused on the cake only, which he ate quickly then got out of his chair to wander off. No recognition of me whatsoever. At that point I was crying. I just can't seem to keep my feelings under control. I took Derek back to his room as I had bought him a bowl of fruit, some sweets and a milkshake. His room was in disarray, with the large wall mirror missing, photos missing from the walled photo frame, furniture had been moved and the bedside lamp gone. I also noticed that on one piece of furniture the laminated wood had been peeled off.

While in his room Derek spilt a little drink on his bed which resulted in him repeatedly rubbing his hands over the spill saying 'sorry'. To be quite honest I couldn't even see the spill. There was no conversation as such. I tried to tell him about the garden at home, but I don't think he understood. I yet again got upset, but surprisingly Derek understood this and put his arms around me asking me what was wrong.

We then went and sat in the garden, which was nice. There was a near fight with two of the male residents, but Derek didn't seem worried about this, which is good. Soon after, Derek fell asleep so I took that opportunity to leave. I did however ask the staff what had happened to Derek's mirror. It took about three staff to find out. Yet again one member of staff doesn't know what the other one is doing.

As I was leaving, one of the nurses made a comment about how she was doing the night shift that night and how she was dreading it! I ask myself, is she in the right job? She was after all a senior member of staff. I was driving home and still upset from my visit. How can two visits be so different? I had my music playing and got the sudden urge to scream at the top of my voice, letting out all my frustration. They say it's good to get it out there. Well I am not so sure, as the following day I woke up with very little voice. Clearly I had damaged my throat, so whoever said let it all out, maybe they were wrong?

***

This week, Derek's CPN phoned to say that she was no longer going to be looking after Derek. She was handing his case over to someone nearer the area. I questioned whether Derek should have continuity, but alas it's out of my hands.

***

The home forgot to phone Thursday to update me on Derek, although I did phone on Monday to ask how he was. For the first time Derek slept in his bed all night. This could be the result of some distant healing that was done the previous evening.

***

The garden has now been turfed over a bit more to make the upkeep a little easier. It looks a little strange, but I guess we will get used to it in time. I have also tidied up the bottom of the garden, even laying bricks to make a hard standing. Hopefully Derek would be proud of what I have done. Singlehandedly, I moved the composter bin which was full. I never imagined that was possible, but in my determination I called out for

Derek's strength and by some miracle I moved it. When I had finished my work in the garden, the builders working next door called out and said what a lovely garden we had. I felt so proud because when Derek tended the garden it was beautiful, but I am no gardener, so when I was complimented it was extra special.

27 May. Bank holiday. For once the weather was sunny and warm. Both girls were home so we went to visit Derek. It was lunchtime and although Derek had finished his main course, when looking at what the others were eating I noted that they had one scoop of mashed potato with a sausage, plus I think it was baked beans – not what I call a good dinner. Derek's pudding was yet again cake with custard. I have never seen any other pudding dished up so far.

We went into his room and sat for a while, Derek eating some chocolate we brought him. We then sat in the garden, but got bored as there was no conversation and Derek was just falling asleep. So as a last minute idea, and as we three had not eaten, we took Derek out in the car. We went through a McDonald's drive-through and we all had happy meals with drinks and McFlurries. I then drove to a beauty spot well known for bikers. As we arrived, for about 30 seconds Derek's face lit up with acknowledgement of the bikes, but then the moment was gone. He did however say it was nice here, and I guess that I should be grateful for that. I can't hide the fact that the outing did not have the big impact I thought it would. I guess the disease has progressed more than I would like to admit.

When we took Derek back to the home he walked through the entrance and he wandered off with no acknowledgment of us being there with him. So very sad.

***

Yet again the manager of the home failed to phone me with an update on Derek. I left it till 11.30am then phoned the home. The lady who answered clearly wasn't English and I had great difficulty in understanding what she was saying. She asked me to phone back in five minutes. I left it for half an hour then phoned, this time the manager was in a meeting, so still no joy. I decided to go visit Derek the following day.

Meanwhile this same day I went to my local shop to post a parcel. The only space available was next to Derek's brother. I parked the car, but no acknowledgement was made to me whatsoever, not even to ask how Derek was.

June 2013
7 June. As planned, I went to visit Derek, taking biscuits, sweets, fruit and a small bottle of coke. I arrived at 10am. We went and sat in his room. I changed the duvet cover to the Manchester United one I had bought him, sorted out some of his clothes, then sat down to do some colouring. I was there till dinner time. At no point was I offered a drink, but more to the point nor was Derek. I so wish I could find somewhere better for him. If I move him, what are the odds of it causing problems for his mental state? And who knows if the home would turn out to be better? I question this home so many times, I just don't need this hassle.

As I was about to leave, Derek put his arms around me and kissed me. He said he wished we could go back and that we had had good times. I couldn't believe he said the words so clearly. He had also thanked me for the items I had brought in. In just that minute in time it was like Derek wasn't ill and this evil disease had not occurred.

13 June. A meeting with Derek's CPN nurse and the new nurse who will be taking over from her was held at the care home. I arrived first and went to Derek's room to sort out the wooden chest that I brought him, and replace it with a large plastic box. This was because Derek was starting to dismantle the chest. I noticed that there were still ants coming into the room after I had reported this the week before. This annoyed me that again no one was taking any notice of me.

I was introduced to the new nurse, and I gave her some insight into our story so far. I told her of my feelings about the care home and that I felt that there was unrest amongst the staff. Although the nurse made no comment, I felt that she knew where I was coming from. The manager then joined the meeting. He was quite elusive. I questioned him on the ants and he said that they were dealing with it today. The manager also said that he felt that we, as a family, had not gelled with him and his staff, which was unusual. I wondered if that was because I will fight for Derek to be looked after the best way possible and in no way will I accept second best for him. After all, he can't question anything that happens.

16 June. Fathers' Day. Myself and the girls went to visit Derek, taking gifts of a tin of biscuits, a chocolate mug, a new sweet jar (as the other one had gone missing) and some sweets. Derek had no idea that it was Fathers' Day. It took a while to make him understand about opening the present and card; so very sad to see and I felt heartbroken for the girls. Our visit was quite uncomfortable because the ant situation had not been dealt with and the ants were everywhere – on the table, a few on the bed and crawling up our legs. I went to see the staff nurse on duty to ask for either lemon juice or vinegar because the ant situation had not been resolved. She gave me some vinegar, so I put vinegar all around the door frame and window ledges. Hopefully that will resolve the problem.

18 June. The staff nurse phoned to say that Derek had been put on antibiotics as his leg was quite swollen. It had been for a while, but I question in my head if this is truly necessary as Derek's behaviour was good and there was no sign of infection.

***

The Thursday phone call from the home manager came at 11.20am when I wasn't home. I had said the call needed to be before 10.45am. He wrote it in his diary and said that if he couldn't make the call he would get a member of staff to call me. The message on the answerphone was he would try to call back!

23 June. Louise and I went to see Derek. As we approached the home we saw Derek walking with a carer. He looked so old it was quite upsetting. Today was a better visit. I managed to cut his hair and his one-to-one carer gave him a shave. The carer was asked to come help with another patient which confirmed my concerns about employing a current member of staff to do one-to-one. Whether Derek gets the full amount of one-to-one care, I do not know. We joked around a bit, he gave me a hug and told me and Louise he loved us. The ants, although gone from the door way, had found their way into Derek's sweet jar, so we had to throw them away. Although the visit was good, both Louise and I left in tears. This pain is just never going to go away.

24 June. Dad phoned me up. This was very rare. His first words were, 'When's the healer going to work on me?' Let me explain. Because dad doesn't seem to be making much, if any, progress I asked a spiritual healer to distance heal dad, with his permission. I must admit that the way dad said it was as if he was depending on the healer to make him better without any input from himself. The fact that dad had phoned me and he sounded better than he had in years suggested that the healing was already taking place. The second question from dad was when am I going away, because both my brother and sister are away at the same time and dad wanted to know who was going to do the food shop.

After the phone call I phoned my brother to ask if he had put an order in for dad's delivery of food. In the course of the conversation he said he had spoken to our sister. In fact she had called a meeting with him to clear the air. After they'd had a talk he asked her if the air had been cleared; her reply was she would let him know. Not only is that strange in itself, but they discussed me and my brother told me that she was hurt by the letter I had written her after the falling out.

After the phone call I found the copy of the letter I had sent and I could not find a reason why the letter would upset her, and if it did that was not my intention. I guess that I have to accept she no longer wants to be my sister or be associated with me.

27 June. Thursday, no call at all from the care home. Guess the manager forgot completely this time.

July 2013
1 July. Donna was invited to my sister's for the evening. Why only Donna and not Louise is anyone's guess. As before it made an uneasy feeling at home. To me it feels like my sister is stirring, why single out one family member? There is no reason for this stupid behaviour. I have had enough of her stupid ways, so I have decided to cut all ties with my sister. I am having her name taken off my will as executor. This opened a whole new problem.

Looking through my will, to my horror it was written in a way that if I died before Derek all savings and the house would be sold to pay for Derek's care. That means the girls would be left with nothing. I phoned my solicitor and questioned this and reminded them that they knew Derek was sick, so why was the will written this way? After a meeting it was decided that the will should be rewritten at no extra cost. I thank god that this was noticed, as not only do the girls lose their dad, but also the house and any savings I may have. But now the will is being changed.

4 July. A phone call from the home. Derek has been seen by the doctor as he has cellulitis again and antibiotics have been prescribed. They said that if the antibiotics don't clear up the infection, then swabs and bloods will have to be done. I questioned why they couldn't do that now. Their reply was that once antibiotics have started they would give a false result. I have since found out that it's not true and when bloods and swabs are done you just take note of the antibiotics.

6 July. Went to see Derek. As soon as I saw his leg I just broke down. One of the staff said she had seen worse! What a comfort that was. Not.

10 July. Popped into the local shop. On my way out was Derek's brother and wife chatting to my next door neighbour. They totally ignored me, not even asking how Derek was.

I phoned the home to enquire about Derek's feet and legs. I was told that they had not cleared and the course of antibiotics had finished. They said they would keep a close eye on the situation over the weekend. I was not happy that they were prepared to go the whole weekend without calling a doctor. I tried to contact Derek's CPN without any success. I was so tempted to drive down to the home to see the situation for myself, but it was the Festival of Speed at Goodwood, so I knew the traffic would be horrendous.

15 July. I phoned the home again and the manager answered. He said that Derek was fine and that his legs were OK now. He asked for us to meet face to face to discuss Derek's one-to-one. The meeting is on Friday.

17 July. The plan today was to pick Derek up from the home and bring him home for a picnic. Louise and I had gone shopping the day before to buy food for the picnic. I made sure the house was tidy and the garden looked good. I was looking forward to Derek coming home.

We arrived at about 2.30pm. Derek was slumped in a chair, he had grazes on his arms. I asked what had happened. The first reply was, 'I don't know' followed by 'he must have knocked himself'. Why, oh why does no one know what happens in this home, be it a removal of a mirror or an open wound? They said Derek had been very active the last few days, and now he was very tired. I said we were hoping to take him out, but the nurse said no. Louise and I went into Derek's room to put away the clean clothes I had washed. The edging strip on the drawers had been completely removed and he had started on the table. His carpet was wet, as was the bathroom floor, also the tap in his bathroom wasn't working. Apparently Derek had flooded his room. He had also removed the rubber strip in the doorway.
Some of Derek's clothes were damp, so whether he had tried to mop up the water with

his clothes is anyone's guess. I have now brought the clothes home to wash.

We went back into the reception area where Derek was sitting. He woke up for a short time and got out of his chair. He was very disorientated and his eyes were out of focus. There was no recognition of us at all and his head was bent over like an old man's.

One of the thoughts that went through my head was has he had a stroke? The nurse said they had done some blood tests, but she hoped that it was just a water infection then antibiotics would sort out the problem.

Both Louise and I broke down in tears.

This evening the home phoned to say Derek was back to his normal self, rearranging furniture in the garden, and he was now in an upright position. I asked that the home phone me when the blood tests results are back. The nurse replied that she was annoyed that the bloods were still in the fridge and hadn't been sent off.

***

Went to visit Derek with his ex carer. I brought with me a new pair of sandals and a new cardigan, hopefully all will fit. On entering the home the first thing the nurse said to us was they hadn't managed to wash or shave Derek today. I asked if they had got the blood tests back and the reply was that Derek was anaemic and another blood test had been done.

Derek was pleased to see us. I think he recognised his carer, but not sure if he knew how. It's the best I have seen Derek in some time. We walked him to his room, and his carer suggested she wash his feet, as they stank. I washed his shoes. I then gave Derek a shave and took him into his bathroom for a wash. With clean clothes and a shave Derek looked good. He had a bit of his sense of humour and chatted a little, which was great to hear. I noticed that the large desk-type unit was missing from Derek's room. At first I thought maybe they needed it for another room, then I noticed that there were some pieces of wood propped up alongside the wardrobe, then realised that Derek must have dismantled the whole unit.

On leaving the home, the manager let us out. He asked if I had seen that Derek had dismantled the unit in his room. My reply was, 'Yes, he did a good job!' I couldn't help but feel the bitter sweet revenge for Derek's actions.

***

My question to the home when I phoned the following Friday, as the manager hadn't phoned on the Thursday, was how long would it take to dismantle a piece of furniture without any tools? And how long is Derek left unattended during the day? The manager's reply was that was his question to the staff when Derek flooded his room.

28 July. Louise and I visited Derek. He was asleep, but was easily woken this time. His foot and ankle have become more swollen and most likely to have another infection. The nurse pointed out that they would be phoning the doctors in the morning.

Derek was in a better place than when Louise last saw him, but not quite as good as I saw him a few days ago. I cut his hair and we played some sixties music, but there was no recognition, which was very sad to see as Derek loved his sixties music. We also played a piece of music that Louise had recorded. I swear there was a smile and I am sure recognition of that. Both Louise and I had tears, although not as much as when Louise went to the toilet and Derek called me to him, put his arms around me and told me he loved me.

That total heart-breaking moment when I ask myself yet again, why is this happening? I don't understand why I have to endure so much pain. On Thursday myself and the girls are going away for a short break, but part of me feels uneasy about leaving Derek behind.

August 2013
1 August. Today is the start of mine and the girls' holiday to Disneyland Paris. We were picked up from home in a taxi at 5.50am. This is the first time we all three have been on holiday without Derek and it felt strange. I felt a real responsibility leaving the house empty, although it was only for four days. But once we were in the taxi it was as though all my responsibilities were lifted.

We didn't realise that it would take us 12 hours to get to our destination, but it was an adventure. I cannot remember the last time I felt completely relaxed. We all enjoyed the break, it was just what we all needed.

***

Once back home, my head seems to be in limbo. It's as though I need to move forward with my life, but I can't. I need to start living my life and to recognise I still have a life. I am starting to realise that the girls will move on as they should, but I will be left with nothing but emptiness. This scares me so much. I feel I need to make major changes to my life, but don't know what.

I hate this feeling of hopelessness.

It's been four years since Derek's diagnosis of Alzheimer's, with the year it took of tests, five years in total, and it doesn't get any easier.

7 August. Went to visit Derek. It was quite a good day. His leg was not quite so swollen. We went to his room and Louise said she could smell wee, then realised that the seat she was sitting on was the cause.

I then went to sort out Derek's clothes. Opened one of the drawers to find that Derek's clothes were wet. He had been using his drawer as a toilet.

11 August. We all three went to visit Derek. We had brought a poster of his favourite bike, had it laminated and was going to put it up in his room. When we arrived we were not allowed in as there was a virus in the home. Shame they hadn't thought to let the relatives know.

16 August. Received a phone call from the home to say all is well with Derek. The call was from a new member of staff who had been instructed to call me as the manager was away.

21 August. Louise and I went to visit Derek. There was recognition for about a minute, then Derek went into his own world. We went to his room which smelt of wee again.

I put up the posters which I had laminated, but Derek took no interest in them. He really did seem to be in his own world. He was having a kind of conversation with an unseen person and also started laughing, even though neither Louise or I had spoken.

Derek was wearing odd slippers of which neither were his, and on searching his room I found six slippers, none of them a pair or Derek's. His two pairs of croc shoes were missing.

On checking Derek's legs, I could see they were red, scabbier and some scabs were bleeding. I asked the nurse to come check on them. She said she had been away for two weeks and had only come back that day and hadn't checked Derek's legs as yet, but to be honest she is not the only nurse there.

The nurse creamed Derek's legs and said she would keep an eye on them. Our visit was not very long as Derek fell asleep in his chair so we left.

22 August. This morning I got a phone call from Derek's doctor asking if I could meet them today at the home to discuss Derek's ongoing problem of cellulitis. The doctor would be calling between 12 noon and 2pm. I was also asked if I would want Derek resuscitated if he had a heart attack, as they had no record of this. I was shocked to be asked this in a phone call, and was wondering if they knew more about Derek's condition than I did, but on questioning this the doctor said that he asked because there was no record of what to do in an emergency. This has made me unsettled and needing to talk this over with someone, but yet again it's me who has to make the decision. Although to be honest, why would you want to prolong someone's life with this evil disease?

On arriving at the home I was surprised that the doctor was a female, and even more surprised that the home had a new nurse who was a trained mental health nurse who I will now call a miracle. Apparently, the head nurse whom I didn't like had left. There must be someone up there looking after us, because this couldn't have happened at a better time. Derek's leg had been swabbed and the results were that he has MRSA. He may have had it for as long as six months, which is one of the reasons why the antibiotics didn't work. The doctor explained that really Derek needed to be admitted to hospital and put on an IV, but unfortunately that cannot happen. Firstly, the hospitals are not geared up to look after patients with Alzheimer's; and secondly Derek would not tolerate an IV. He won't even leave a bandage on.

The doctor contacted the hospital who advised on what medication to use, and it's now a case of trial and error as to whether they can get rid of the MRSA in his leg. Derek has been itching his body, mainly his upper body. My concerns are what if the MRSA is in his system?

30 August. Went to visit Derek. He was quite agitated and not quite himself. My concerns are more so due to the fact that in my heart I feel that the MRSA might be what ends his life, I feel I am trying to prepare for the worst, but I hope I am wrong.

The new nurse has asked for the water to be put back on in Derek's room, as hygiene is very important in MRSA cases. Not sure if this will get done as the home seem to care more about the decor than the clients.

September 2013
3 September. I phoned the home to ask how Derek was. There had been an incident at the home. Oh, how I wish I didn't have to hear that sentence again. Derek had become more agitated and hit a resident again.

On the other occasions when Derek had hit out it was because he had an infection, and although he does have MRSA he is taking antibiotics, so I am not sure why this has happened. I have asked the mental health nurse to do some blood tests to see if the MRSA is in his system. Hopefully this is being done.

6 September. I went to visit Derek on my own today, as Louise is becoming stressed through college work. Also, I feel that because she has been with me the last few visits I think it's also affecting her, seeing how her dad is deteriorating.

At home we had made a large collage of bikes to hang in Derek's room. It's quite an impressive size. I hope he likes it.

On arrival Derek was wandering the lounge, so I went to his room to hang up the collage. Then I went to the lounge; it was lunchtime and Derek was given his pudding, but he insisted that he stood up. I tried to coax him to sit down so he could eat his pudding, but it was quite difficult to reason with him. Derek was quite agitated; another resident was cursing after Derek calling him names and saying what a prat he was wandering around moving furniture. I had to stop myself from biting back at her. I just continued to stare at her hoping she got my thought message. As I walked past her she made another comment about Derek, but this time I couldn't stop myself. I turned around and said he's a very sick man. I walked Derek into his room to show him the collage of bikes, but there was no reaction. I gave him the sweets I had bought him – liquorice allsorts, his favourites, but he didn't want them.

Derek's behaviour was very strange. He kept saying 'Let's go, come on!' Over and over again, 'Let's go'. But every time I said no, or I didn't understand, he got more angry, he was crying, slapping his face, pulling the skin on his face, saying I hated him. There were also signs of paranoia. He then started to grab my wrists to pull me along. I went into the hall way so I could find a nurse. Derek had hold of my wrist in a tight grip. I was crying by now and one of the visitors asked me if I wanted help. She then went and got the nurse, who then took Derek into another part of the home. I had a long talk to the nurse, who informed me that they were keeping a watchful eye on Derek, as they had also noticed a change in him. They were hoping to get a urine sample from him as this behaviour may be because he has a UTI (urine infection) or at worse, a decline in his Alzheimer's. The last time Derek was anything like this was when he was taken into hospital.

***

I thank god that Louise wasn't with me to witness what happened, as this would have stressed her out more. For the first time ever when I came home and Louise asked how dad was, I had to lie and say he was fine. I am now waiting for the home to phone and say they have done the urine sample. Hopefully I won't have a long wait.

***

I received a phone call tonight to say that Derek had a UTI as suspected so they were hoping to get antibiotics in the morning. This may have been the cause of his behaviour today. I have such mixed feelings about the results; part of me maybe wanted it to be that his behaviour was due to a decline in the Alzheimer's which makes no sense to me other than maybe I have had enough of this roller coaster of emotions. It's not that I want Derek to pass, it's that I no longer want to see him decline into a person I don't know. This never-ending nightmare, the unknown of what will happen next is taking over my life.

Louise and I had tickets to see *Nil by Mouth*. It was being performed by the 6th form at Louise's youth theatre. As a member, she has to attend the show.

When we arrived, a parent of one of Louise's friends said the show was very good, but

161

might be a little too close to home. I just thought it was because it was staged in a hospital ward.

Within the first five minutes of the show, one of the patients was an Alzheimer's case. I have never wanted a show's interval to come so quickly. Both Louise and I felt so uncomfortable. We walked out in the interval and came home. I can't believe that the director, who knew perfectly well of our situation, didn't have a thought to forewarn Louise about the play. Never in my life have I walked out of a show.

13 September. Most days this week I have been phoning the home to ask how Derek is. Still he is agitated. Today I phoned and the nurse said that the blood tests were back, but because the home needed to phone between a certain time to obtain the results and that time had passed the results would not be given until Monday. Well in my eyes that is totally unacceptable, so I decided to phone the doctors myself. The receptionist said she would get the paramedic to phone me back after 2pm. Just before then the receptionist phoned to ask if I could come into the surgery to see the doctor for the results. I explained that I lived 14 miles away and that I wouldn't drive that far for information they could give me over the phone, so they agreed to get the doctor to phone me. At 5.45pm still no phone call. I was worried they had forgotten me and I didn't want to wait over the weekend, so I phoned them again. This time I spoke to the paramedic. He said all blood tests were clear, which is good news.

No sooner had I put the phone down and the doctor phoned. He questioned if Derek would mind me having the results. Can you believe that? Derek wouldn't mind if I dropped down dead, to be quite honest. The doctor went on to say that Derek was anaemic and asked is his diet good and could I bring him down to the surgery! Hello, is anyone out there in doctor/hospital land who ever reads their notes? Feeling very angry at the moment, why is everything such a battle?

14 September. Today Donna walked the 10K memory walk in Southsea. I went to see her off. It was such an emotional time, I didn't expect to feel so upset. The organisers had put up a tree for people to hang messages on. I couldn't bring myself to even read them. I am so proud of Donna for doing the walk, it couldn't have been easy for her.

17 September. Went to visit Derek. He was very pleased to see me, but still there was that agitation. The all clear has been given on the MRSA and Derek no longer has a UTI. This is all good news, but unfortunately Derek is still agitated and unsettled. This means that he has progressed further down the ladder of the disease.

The doctors are going to revamp his drugs to see if there can be any improvement in his behaviour. I received a newsletter from the home this week. On reading it I was shocked to see that the home had a suspected case of scabies. When I phoned the home, it seems that a notice had been put up, although I hadn't seen it; and there were four suspected cases of it, but not confirmed. I asked if Derek was one of the cases. Luckily he was not, but I am concerned especially as Derek has terrible problems with his leg, with cellulitis and with the MRSA.

***

This week has been one of my worst with regards to myself and my emotions. I have been feeling really down, as if a cloud has formed over my head. I broke down in front of Louise, which I am so sorry for as she is finding it very hard at the moment. I just can't seem to find a way out of this sadness. I am hoping I will bounce back very soon, I need to be strong for my girls.

23 September. Just when I think I can't feel any lower, Donna had a doctor's appointment, the results of which were the discovery of some brown marks behind her eyes. These need to be looked at by an optician. Also, she is being referred to a neurologist because of her continuing headaches. Probably because I am feeling low myself, but in my head I feel like the end of the world is about to happen. I just don't think I can continue to hear any more bad news. I just want to pack my bags and run, run from anything that's trying to destroy me and my family. It's like a never-ending whirlpool that keeps trying to pull me under, and I feel that I am slowly drowning.

27 September. Donna had an appointment at the opticians today and got the all clear. Apparently she has always had these marks in her eyes. I felt so relieved that there was nothing untoward happening.

This evening Louise had a panic attack. I was at home with her when it happened. She too has not been feeling well, with dizzy spells and great tiredness. I am wondering if this is stress.

28 September. Went to see Derek as I hadn't seen him for a while due to my own problems. I felt I couldn't cope seeing him. When I arrived at the home Derek was wandering around the lounge zipping and unzipping the seat cushions. We walked back to his room and I managed to get him to lie down for a while. Then I did some drawing for him. He seemed to be in quite a good mood.

29 September. Received a phone call from the home to say there had been two incidents involving Derek whereby he had hit a patient and also tipped a hot cup of tea over someone. I decided at that moment to go down to the home to see for myself how things were, as they had called the doctor out. I didn't want them to just drug him.

On arriving at the home Derek was wandering the lounge. We walked back to his room where he was given his tea. Later the doctor arrived. I asked if anyone had checked if Derek had a UTI. They hadn't, so they went and got a sample pot and a stick so I could try and get a sample from him. This was quite a difficult task, trying to get Derek to understand that he needed to wee. I was slowly losing my patience as I was desperate that the doctor didn't medicate for aggressive behaviour when in actual fact it was a UTI.

In the end I threatened Derek, saying I would go home if he didn't wee in the pot, and somehow after that he did wee. Turned out that Derek did in fact have a UTI.

The annoying thing is the care staff should have realised that Derek had an infection straight away instead of thinking the aggression was something else.

30 September. Phoned the home to see how Derek was overnight. 'Disruptive' was the reply. He has now dismantled his table. But now he is fast asleep.

Yet again I phoned Derek's CPN to update her on what's happened at the weekend. She agreed that the home will have to learn to work with Derek as he's of a younger generation with Alzheimer's and is not willing to spend his days sat in a chair waiting for god (my words).

October 2013
2 October. Louise's 18th birthday. Yet another milestone Derek has missed.

5 October. Louise had her 18th birthday party. All went well, everyone seemed to have a great time. The theme was Disney/Hollywood, so everyone dressed up as Disney characters. If anyone had said to me five years ago I would organise an 18th and 21st party on my own I would probably have freaked out, but it seems with everything that has happened I take it all in my stride.

***

I have not been to see Derek in over a week. I have phoned the home and they say he's fine. I have been so worried about the girls, I just couldn't bring myself to visit him.

8 October. I had a meeting with the outreach dementia team at my home to discuss Derek's care plan. This turned out to be an interesting meeting. They wanted to have some background information on Derek before the Alzheimer's. This team go into care homes and study patients to find out their needs. While watching Derek they noticed he was a caring man, who was very precise in his work.

They realised that what the care home took as problem behaviour was in fact a caring nature. For example, if someone needed a small table to put their cup on, Derek would go and get one, but was unaware as to if the table he took belonged to someone else. The team said that there were to be changes made to the care home. I replied that once the team left the care home, nothing would be done. Their reply was, 'Yes, it will'. If not they will complain to higher management.

The list included better lighting, more room needed for residents, Derek to have an old chair he could sand down to keep him occupied, to change Derek's room around so he can identify the toilet in his room better, to not have the door alarm going off every few minutes (which does unsettle the patients), more activities and access to the conservatory, which has since been made into another office. I must admit I was very impressed with the ideas they had to change the home.

The outreach team are at the home till January, so fingers crossed all will change for the better. The team said that the home wanted Derek to go back to the psychiatric hospital. The outreach team said, 'No, you have to learn to work with Derek.' I call that a result at last.

9 October. A phone call from Derek's CPN nurse to say that Derek will be getting a new CPN nurse again. What happened to continuity? I have this feeling of being lost at the moment, I think it's about not belonging to anyone. They say I am in a grieving process and maybe I am, who knows, but I am sure when Derek is no longer around my grieving will be more so. I recognise now more than ever that all the time I can keep some normality in my life I can cope, but too much time on my own, or having to talk about Derek and his illness, is when I just break down. At times I feel so alone, as if no one really understand just how I feel. Not only have I lost a husband, but a friend and someone I trust completely to share my worries, dreams and life with. The thought of being alone for the rest of my life is so scary, sometimes I can hardly bear it. I tell myself that when this nightmare is over I will pack up and move, possibly abroad, but maybe that's a dream to keep me going, who knows. I like to think that I will be brave enough to do just that.

11 October. Went to visit Derek with my friend Maz. She hadn't seen Derek since he was in hospital and was interested in the home he was now in.

When we arrived, Derek was in the lounge, sitting on the arm of a chair and bent right over fast asleep. I had trouble waking him, and when I finally did manage to wake him up I guided him to his room so he could lie on the bed. Why the carers could not have noticed I just do not know. Maz was not impressed by the staff at all.

15 October. I visited the home again, as I wanted to see if Derek was still sleepy. When I arrived he was slumped in a dining chair, bent over again. With the help of a member of staff we got Derek into his room, and I managed to lie him on his bed.

Derek was unshaven and scruffy. While he was asleep I went to my car to get the scissors, comb and razor I now keep there. On checking his leg, I noticed it looked a bit weepy. The nurse came into the room and I pointed out that Derek's leg didn't look too good. She agreed and phoned the doctor, who will now swab the leg and then possibly prescribe antibiotics again. If I hadn't turned up today, how long would Derek's leg have gone untreated?

When Derek woke, I managed to sit him in a chair and cut his hair. I then tried to shave him, but he got very angry and grabbed the razor out of my hand and scraped it down my hand drawing blood. I think he was trying to tell me that it hurt to be shaved.

The next challenge was to wipe the loose hair off him without any facecloth or towels to hand. I have no idea why there are neither items in his room. Next I needed to put clean clothes on him. The t-shirt wasn't too difficult, however the trousers were a different story. I couldn't make Derek understand that his trousers needed changing because of all the hair over them. I had quite a battle on my hands trying to get him to change, to the point he got very angry with me, and I believe that if it wasn't me trying to get him to change he may well have hit a carer. I came home with some of Derek's clothes to wash as clearly the person who does laundry must have a sight problem. Yet again clothes not belonging to him were hanging up in his wardrobe.

18 October. Went to visit Derek as I had some clean clothes for him which I had taken home the previous visit. Derek was wandering around the lounge so I went into his room to hang up the clothes. One of the carers brought him into his room to see me. He seemed yet again very sleepy. I sat him in a chair and attempted to shave him with the electric shaver I had brought from home, but it was not successful. I noticed he was wearing socks, even though I had told the home before to make sure he doesn't wear them as they are too tight on his legs. In fact, I thought I had brought all of his socks home, but alas I am not even sure if the socks he had on were his. I managed to prise the socks off, and was shocked to see that his leg was double the size it was on Tuesday. It was hot and red and clearly infected. I went to find the nurse; she was outside having a smoke. I told her about Derek's leg and she said that they couldn't do anything until the swab results were back on Monday. I said that wasn't good enough and that if he wasn't put on antibiotics he would become aggressive again over the weekend. Her reply was. 'Let me finish my cigarette then I will phone the doctor.'

I went back into Derek's room for a while. He was fast asleep. I later went to check to see how the nurse had got on about calling a doctor. She said she had to fax them and wait for a phone call. Not good enough. I asked for the doctor's number and called them myself. The doctor/paramedic who knew of Derek's case asked why the home hadn't phoned him about Derek's leg. I replied, you tell me why! He was annoyed that he hadn't been told and said he was going to talk to the manager. I told him there was no point.

Anyway, within 20 minutes I had the prescription from the doctors. I had to drive round and pick it up, otherwise it would still be there waiting. I think it's terrible that a nursing home at the end of the day lacks nursing. I just don't understand why there is a lack of care.

When I walked back into the home, another resident's relative said, 'I see you have just done what I did the other day and had to pick up medication from the doctors.' Turns out it's the norm for this home, no sense of urgency whatsoever. I commented on the fact that I had been thinking of looking at other homes, but apparently they are all the same in their opinion.

Waking Derek up to give him his tablet was a task. He was so sleepy. Eventually when he did wake he was very disorientated. He took off his trousers, then tried to put them back on again, but with both legs in one trouser leg. When I tried to help he got very angry with me. I think the agitation had started.

As I went to leave I moved Derek's box which holds his books and colouring pencils. I noticed it smelt of urine. On further investigation, his Man Utd scarf, which was also in the box, had been weed on. Again, why didn't the carers notice this?

I think it's time to make waves in the home. I am very angry at the lack of care in this home. On Monday I will make a complaint.

21 October. Made my complaint to the in-reach team, who asked me to put it in a letter to the manager and also to the area manager. I then phoned the home to see how Derek was. The nurse said Derek was very quiet and of low mood.

22 October. Phoned the home to see how Derek was. The nurse on duty didn't speak clear English so it was difficult to understand what was being said. I understood about the doctor coming to see Derek, but that was about it. Later that afternoon I phoned the doctors who said they would get back to me. In the meantime, when I got home there was a message from the manager of the home. I phoned him back and he said that Derek was booked into St Richard's Hospital for a leg scan, to rule out DVT. A nurse will come to the home to inject Derek, then he will be taken by ambulance to the hospital for the scan.

It's typical that of all the days I am free, tomorrow I am going to Guildford with Donna for her Camp America interview, but I will visit Derek at the home when I return.

When the doctor got back to me she said that they were unsure about what was happening with Derek's leg. He did however have MRSA again. If Derek has DVT he will be put on Warfarin, but if it's just the MRSA they will have to consult with the microbiologist again.

23 October. Louise wasn't feeling too well, so she came to Guildford with us. To be quite honest, I think she had got herself into quite a state, because she knew if she had a panic attack at college I could not be there for her without travelling for an hour. It was best she came with us, then I also wouldn't worry in case she was ill. I admit she did look washed out.

Anyway, Donna went to the interview. We then planned to do some shopping in Guildford, but we couldn't find where to park, so we landed up driving to Southampton. Crazy I know, but at least I managed to buy Donna's Christmas present.

On the way home I stopped at the Chinese to get some chips for tea. While Donna was in the Chinese I phoned the home to see how Derek had got on. Their reply was that

Derek was still at the hospital, waiting for transport home. This was at 6.30pm. Derek's hospital appointment had been at 3pm. The home said they would phone the carer with Derek to see what was going on, and phone me back.

When I got home I phoned the home again. They gave me the carer's phone number. I phoned him and he said that the hospital couldn't do the scan because Derek became aggressive when they wanted him to take off his trousers. I realised afterwards that Derek wasn't wearing pants, so that may have been the reason, but then surely the home should have checked that before taking him to the hospital.

The doctors decided to do a blood test instead to check for a blood clot. After I dropped the girls off home I went straight to the hospital. Derek and his carer were still waiting for the blood test results. It was now 7.30pm. I complained that the hospital should never make an Alzheimer's patient wait in a hospital for so long and pointed out that they were lucky Derek was so calm, because at this time of evening he becomes agitated. The nurse agreed that this should not have happened.

The good news was that the DVT blood test showed no blood clots. The nurse then phoned for a taxi to take Derek and his carer back to the home. I interrupted the phone call to say not to bother as I would take them back. We arrived back at the home at 8pm, five-and-a-half hours after Derek departed for the hospital.

24 October. I phoned the home to ask if they had been in contact with Derek's doctor. The reply from the manager was they hadn't got the results back. I replied that we'd had the results yesterday – all clear on DVT, but he needed to get the antibiotics for the MRSA. What the hell does the manager do at the care home? Clearly not care.

The manager said he would get someone to phone me back. I said not to bother because I cannot understand half the words she says due to her accent. The manager said he understood and that he would get one of the carers to phone me.

Still waiting.

I have just phoned the paramedic at Derek's doctors, because I don't know who to turn to. I need someone who can sort Derek's leg problem out now, not when it's too late.

The paramedic said that the blood test would not be accurate because Derek was given a blood thinning drug for the scan. The paramedic is now going to visit Derek to see what he can do. I am now waiting for his phone call.

Still waiting for the call, but I have just received a call from social services saying they had been advised by the in-reach team about a complaint I had made about the home. I told them what had happened yesterday and so far today. They said that they were now going to look into it .

At 5.30pm I phoned the doctors to see what was happening with Derek. The doctor thinks that Derek has a skin infection, not DVT. The doctor contacted the microbiologist at the hospital and now Derek has a prescription for an antibiotic to hopefully combat the MRSA. I questioned the doctor as to why Derek either has a leg infection or a urine infection, asking if this was a sign that the body has some kind of infection going on. He said maybe, but they have now gone to the top in regard to medical information; it's the best they can do.

I find this quite worrying, as I am not convinced this problem is ever going to go away. I worry that the home is too laid back to see the urgency of getting antibiotics when Derek shows signs of infection, for if they do not act quickly it could turn to septicaemia.

There has been a lot in the news lately about misconduct in care homes. I am so worried that if something happens to Derek due to the home's neglect there will be an investigation and possible court hearings etc. I just don't think I could cope with this on top of everything else. I pray this never happens.

25 October. Phoned the home to ask after Derek. All is OK, still a little sleepy but that could be because of the infection, who knows? Apparently, he is still on observation.

30 October. Louise and I went to visit Derek at the home. When we arrived, Derek was in the lounge sitting at the table eating cake and having a cup of tea. I had brought with me some Actimel, with the assumption that Derek needed some good bacteria to help with all the antibiotics he has been having recently. Ideally I would have left a stock of them there, but I am not convinced that the home would remember to give them to Derek on a daily basis.

When Derek got up from the table I noticed he had wet himself. I pointed this out to a staff member, but in the same breath said don't worry I will change him. I was so annoyed that Derek was in that state. I must admit it took some time and a lot of encouragement to change Derek's pants and trousers, but it was doable. I then hunted for his Man Utd duvet cover, put that back on the bed, sorted out his dirty washing to bring home to wash. Then I moved some of the furniture around so that the commode was in a better position to be used. Hopefully it will help Derek.

Also we noticed that Derek's feet were black from walking around with no shoes on, so I found a bowl and with soap from the soap dispenser soaked his feet. Apparently Derek's feet get washed on a daily basis!

One thing is very obvious, Derek's teeth never get cleaned. I was going to try but the toothbrushes were missing. When I questioned about Derek's teeth being cleaned, the reply was he won't let anyone clean them. To be totally honest, I don't think I have ever seen such disgusting teeth. They are grey, borderline green. Care homes should be prosecuted under the trade description act for 'care'. Derek was saying in his own way about how he just sits around doing nothing. He kept asking to go, to where I don't know.

31 October. Phoned the care home. Spoke to the manager and mentioned the fact that Derek had wet himself and no one had noticed. His reply was that Derek had been found weeing in different places as he couldn't find the toilet.

I then mentioned that Derek said he wanted something to do. His reply was that he was quite annoyed that this hadn't been put into practice yet and they must sort out some better activities for Derek. I felt that he was passing the buck somewhat, as I still am not sure what his role in the home is – manager?!

Went to a carers' meeting at the psychiatric hospital and received some sad news – the SWACAS team are no longer running carers' groups due to them losing their jobs. Considering everyone keeps saying that Alzheimer's is on the increase, still important people vital to this service are losing their jobs. This means that the nurse who was our first nurse will no longer be able to help with Derek's case.

November 2013
5 November. Attended a meeting at the care home. About 13 people attended including the in-reach team. I had a list of questions for the manager which included the food, smoking, clothes, hygiene, staff ID board.

After commenting on what I had witnessed Derek being served up, one of the relatives of a resident said that she thought the food was good and that the sandwiches were lovely. In respect of the clothes, yet another relative said how well the clothes were ironed. I mentioned about the smoking and the full ash trays. The manager replied that the ash trays were emptied regularly.

I asked about the staff photo ID board. This was at least the third time I had asked, and again the manager said, 'Oh yes, I will get round to that.' Needless to say, I came away from the meeting feeling disheartened. I felt I had wasted my time and more than that I felt it was me against everybody else, as if I was nit-picking.

Derek was the best I had seen him in a while, although I did notice that his swollen leg did have a sore on the opposite side to the infected side, so I will have to keep an eye on that.

14 November. Received a phone call from the home today to say Derek had another urine infection and he is now on antibiotics.

It was decided that it would be good if a meeting was set up with Derek's doctor to find out if any more can be done about Derek's continuous infections. After a couple of phone calls, a consultation was held between myself and a nurse at Derek's surgery.

The outcome was that there are tests that can be done, which are quite invasive, and to be quite honest Derek would never be able to tolerate such investigation. It was then decided that when Derek finished the antibiotics another urine sample would be taken, and this time sent to the hospital to see if anything can be diagnosed there.

24 November. Louise and I went to visit Derek. When we arrived, Derek was fast asleep in a chair. The nurse said he hadn't slept for about four days, neither day or night. I can't understand how he keeps going without sleep. I asked if a urine sample had been done yet, but apparently they hadn't managed to catch Derek having a wee yet.

Louise was sitting in Derek's room waiting for us, as she doesn't feel comfortable in the lounge with all the other residents. After talking to the nurse, Derek woke up. I asked him to come with me to his room as Louise was waiting for him. To be quite honest, I don't think he understood me at all. But anyway he got up from his seat, and was fiddling with his trousers. I realised he wanted the toilet so I called out for a member of staff for the sample pot. Would you believe, they didn't have one close at hand, even though they were supposed to be getting a sample from him? I guided Derek towards his room, but on the way he had started to wee himself. Just as we got to his room one of the staff produced a kidney dish for the urine. I wondered when Derek was going to stop weeing, he almost filled the dish up. We then had to change Derek's clothes. He had stripped from the waist down, standing in the corridor, but trying to put clean clothes on him was very difficult. It took two of us to achieve this, with Derek getting very angry, swearing and trying to hit out. Unfortunately, Louise witnessed this. It's so sad to see this happen.

After this ordeal, Derek fell asleep in the chair in his room. Louise and I sat talking to each other for a while, then out of the blue she said to Derek, 'Oh by the way, I have a main part in the musical Peter Pan! I am Wendy!' At that point my heart broke, for Derek would not have understood what she was saying even if he was awake. I was reminded yet again how Derek's illness has made a massive impact on not only my life but also the girls' as well. After a while, Louise and I managed to get Derek into bed, and then we left.

27 November. Louise had a bad panic attack, the worst so far. I felt so helpless, I wanted to take her suffering away. This has made quite an impact on me and has reminded me yet again how vulnerable we all are.

28 November. Received a phone call from the care home. There had been an incident involving Derek. He had gone into another resident's room while they were sleeping and barricaded himself in. I immediately said he must have a urine infection, as he had been off antibiotics for seven days. I asked if the results had come back from the sample we took on Sunday. The reply was that it hadn't been sent off. I was so angry that the home hadn't even bothered to walk the sample a few yards up the road to the doctor's surgery. I told the home I wanted to put in a formal complaint.

Now the crisis team are involved because of the room incident. The story unravelled: with a few phone calls from other health professionals I found out that Derek had gone into the room next door to his when the resident was asleep. He urinated over the bed, barricaded himself and the other resident into the room, and when the care workers finally managed to get into the room, he was holding a chair over the other resident's head. This was seen as threatening behaviour, hence the crisis team were called. They have also given Derek another drug to see if they can control the aggressive behaviour.

The problem is Derek has got back into the no sleep at night routine, but also the aggression comes with this. Since all of this happening, Derek continues to try and get into the room next to his, and is still aggressive to staff, even trying to bite them.

As this has happened near a weekend, Derek has been given one-to-one night cover until Monday. The home are trying to get funding for him to receive one-to-one night cover on a permanent basis. Hopefully this will happen on Monday, if not I am not sure what will happen. It is possible that Derek may have to move, which causes another dilemma, where will he go? It might be that he has to go back to hospital.

30 November. I went to see Derek. He was wandering around, head bent over. He looked like an old man. I guided him back to his room, his trousers were wet through, his t-shirt covered in food. I managed to get him changed without too much of a problem. I am not sure that he recognised me, it's hard to say. He ate a few sweets, then fell asleep in the chair.

December 2013
1 December. I feel our lives are in turmoil, not knowing what's going to happen about Derek. Will he get the funding or will he be classed as a threat to himself and the residents of the home? If so, he will be removed and maybe sent back to the hospital, which I find scary, especially if they start playing around with the drugs again. I don't think I could bear that again. I find myself asking the question how much longer is this going to go on? The situation is taking its toll on both myself, the girls and of course on Derek, although Derek is unaware of how his illness is affecting us.

***

I was thinking of booking a holiday for myself and the girls. I even had everything saved on my laptop, but I just couldn't push the 'book' button. I just don't want to be too far away from Derek in case another phone call comes. A friend said I can't put my life on hold. But that's just it, I have to.

3 December. Phoned the care home this morning to see how Derek was. He has only had about three hours' sleep, and is still a bit agitated. At 3pm today I received a phone call from the crisis team to say there had been three incidents involving Derek. He had hit a carer, thrown a drink and has become uncontrollable. The home are now waiting for the doctor to arrive to section Derek and take him to the psychiatric hospital. I am very worried that if they start giving him a cocktail of drugs again it could finish him off. I am scared to tell Louise in case it upsets her too much. Luckily she wasn't at home when the phone call came. I understand that Derek needs to go into hospital for his safety, as well as for the other residents' safety at the home, but I do worry after last time as to what drugs they will use. My other concern is how his reaction will be to being in the hospital again.

At 9pm Derek was admitted to the psychiatric hospital. He was sectioned under the Mental Health Act and taken by ambulance to hospital. I was informed by various health professionals throughout the evening of the progression of Derek's admission.

Derek showed no sign of agitation or aggression throughout the move, although he didn't sleep that night. He was calm throughout the night.

4 December. Went to visit Derek. He was fast asleep in the chair. He was very difficult to wake. I guess that the accumulation of the new drug might be catching up with him. When he did wake up I am not sure he recognised me, he was mumbling in his own way, walking around with his head bent over. He looked so old and frail today. For the first time I felt that this was no longer my husband, but a sick man who just belongs to the system. So very sad.

The upside to Derek being in hospital is the amount of space there is for him to walk around in and at the moment there are only five patients. I am now wondering if Derek would benefit from a care home with more space, as maybe this is why he gets agitated.

5 December. My birthday. I can't believe how quickly the last year has passed. Phoned the hospital this morning to see how Derek's night had been. Derek had not slept all night, he was moving furniture around, he had become incontinent, and when staff tried to change his clothes he was aggressive. The staff had to restrain him and medicate him.

Yesterday I had hoped that Derek's aggression was due to the staff at the care home, but clearly that is becoming untrue as he is still showing signs now. This is sad because I don't know how this is going to progress. Will it be a case of medication again? I hope not as I am worried his body may not be able to cope.

The hospital are trying to get a urine sample from Derek to check he hasn't got a UTI. This is more challenging than it sounds.

7 December. Went to visit Derek at the hospital. Yet again he was fast asleep, there was no way of waking him up. I spent a while there, and as I was about to leave Derek woke, wandered around the ward a bit, but there was no recognition of me being there. It seems to me that he has also started to age. Something I didn't realise was that with the deterioration of the brain also comes premature ageing. I was very surprised and a little shocked that this was the case.

9 December. Had a call from the hospital to say there was going to be a meeting at 10am tomorrow to discuss Derek's case.

Today I made a visit to a purpose-built centre for Alzheimer's located in Portsmouth. I had visited this home before, but was impressed with how they handled a resident who became agitated on my last visit. This was the home open to Portsmouth residents, but under the circumstances I felt I may stand a better chance of applying as clearly Derek needs specialist care. I was still impressed with the home, lots of walking space for Derek, nice areas to sit, activities, very quiet, but I am not sure if it's the right place.

10 December. Arrived at the hospital at 10am. Derek was fast asleep again, and I still couldn't wake him. At the meeting was the staff nurse, social worker, a young doctor, a lady from the crisis team and a consultant psychiatrist. The meeting covered all aspects of Derek's care, including the care home. I was asked if I was happy with the care home. I pointed out about the incidences at the home, not calling out the doctor when needed, and the lack of personal hygiene with regards to cleaning teeth. Also the state Derek's leg was in and that I didn't think the cream supplied was being used when needed. The lady from the crisis team also backed my story with regards to the leg and that I had to change Derek's clothes because he had wet himself.

It had become apparent at the hospital that Derek was aggressive when personal care was needed. For example, when Derek had wet himself and needed clean clothes, it takes three staff members to take on the task. When Derek has been changed, he then sometimes strips off his clothes and walks around naked. This was new to me. Derek then becomes aggressive because the staff are trying to re-dress him.

The staff nurse then asked if Derek was like this before. My reply, 'What walked around naked?' then I laughed, 'Or aggressive?' At this point I got upset and replied to the nurse I can't believe you could even ask me if Derek was aggressive, he wouldn't hurt a fly, and that she should know it's part of the illness. With that the nurse turned a little pink. At the end of the meeting she apologised, and said she had worded it wrong. I then apologised for snapping at her. The consultant psychiatrist asked if I wanted Derek to return to the care home. My answer was no.

***

The outcome of the meeting was to lower the dose of Risperidone and add another drug to hopefully reduce the agitation. Meanwhile I need to look for a new home. Two of the suggestions were the one in Bishops Waltham which I had looked at before, and a unit which was part of a forensic science hospital, which I had also looked at before, but not the hospital side. I will take another look as Derek's needs have changed, but it's sad to think that he now has to go to a specialist care home for difficult patients. I never wanted this to ever happen; in my head it's like putting Derek into an asylum.

14 December. I went to visit Derek at the hospital. It was just before lunch so I stood a good chance of seeing Derek awake.

On arrival Derek was asleep, but after a few minutes he woke up and was unsteady on his feet. The staff realised he needed the toilet so guided him into the toilets. Derek was feeling cold so one of the nurses went and got a jumper from Derek's room. With great difficulty she was trying to get Derek to put the jumper on, but Derek had taken off his trousers and was trying to put the jumper on his legs. It took three members of staff with great patience to re-dress Derek. I was very impressed at how they managed Derek, if not a little upset at how Derek has deteriorated.

I went into lunch with Derek who ate a good meal, with pudding, without any trouble. When he got up from the table he looked at me for the first time, put his arms around me and kissed me. This is the first time in the last four visits that there has been any acknowledgement of knowing me or of being aware I was there. I gave Derek his Christmas card from me, but he had no idea what it was. He wouldn't open it and in the end I opened it up and placed it on the windowsill in his room. Derek then went back to the lounge and fell asleep.

***

At this moment in time I wish Derek could stay in the hospital. The staff are so caring and Derek has had no infections since being there. His leg has actually improved, it's no longer scaly, as it was at the care home. This, I believe, is because the hospital are actually using the cream supplied to treat his leg unlike the care home. I think that's proof enough that it is not the right care home.

16 December. Went to visit the Waterlooville care home today. Although I had visited it before, I realised that Derek's needs are now different, and this home was on my top list before. We were greeted by a different manager. I explained the difficulties that the care home were having with Derek and his needs. The manager asked how Derek was funded. She then went on to explain that the QCC had found that the paperwork in the care home was in disarray and that therefore the funding people would not be happy placing Derek in their home, which was honest and direct, I can't ask for more. This, of course, could change so it wasn't a definite no. We were given a very quick tour, basically in the lift, down a corridor to the lounge, then back down again. We were not shown around any rooms or told about activities, meals or anything. The manager did recommend another home in Southampton. I did get the impression that Derek wasn't really wanted there.

18 December. Today I went to visit the forensic science hospital in Surrey. It's a long trek and very much off the beaten track – a single track, in fact, in the middle of the woods, leads up to the unit and the hospital. A post van was coming towards me so I pulled over only for my wheels to get stuck in the mud. Quite scary when you're on your own in the middle of nowhere. Anyway, I managed to spin free out of that situation.

I went to the reception, but was told that they do not show visitors around because it's a secure unit. I was taken to another building which was part of the unit, I believe. I was made to feel very welcome. I told them about Derek and the problems we were having. I told them that the doctor had recommended the unit to me. They were confused as to why he recommended it, since that unit was for very difficult cases and a locked unit. It catered for all aspects of mental health, some had been through the prison system.

It was suggested that another unit, which was also on the same site, may be the better option for Derek.

We walked over to this unit, which looked new. It only had 18 residents; inside it was light and airy with lots of room to walk around. The downside for me was that all the residents wore wristbands which opened certain areas of the building that they were allowed in. I questioned how the residents knew how to use the bands on their wrist. The reply was that they learnt. I question this in my head – can someone with Alzheimer's learn new things?

The biggest thing about this home which doesn't sit well with me, was that to visit Derek we would have to make an appointment, and on arrival we would meet Derek in a family room. Only one family meet in this room at a time. This means we don't get access to Derek's room, or get to walk around the home, only the places allocated to us.

This also means I would lose control to some extent of Derek's care, and it would feel like visiting him in prison.

After the visit we walked back to the original building and had a further chat about the care the home offered, with alternative homeopathy, reflexology and also they had a sensory room with lights, which caught my attention. I was asked what I would do when Derek was no longer around, and it was put to me why I couldn't do those things now. My reply, I won't let go until Derek is no longer living. I was asked how they could help, suggesting that I could help out at the home, which may sound ideal and if it wasn't so far away maybe an option.

The idea of three units at the site was that if Derek became ill there was a hospital there when he became bedbound and he could be moved to the appropriate part. So ideally he would not move off this site, as all eventualities are catered for. It's just that I don't want to let go, and sending Derek so far away, I feel I am sending him out of sight and out of mind.

On my way home I stopped in at the hospital to see Derek. Today he was awake and walking around. He'd had no sleep last night or the night before, he also hadn't slept during the day. Surely at some point he will need to sleep.

19 December. Another day, another care home, this time in Southampton, the home that the Waterlooville home had recommended. It was a very large house which was having building work done.

Again, I was made very welcome and was shown around the two floors. There was access to a large garden, the men and woman are separated but come together for activities, the staff seemed very friendly, and I witnessed a family going to visit with a picnic which I thought was lovely. This home may be a contender. I have decided to visit a couple of other local homes, as I pass them every day. Maybe the home I am looking for is on my doorstep?

20 December. Started another lot of counselling – my fifth now. I only have six weeks though. I guess that will have to do, after that I guess I am on my own.

21 December. Went to the old care home to collect some clothes for Derek. He was running short of jogging bottoms. A couple of the care staff said how they missed Derek; one said she was surprised Derek was in hospital.

From there I went to the psychiatric hospital to see Derek and to cut his hair. On arrival Derek was asleep so I took the opportunity to start cutting his hair. I was almost finished when he woke, stood up and started to walk around, not acknowledging me at all. He then went into dinner. Eventually I managed to sit him back in a chair and finished off cutting his hair. At no point did Derek acknowledge me. Whilst talking to a staff member, one of the care homes near me was mentioned again. This is the fourth recommendation I have had. I thought it was just a care home, but apparently it has a dementia unit, so I must visit.

23 December. Derek's social worker phoned this morning. She asked if I had seen any homes and said about the forensic science hospital. I told her I'd been to look around, but wasn't allowed in due to it being a secure unit. I said I wasn't happy with having to make appointments to see Derek, and that it was like a prison. She gave me the name of another home to look round in Littlehampton, so I have added that to my list. I said to her that I didn't think Derek was so bad that he needed to go to a secure unit. Her reply was, 'Yes Angela, he is that bad.' To hear her say that broke my heart. How the hell did someone so kind, loving and gentle turn into this other person. This disease is just pure evil.

24 December. Myself and the girls decided to visit Derek today instead of Christmas Day. Derek I believe was unaware of what day it was. There were a few more patients on the ward today so we went to his room. The staff brought his tea into his room. Derek needed a little encouragement to eat. We gave him his Christmas presents – a chocolate tool kit, which he thanked us for, and a sensory cushion I'd made him.

Although I wasn't sure if Derek recognised us, he did give me a big hug and a kiss, the best Christmas present ever. There wasn't much recognition, if any, of the girls being there, although there was the occasional smile from Derek. I feel the loss of Derek even more so at Christmas. This is the second Christmas that Derek hasn't been at home with us.

25 December. The strangest Christmas ever. We stayed in our night clothes, eating Christmas dinner on our laps in the lounge, watching a film. Never in my whole life have I done this, but the girls were happy. We got dressed at about 4pm to spend the evening round at my brother's.

27 December. I called into the local care home to see if it was a possibility for Derek, but they said that they were closing down one of their homes and all vacancies were for the other residents. But I also felt that it probably wasn't right for Derek.

I then went to the home in Littlehampton. Although only 22 miles away the traffic jams were doubling my journey time. My first impression was OK, but when entering the building and seeing the residents, I was a little shocked at how old and frail they looked. Apparently, this care home takes the patients when no one else will. This is not the place I want Derek to go to. I am now at the point of despair. I only have one other place to look. One of the staff nurses mentioned it again and said to speak to the person in charge to see if they would consider Derek. I feel the decision of care home for Derek may be taken out of my hands because of his challenging behaviour. I just can't accept that he has got this bad.

The total number of homes I have now looked at is 30 and that's not including the ones I have visited more than once.

2014

January 2014

2 January. Went to visit Derek. He was sleepy as usual. The ward was very short-staffed. I felt sorry for them, only two nurses on the floor with 8/10 patients, and one of them was needing one-to-one. I just don't understand why mental health provision has to struggle with funding, staffing etc. Does no one listen to what's happening?

Derek wasn't aware of me being there. This seems to be happening more often. Towards the end of my visit the psychiatrist who was Derek's original mental health doctor came onto the ward. He kindly gave me an update on Derek's situation. Apparently they are trying out a drug which has a good effect on aggression. They have started Derek on a low dose, but will up the dose from now, and hopefully it will have a good effect on him.

This psychiatrist is now taking over Derek's case as his previous one has moved on sadly. The psychiatrist said that he sees no reason why Derek cannot be transferred into a home now. I am keeping a low profile as the longer Derek is in hospital the better. At least he is being looked after properly.

10 January. Took a second look at the other care home today. I needed to see the size of the bedrooms and the dining area. My one concern was that there were several staircases which were fire escapes, and Derek's room would also be upstairs. Now Derek hasn't used stairs for 18 months, so I would be very worried about this, but these things could be resolved. One idea would be to put pressure mats outside the door of Derek's room which would sound an alarm if he left his room.

When I got home I phoned the social worker to say that this care home is a possibility, but the stairs were a concern. The social worker's reply was that this home would not be able to deal with Derek. This puts me back at square one again. The social worker gave me the name of another care home, this time in Hayward's Heath. I said I would take a look.

11 January. Today I went to visit Derek with his ex carer. When we arrived the staff said that Derek was asleep in a chair in his room. No matter how much I called him or tapped his arm he didn't wake up. I went to sit on his bed and noticed his bed was wet, as was his pillow and the sweatshirt on his bed. I stripped his bedding off the bed and advised the nurse that he needed new bedding.

When the nurse came into the room she said that Derek's trousers must need changing because he doesn't pull his trousers down to go to the toilet, he just wees himself. She then went into great detail about how he doesn't sleep, paces up and down, and now poos his trousers and then smears it everywhere. She then went on to say that Derek had even had a poo in his hand, offering it to another patient who was blind. She then said about how Derek tried to wee into another's cereal bowl while she was eating it, then about how Derek had kicked her and head-butted another member of staff. This time I had heard enough and turned round and said to the nurse, 'What do you suggest we do, put him down?' The nurse was shocked, I believe, to hear me say such a thing, but the way she was listing all these things that Derek does, I just flipped. I told her I had been to 30 homes and they didn't want him either. By this time I was in tears. I just don't know what to do any more.

I did try to change Derek's trousers when he woke up, but he became angry with me. No amount of persuasion could get him to change his trousers. He seems very distant, his eyes unfocused, and I believe he doesn't know me, not today. I believe that something isn't quite right. Derek seems more agitated and he is scratching his legs constantly. I mentioned to the staff nurse that Derek's leg seems to be more swollen and spreading further up his leg, so they asked a doctor to come and look at it. After waiting a while the doctor had not arrived, and I had to go as I was watching Louise's show.

When I got home late tonight I phoned the hospital to see what the doctor thought of Derek's leg. They prescribed ibuprofen and if he becomes breathless they are to take him to St Richard's Hospital. What all this means, I do not know, but I am worried.

13 January. Visited Derek today. He was wandering the corridors, with no recognition of me being there. The nurse told me that Derek was booked in to have a scan the next day to make sure he hasn't got a blood clot. I went into his room and noticed there was poo on the seat. The nurse went to clean it up, and I asked her about Derek now playing with his poo. She said that they had just cleaned Derek up as he had smeared it up the walls of the corridor. She said that Derek believes its putty, as he tries to fill up holes with it. If it wasn't so sad, it would be funny.

After I had been there a while, Derek sat down with a cup of tea. I sat in the chair next to him. He looked at me and smiled and said 'Love you'. He also mentioned the girls, saying 'Good girls'. I thought I would tell him that Louise had been in a show, but as I said the words that moment had gone.

14 January. I phoned the hospital to ask how the scan had gone. The hospital had managed to scan three major arteries out of the five and they were clear, which is good news. It was decided that Derek has lymphoedema, which is not life-threatening, but he will be more susceptible to infection. Hopefully he will now be put on a low dose of antibiotics.

18 January. Went to visit Derek. He greeted me with a hug and a kiss, quite unexpected. He asked me if I had anything for him, which made myself and the nurses laugh. On previous visits when Derek was in the care home I had brought along sweets and drinks, but because of his unawareness of me visiting him I hadn't brought him anything this time. One of the staff went and got him a chocolate cake.

22 January. I phoned the hospital to see how Derek was. There was no change. They had just given him a bath, but he was now walking around the ward with his pants on over the top of his trousers like Superman.

24 January. Received a phone call from the hospital. Derek's doctor would like a meeting with me to discuss options for drugs to try on him. I am not sure if the drugs are for his lack of sleeping at night or for his aggression. Apparently there hasn't been a member of staff that hasn't been hit by Derek. The meeting is on Tuesday.

***

In the last week I have had two incidents with dad. Firstly, when phoning to ask how he was his reply was that he was not well. He said he couldn't go to the toilet and that he couldn't eat because he was full, which was causing him chest pain and that he would die if he got too full.

On the second occasion dad phoned me to say he had broken a bone in his foot and that he couldn't walk. I asked if he had seen a doctor and his reply was that he needed an ambulance to take him to hospital. I explained that I was unable to take him, as I had a dental appointment and then a meeting at the hospital for Derek. I asked him to ask my sister. I then phoned my brother to ask his advice. He said that he had slipped on the stairs but his foot was OK. It seems that dad was trying to play for sympathy from me at a time when I am trying to deal with Derek. Such a sad situation.

28 January. The meeting at the hospital was, I feel, a waste of time. We talked about all the drugs Derek had been on. The doctor wanted to know if he had been on a particular drug, which I couldn't answer as since Derek hasn't been at home I have lost touch to some degree of which drugs have been used. I felt the conversation was going round in circles. To be honest the doctors have no idea how to treat Derek. The drug lithium was mentioned, but I do seem to remember there being bad press about that drug.

I asked what would happen if Derek was taken off the antidepressants. The answer was they didn't know. I mentioned that the side effects of antidepressants can be depression, but as I said I don't feel the meeting achieved anything.

I told the doctors that I wanted Derek to stay at the hospital because at least he was being looked after there and the staff knew him. I asked if he would be moved on because of his aggression. The doctor replied they had never moved anyone because of that and usually they are moved to the psychiatric hospital for that reason

I asked again about Derek's lifespan. He was very reluctant to reply. I said to him he must have some idea, as the Alzheimer's Society say when diagnosed younger the average life span is ten years. The doctor replied, sometimes only two years. I said that Derek was now in his sixth year, and the doctor said that he was surprised that Derek had survived this long.

After the meeting, I went to see Derek. He looked at me and said, 'My wife.' He then asked if I had anything for him. Luckily I had brought him some Christmas cake. With a big grin he ate the lot and said it was nice.

I noticed that the bottom of Derek's trouser leg was wet. Apparently his swollen leg was now oozing fluid. On one occasion there was a puddle of fluid on the floor where he was sitting which had come from his leg. Derek is now on antibiotics full time, as he will now be more prone to infection due to his leg.

February 2014
3 February. Visited Derek. He seemed very agitated today. His leg looked like it might be infected, so the staff nurse asked the doctor to have a look at it. The hospital are keeping a close eye on it.

***

To obtain some normality in my life I am taking a training course to become a home start volunteer. The reason I mention this is relevant only to what I am about to describe. I am into the fifth week. I arrive early because parking is a pain. The lesson starts and we are told that today's lesson is about illnesses, depression, mental health. We are told that if this subject is too upsetting then we can leave the room.

We were only into the discussion about ten minutes and the talk was about how they used to put women into asylums when they were suffering postnatal depression. Just the word 'asylum' started the tears. I got up and left the room. I was so upset, but at the same time angry at myself for getting upset. The organisers were very supportive, and gave me the option to leave the lesson if it was too much. They then said that they thought that the afternoon session should be missed because it was about grieving.

Great, I can't even face that subject. I think what hit me hard was the realisation that after all we have been through as a family I don't think I have truly realised the implications of how this will end. Instead of going home, I felt a great need to go to the hospital and see Derek. Unfortunately, it was a bad day for him too and he didn't acknowledge me at all. I left the hospital on a real low, unable to see a positive in my life.

12 February. Today I went to visit Derek. He was up and about and not so sleepy. Not long after I arrived he was peeing against the wall in the hallway, too late to guide him towards the toilet. I then realised he had messed himself, so the nurses took him off to the bathroom to wash and change him.

I then walked Derek to his room as I wanted to cut his hair. After a lot of persuasion, we managed to get him to sit in a chair. Cutting his hair was easier than I'd anticipated. Derek fell asleep just before I'd finished. I always shave his neck, to make him look tidy. I put shaving foam on my hand and went to apply it to Derek's neck. He woke up and got quite angry with me. He grabbed my wrist very tightly and tried to pull my bracelets off. I managed to loosen his grip on me, but it did bring tears to my eyes. I don't think he realised it was me cutting his hair.

After I had finished, Derek got up and peed on the floor in three places. He also messed in his trousers again. I can't believe that in a short space of time he needed the loo so many times. It's a full-time job just keeping him dry and mess free.

I also noticed that the lovely cushion I had made for him had poo on it and on closer inspection realised he had weed on it too. So sad, all that hard work gone to waste.

I decided to take Derek's suitcase home with me so I could collect Derek's remaining items from the care home on Friday. That too had been used as a toilet.

When I left the hospital I decided to go straight to the care home and collect Derek's items, instead of leaving it till Friday. When I arrived at the home I noticed that a few subtle changes had been made. A wooden wall plaque had been put up to welcome visitors, a weekly 'tea and chat' was now taking place, and there were wall art transfers with little sayings put up on the walls. Again, all for appearance. Still, they don't get the concept that care is more important than appearance.

Not one member of staff asked how Derek was, that just about says it all.

14 February. I realised that when I called into the care home to collect all of Derek's belongings, it was exactly a year ago to the day that Derek first moved into the home.

Today is Valentine's Day and its 25 years since I first started going out with Derek. I felt I should go and see him. I gave him some chocolate hearts, not that he was aware of what they were, he just ate them. I noticed that Derek's leg looked very sore and fluid was running out of it again. The nurse said that Derek had cellulitis back again. He also has a urine infection to which he is on more antibiotics. That's two types of antibiotics at once.

The staff nurse was talking about how she thought Derek would be better off in a home. I replied that there is no home out there for him. She said that the forensic science hospital unit was full. I couldn't help but feel relieved about that. I mentioned another home and said that the social worker commented on it costing £1,700 a week. Her reply was good luck with trying to find that funding. I replied that they may not have any choice, there is nowhere else for him to go. I so wish he could stay in hospital, it's the only place I trust to look after him.

20 February. Went to visit Derek. As it was half term, Louise wanted to see him too. I was worried that her seeing her dad might cause her to start having panic attacks again, but I felt I couldn't say no, because what if Derek were to die after I had said she couldn't come with me to see him. I just couldn't deal with knowing I had stopped her from seeing him.

As it turned out, Derek was in a good place. It's the best I have seen him for a while. He was quite chatty in his own way, though we didn't understand what he was saying. He looked at Louise and said, 'Beautiful girl.' I am not sure if he knew who she was. We gave him some chocolate which he ate. He then walked off down the corridor. He was gone a while. I went to find him and he was having a conversation with one of the female residents. I don't think that either one could understand the other. They then both walked back into the lounge where Louise and I were sitting, but they sat at the other end of the room to us. Apparently, the lady has become quite attached to Derek. She must be at least ten years older than Derek, not that age makes any difference.

After a while Derek looked across the room at me and motioned as if to say do you want me to come and sit with you. I replied yes, so he got up and came and sat with us. Derek then planted a kiss on my cheek. Later on, the lady whom was attached to Derek came over and said that Derek was her dad. That would have been technically impossible. Louise was very quiet throughout the visit. I noticed once sat down she was very rigid, almost as though she was scared to move. We didn't stay long, and once back in the car I noticed that she was silently crying. My heart went out to her. I feel so hopeless in these situations as we are all going through this nightmare in our own way, myself losing my husband who should have been my life partner until old age and beyond, and for the girls losing a dad who could help them through life's difficult journeys, be there on their wedding day to give them away, and so much more.

The last few days after the last visit with Derek I have been very emotional. I can only put it down to the fact that seeing Derek in a better place mentally and acknowledging my being there with the kiss, gave me a false sense of the old Derek and how he used to be.

25 February. Derek was seen by the lymphoedema nurse and prescribed a spray-like plaster to help his leg. She wasn't too concerned. I guess she has seen worse leg conditions, but to me it looks bad.

March 2014
1 March. I can't believe how quickly this year is going. Went to visit Derek. When I arrived it was very obvious the ward was short-staffed. Derek was wandering around. When I walked up to him I could see he had messed himself and also weed. I then noticed that there were small pieces of faeces on the carpet around the lounge. I don't know if they were Derek's or from another patient, even so I do think that was unacceptable. I went to report this to a staff member, also to say Derek needed cleaning. After about 20 minutes, maybe half an hour, staff came to take Derek for a bath and change of clothes.

On this visit Derek did acknowledge me, not straight away, but I had brought him some sweets, and while he was eating them he gave me one of his mischievous looks, as if to say there was still some of himself here. He also put his arms around me and gave me a kiss.

2 March. Today I received a phone call from the hospital to say there had been an incident involving Derek, which led to Derek being safeguarded. The incident was that Derek was in the lounge, got his penis out to do a wee and another patient touched it. Not something you want to hear about your husband, but sadly this is just another thing I have to accept in this long road to Derek's end of life.

I say end of life because this is sadly the only outcome Derek has from this disease. I am starting to look at end of life now, because I have to accept that this will happen. I only hope that it is sooner rather than later. Derek has lost his dignity, his understanding, his speech, his freedom, his love of life. There isn't much more left, just a body fighting to stay alive. Derek's illness is starting to take its toll on us as a family now, with both girls having panic attacks, headaches, stomach aches, and just recently I am having what I think are anxiety issues, which make me feel breathless. I have been booked into the doctors for blood tests and an ECG just to rule out anything else, but I suspect its anxiety. I was offered antidepressants but I turned them down again.

***

It is Derek's birthday next week; on 16 March he will be 68. I have bought him a new jumper, not that he needs one really but I just don't know what else to buy him. I think I will buy a small cake for him, otherwise it will feel that we have not celebrated his birthday. I don't know if the girls will go and see him. It's so difficult for them to see their dad in this state, my heart goes out to them.

I am finding myself having more sad days recently. This worries me a little because I don't want to get to the point that I can no longer cope. I have two daughters to support and who rely on me.

7 March. Received a phone call from the hospital to say that Derek has broken his electric razor, the one I had bought only a couple of weeks ago. I was told that Derek had smashed it up.

11 March. Went to visit Derek with shaving gel and two razors. One of the members of staff said that he was to blame for the broken razor. Derek had taken the top piece off the razor then apparently he went to hit one of the nurses and the razor was placed on the radiator and two of the blades fell down the back of the radiator. Either way, Derek no longer has an electric razor.

Derek was very sleepy when I walked into the lounge of the hospital. In fact, he didn't acknowledge me at all on this visit. I was shocked to see the state of his leg, most probably the worst I have seen it. The doctor came and had a chat with me. Derek has MRSA again and the cellulitis is causing his leg to be very red and oozing liquid. Derek has become immune to the antibiotics, and I was shocked that this had happened over such a short period of time. The doctor asked me what I wanted to do about trying another antibiotic, but of course Derek may become immune to that in a short time too. Then we could be on difficult ground because if Derek needed antibiotics, for say pneumonia, they wouldn't work.

A meeting is being held this afternoon to discuss Derek's case.

16 March. Today is Derek's birthday he is now 68 years old.

Although Derek is unaware of what day it is, I am disappointed that he only received four birthday cards. His brother and sister didn't bother, neither did any of my family. Just myself, the girls and two of Derek's cousins gave cards. It's almost as though they have written Derek off already. I am feeling quite angry as well, wondering if when Derek passes, will they still ignore him.

Myself and the girls went to the hospital to see Derek with a large birthday cake for everybody, and presents for him. When we arrived, the staff were waiting for more staff to arrive so they could change Derek as his shorts were wet. We were given access to the smaller lounge so we could be with just Derek.

We sat Derek down, but he started to put his hands down the back of his shorts. Unbeknown to us he had pooed his shorts and was now playing with it in his hands. He took his hands out of his shorts to show us, unfortunately this was done in front of the girls. I felt sorry for them having to witness their dad acting this way. I went to get help. The nurses came and took Derek for a wash and change of clothes.

Later we went into Derek's room to give him his cards and presents, but I had to open the cards for him as he wasn't interested at all. That also applied to the presents. I cut the birthday cake and gave Derek a piece, but while eating it he just fell fast asleep as though someone had just switched a switch.

We sat in his room for about 20 minutes. He felt cold so I put on his new jumper I bought him. We then left. Derek was still fast asleep. I am not sure that Derek had any idea of what went on today, there was no recognition of the girls, or that he was eating birthday cake. I so want to make this nightmare go away. Derek's leg is looking so bad I don't think it will ever get better, even Donna was shocked at how bad it looked.

18 March. Today I received a surprise through the post. About a week ago I sent back Derek's electric razor which he had broken. I had written to the manufacturers to explain how it had got broken and asked if they could repair it, as it was only a few weeks old. To my surprise, they replaced it with a new one, free of charge.

19 March. Went to visit Derek as Louise had an audition at Chichester University. Derek was walking around with his box of Turkish delight that Donna had bought him for his birthday. He recognised me straight away and gave me a big hug.

Derek was very talkative, in his own way. I could pick out a couple of words he said. The one phrase that was very upsetting was 'I am frightened'. I just wish I knew what he was frightened of. Maybe he just didn't mean frightened in the way that I took it to mean, I will never know, but it gave me a sad feeling to think that he was frightened for whatever reason. I wish I could just tell Derek that whatever happens next that it won't be as frightening as what he has already been through. But unfortunately he wouldn't understand.

Just before I left the hospital I noticed that Derek's leg was weeping, but this time it was pus, not just fluid. The nurse took a look. His leg had become more itchy which suggests an infection so they are going to take a swab and increase the painkillers. I asked the nurse what's to stop the infection getting into his blood stream, she replied I would have to ask the doctor.

***

I managed to get hold of Derek's social worker at last to ask what was happening to Derek in regards to him being moved on. Her answer was that we are no longer looking for a care/nursing home but at a private hospital. But that takes time to set up, so meanwhile it's the psychiatric hospital which to me is good news.

***

Between my last visit to see Derek and my next visit on the 28 March I had started to experience some difficulty in breathing. I went to the doctors who did a series of blood tests and an ECG, but all came up clear, thank god. But on the 21st I experienced a great fear. I felt I couldn't breathe and had a feeling of dread. Out of complete desperation I phoned my tutor of spiritual healing. He asked me to come to his house straightaway. On arrival I just broke down. We chatted for a while then he gave me some healing. The stress of my life had taken its toll on me. Without my healer I don't want to think what would have happened, but it sure scared me. The outcome of this scare has taught me that I need to look after myself, something I hadn't been doing; in fact I feel I was on a mission to self-destruct.

This experience has scared me into realising that I cannot help Derek any more. I need to, in some way, detach myself from him. I will still visit, of course I will, he's my husband and I love him, but I need to realise that I need to live my life as best I can, for I have two daughters who have no one else to look out for them. Derek is in the best place for care, I couldn't ask for anything more.

28 March. Went to visit Derek. I was very worried how this visit would go, after the last few days and how I had been feeling. Derek was awake and chatty in his own way. He did seem a little agitated. I noticed that he was very much in the nurses' faces. I questioned this with the nurses and they said that when Derek does this it's due to agitation. I looked at his leg – it was bad. In fact, there had been no improvement since I last saw him, His leg was like an open wound with no sign of healing. The nurse said that the doctors were talking about IV antibiotics, which is a joke really seeing that Derek won't tolerate wearing pads, let alone a needle in his arm. Sometimes I do wonder what goes through the doctors' heads.

My biggest worry is that Derek will get septicaemia, and if the antibiotics are not working this may well happen. Derek did seem to be in a little pain. I pointed this out to the nurse. His painkillers had already been increased. He is on painkiller patches and oral painkillers.

I pray to god that Derek doesn't suffer any more then he needs to. He doesn't have much of a life. It's been four months since he has been outside; he just wanders around the ward, naps and eats, that's no life, is it? I also noticed that Derek looks like he is losing weight, his collar bone seems to be more prominent. The hospital is finding it difficult to weigh him and he will not cooperate.

April 2014
9 April. I haven't been to see Derek in a couple of weeks due to picking up some virus. Knowing it could be lethal to Derek I stayed away from the hospital.

I had been phoning the hospital to ask for updates, the doctors were supposed to phone me back on several occasions, but never did. I was getting worried as to how Derek's leg was. I arrived at the hospital and Derek recognised me straight away and he gave me a kiss.

I was shocked to see how thin he looked, his clothes were also very dirty, with food stains down his t-shirt, which by the way was back to front. We walked to his room and after about half an hour of persuasion managed to get Derek to sit in a chair so I could give him a much-needed haircut. I noticed that his room was depleted of curtains, chest of drawers and a chair. I questioned why. It was because Derek was dismantling things on a bigger scale now. He even tries to dismantle the bed.

Derek was given his lunch in his room, so I could finish off cutting his hair. He had spilt some food on the table so I got him a paper hand towel. He proceeded to wipe the gravy from his plate with the paper towel, then put the towel in his mouth to eat, luckily my quick action stopped him from swallowing it.

Then came the nurse to give Derek his tablets. She put them on a spoon for Derek to take. He started chewing them up, then he spat two out which shot across the room on to his bed. It was like watching a naughty two-year-old.

After lunch I tried to get Derek to change his t-shirt, as there was also hair on it, and speaking from experience that's going to itch for the rest of the day. But I had to give up in the end because Derek got annoyed with me.

***

After my visit I was left feeling sad that Derek was now only living an existence of food time and lots of pills to help with the pain and infection of his leg. I feel so sorry for him, this is no way to live.

Although Derek's leg in parts had started to scab, there were areas where the leg still looked infected, but today Derek started another antibiotic.

16 April. Today's visit was very emotional. Derek clearly didn't recognise me to start with. I had been there a while before he gave me a smile of recognition. He was wearing jogging bottoms with shorts over the top, which were very dirty.

Derek's leg clearly was still very sore, with an open wound. The worrying thing is that he has finished the antibiotics. I asked to speak to the doctor about this, but the doctor had left the hospital for the day.

Derek was clearly very agitated, he was talking gibberish all the time. I mentioned to the nurse that Derek seemed agitated. He said that Derek had an infection in his genitals, due to him scratching his leg and then touching himself below. I find this quite worrying that there is no way for this to be avoided.

Derek and I were sitting alone in the quiet lounge just before tea was served. I placed my hand on Derek's leg and said, 'I love you, the girls and I will be OK. I will look after them, it's OK to leave, stop fighting.' I feel guilty for saying this, and I don't know if he understood at all, but I don't want him to suffer any more. I don't want him to be moved to another hospital where I can't be sure if he would be looked after properly.

I stayed a little longer after that to help feed Derek, as he will not sit still to eat now. I followed him around feeding him. The nurse said that getting Derek to feed is more difficult due to the fact he will not sit down, so a member of staff has to spoon feed him while he is on the move.

I see in Derek's face how he is ageing; his eyes are not focused and the pupils of his eyes are just small black dots, his upper arms are thin and frail looking, his posture is of an old man. Not only has the disease taken away his brain bit by bit, but also his physique, this evil disease.

17 April. At last I managed to speak to the new doctor on the ward. I was pleasantly surprised at how informative he was. He explained that Derek's painkillers were morphine. I questioned whether this would make him more confused, but the doctor explained that due to Derek's pain they had to outweigh the side effects of the morphine drug. I asked the doctor if the infection Derek had in his genitals was the same as the infection in his leg. The doctor said no, the infection in his leg is bacterial and the genital infection is fungal.

20 April. Today is Easter. Myself and the girls went to visit Derek. He was fast asleep on his bed. We waited a while for him to wake up. The staff asked if Derek would like his dinner in his room. We tried to wake Derek with some mashed potato on a fork. He was eating it while half asleep. He then woke up, sat up then got quite agitated because we were trying to put the table close to him so he could finish his dinner. He tipped his drink over, wandered around his room, then weed in the corner. All this witnessed by the girls. His dinner was taken away and he was given sandwiches which he ate while lying on his bed, Derek seemed quite agitated and was continuously trying to put a cover on his bed. He then went back to sleep. We didn't manage to give him his Easter egg so we brought it back home with us.

24 April. Today's visit turned out to be longer than anticipated. I arrived just after lunch. Derek seemed OK, he was smiling and although he had his t-shirt on back to front he seemed contented. I gave him some of his Easter chocolate which I had to put in his mouth for him, but I think that was just laziness on his part.

Derek's leg at long last was starting to look better. It was starting to scab over which is a good sign.

After a while Derek seemed to want to go to the toilet, so I walked him to the bathroom. He seemed to be struggling to wee. I turned on the tap to see if that would help. Derek then bent over in pain. I noticed that his lower abdomen was very hard. Derek winced when I touched that part of his body. He was showing intense pain by his facial expression, to the point of tears. Knowing Derek, his pain threshold is very high, so to show pain in his facial expression shows me he was in great pain. I asked to see a doctor. I was taken into a meeting room and I explained my concerns and made sure the doctors were fully aware that he was in pain more than I had ever seen. While in the meeting, the doctors asked me about re-sectioning Derek. I asked why, but they were not sure, something to do with Derek moving on to a home. I told the doctors that I was told he would only be moved to a private hospital. The doctor replied that maybe that's why Derek needed to be re-sectioned, crazy I know, but the whole system of mental health is crazy. The result of the meeting was that another meeting needed to be arranged, but with the social worker present.

I told the doctor that I didn't want Derek moved from the psychiatric hospital and that I would fight to keep him there. I asked that they give him a year, because I believe he will not live longer than this. I understand it is out of the hands of the doctors as to how long a patient stays, and after all the hospital is an assessment ward only.

The pain that Derek was experiencing could be a urine infection, so a wee sample was needed. I went back on the ward to see Derek. He was clearly still in pain, with him bending over with his face screwed up, and he was getting very upset. The nurse and I managed to get a very small sample of wee, which is now being sent to the hospital for tests. I have never seen him in so much pain. It reduced both myself and the nurse to tears. I felt so useless knowing Derek was in pain and there was nothing I could do to help.

While walking the corridors with Derek he started to drop small pieces of poo on to the floor. He then picked them up and started to fill in the gaps between the skirting board and wall. I must admit he was doing a good job of it! Clearly he thought he was grouting tiles or filling gaps with filler. So sad to see him do this.

As the hours passed by I also noticed that Derek's leg was starting to seep fluid again, and his leg was looking a purple colour. I can't believe that in such a short space of time his leg could change so much. Even the nurse noticed this change, so it wasn't my imagination.

The doctor asked me to come back into the meeting room to discuss Derek. This is unusual to be called in twice in one visit.

It turned out that Derek's pain relief patch was not replaced last Friday, almost a week ago. It's supposed to be changed every Friday, but for one reason or another it had been forgotten. It was assumed that's why he was in pain, but I question this as the pain is clearly in his abdomen. Ideally he should have a blood test to see what's going on, but because of his agitation they won't do a blood test. I asked why they couldn't take blood when he was asleep. Their answer was that it's unethical. I told them they have my permission to do the test when he's asleep, but I guess that they won't.

I phoned the hospital tonight just before bedtime. Derek is calm and quiet and now has the pain relief patch on. Let's see what tomorrow brings.

25 April. Today I started my first home start job. Just as I was finishing I received a text from Donna asking if I was busy. As I was on my way home, I didn't reply. As I started driving my phone started to ring. I pulled over, it was Donna. She had been involved in a car accident. My heart just stopped, my worst nightmare. I asked if she was OK, asked where she was, then proceeded to find her. Thank god she only suffered whiplash. The car which she only bought three weeks ago was in a poor state, but I don't care about a piece of metal. I question yet again why are bad things happening to us, as if dealing with Derek's illness is not enough.

26 April. Popped in to see Derek. He was fast asleep so I didn't stay long. I just wanted to check that he was OK and that he was no longer in pain. Sadly, he didn't know I was there.

May 2014

2 May. Went to see Derek. He was walking the corridors. I couldn't help but notice the two pieces of poo in the corridor and couldn't help wondering if they were dropped by Derek.

Derek was very talkative in his own way. His leg seems to be clearing up nicely. We went and sat in the lounge. I felt that Derek was trying to communicate to me, but the only words that were very clear were 'I love you' and the name of Donna's boyfriend. Derek also said 'Pain' and pointed to his lower abdomen again.

I went to the office and reported that Derek was saying 'pain', they then got him some more painkillers. The nursing staff also told me that Derek had hit one of the nurses and she had to go to A&E.

3 May. Phoned the hospital to ask the staff nurse about Derek's pain. She was very informative. Derek is on two types of morphine painkillers plus other painkillers as and when. She said that he was becoming more aggressive and that he had hit one of the staff who had to go to A&E. Clearly Derek didn't know what he was doing, but I was surprised that the nurse he hit was the same nurse who a week ago was in tears because Derek was in so much pain. I feel so sorry for her, for Derek would never have hit anyone ever. This evil illness is destroying any dignity Derek had, and I am so upset that this is happening.

I am extremely worried that Derek is in so much pain. I know the hospital is doing their best to control the pain, but I worry why he is experiencing so much pain.

Derek was also a little tearful. I can't help wondering if he's tearful because he knows this is it for him, he's lost so much, never seeing his daughters get married, seeing any grandchildren that may come along, see how his daughters achieve their goals, and I will never get to go travelling with him as we hoped we would one day, and we will never grow old together.

Later that afternoon I received a phone call from the hospital to say they were sectioning Derek under the Mental Health Act section 3, and how did I feel about it. How do I feel? From what I understand, I cannot object, knowing how Derek is and that it's for his safety. I won't pretend to understand how this works, but I feel it's all in Derek's best interest.

Over the weekend I researched more information about lymphoedema. I found out that this can occur in the groin and genital area which got me thinking that maybe that's why Derek is in pain down there. I phoned the lymphoedema help line who gave me lots of information on this condition. She told me that lymphoedema should be treated with massage and dressings, both of which are impossible to do with Derek.

6 May. Next plan of action was a visit to the hospital and to ask the doctors if they think Derek has lymphoedema in his groin and genitals. I had a long meeting with the doctor about Derek, he suggested that it was unlikely to be lymphoedema in Derek's groin because the lymphoedema was not all the way up his leg. I asked why Derek seemed to be in pain still and why his lower abdomen seemed to be hard. The doctors are looking into Derek's case, which I understand is very complex. There is a possibility that Derek has an enlarged prostate, but because Derek is unwilling for anyone to examine him it's very difficult to know what's going on. Clearly Derek is unwell, his lower abdomen is hard, he has become more aggressive and clearly he is losing weight. The hospital are trying to seek out help from someone in the medical profession who may have answers to Derek's problem. Meanwhile the drugs are being changed to make Derek as comfortable as possible.

One thing I will say about Derek, he is a true fighter against this disease.

14 May. The hospital phoned to say that it has been agreed that Derek will have a scan today. The plan is to sedate him and then at 2.10pm he will be scanned. The hospital have forewarned me that the scan may be inconclusive, but at least they are doing all they can to help him.

Later that afternoon I phoned to ask how things went. Their reply was it didn't. Derek had been given 5ml of the sedative, normally 1mg would work, but the 5ml had no effect, so the hospital were unable to scan Derek.

16 May. Went to visit Derek. He was walking around the ward when I arrived. Luckily the doctor was still there so we had a catch up on what's been going on. It has been decided to treat Derek for an enlarged prostate as it's better to start some kind of treatment than for him to remain in pain. The hospital are hoping to have a specialist attend next week in the hope they can give Derek a scan with a handheld scanner.

After I had spoken to the doctor Derek was sitting down in the lounge. I went and sat next to him, giving him the remainder of his Easter egg, which he ate quite readily. Derek then dropped off to sleep. When it was teatime the staff brought Derek's food into the lounge for him. I tried to feed him the soup, but it was hard work. One of the nurses came with a lamb casserole and mashed potato. She had the knack of spooning it into Derek's mouth and he ate a good portion of it, followed by a yogurt which had been fortified with a supplement to help Derek gain some weight.

Derek's general appearance was not good. He is clearly losing weight, his face looks drawn, he looks tired, his clothes were very dirty, but I now understand that to handle Derek in any way is traumatic to him and to the staff. He just hits out all the time when any kind of personal care is attempted. I witnessed this again today when he started to play with his feet, which were very dirty with who knows what on them. Because he was about to have his tea, one of the nurses tried to wipe Derek's feet with a wet wipe and straight away Derek tried to hit out. I fear that Derek's time is coming to an end. I watched my mum lose lots of weight towards the end of her life, and sadly I now have to watch my husband.

All I keep thinking about at the moment is planning Derek's funeral. It's almost as though I am being pushed into getting things sorted because it will soon be time, and although I know it's inevitable, that's what will happen. It's starting to feel more real and very scary. I keep telling myself that we have lived at home for two years without Derek and that we will be OK, but not being able to see him is breaking my heart.

17 May. Just received a phone call from the hospital to say that last night Derek was given a wrong drug by mistake. It was a drug that he had been prescribed before but was given in error. Derek has had no side effects from this. An incident report has been filed.

20 May. The visit today with Derek went well. He didn't seem so agitated, but did say he was in pain and pointed to his lower abdomen again. At one point Derek had wandered off. I went to find him, he was in the toilet. He had pooed on the floor and was picking it up. He put it into the toilet then washed his hands in the toilet bowl. As much as I tried to put soap on his hands, turned the sink tap on, I could not get Derek to wash his hands in the sink. This again makes me worried that his personal hygiene is almost impossible to deal with, as Derek not only does not understand but if you try to insist that he does things that are beneficial to him he gets very agitated and will hit out.

My visit went through lunchtime so I decided to stay so I could see how much food he was eating. He managed his lunch, no problem. When it came to pudding Derek hesitated. It was sticky toffee pudding with cream. Derek lifted the toffee pudding out of the bowl as if to say he can't eat it, then I realised it looked very much like the poo he picked up and put in the loo. That must be very scary for Derek to not be able to distinguish between the two items, although I had a little chuckle to myself that I also could see the resemblance.

23 May. Phoned the hospital to ask how Derek was. He has been quite settled. They had managed to get a specialist in who sedated Derek and she managed to feel all around Derek's tummy and take bloods. Also his leg was given a really good wash, something they couldn't always do before. No problems were found with Derek's tummy, and the blood tests came back all clear, so the doctor has requested for more tests on his blood as the opportunity for Derek to have blood tests doesn't often happen now. Although the blood tests were clear, this still hasn't given us any answers as to why Derek is in pain.

Later on today I phoned the hospital as arranged to chat to the doctor about Derek. He explained that his bloods came back negative, which also surprised them. Derek's bladder is enlarged and the only way to alleviate this would be to fit a catheter, which he would not tolerate, or to have an incision in his bladder which would make him incontinent. But that raises the problem that Derek will not wear pads so surely that's not an option either.

The doctor also suggested that they use a slow release drug which is injected into him once every one/two weeks to keep Derek calmer. The drug is called Olanzapine. It's an atypical antipsychotic. This would have to be agreed by the ward pharmacist and by myself as well. I told the doctor I needed to look into this drug.

When I googled Olanzapine it said that it increased the risk of a stroke and the UK had issued a warning that it should not be given to elderly patients with dementia. In the USA this drug comes with a black box warning for increased risk of death in elderly patients. It is not approved for use in patients with dementia-related psychosis. However, in June 2008 a BBC investigation found that this advice was being widely ignored by British doctors.

28 May. I went to visit Derek with his ex carer. I was surprised at how good Derek was. He was happy and smiley and although not making much sense he was saying some words. It seemed there was some recognition of his carer, although very brief. She said she could see that Derek had lost weight; she also noticed, as did I, that Derek had a very faint tinge of yellow to his colouring.

It never ceases to amaze me that when on the very rare occasion someone comes to visit Derek with me that there always seems to be an improvement in him.

June 2014
1 June. Myself and both girls went to visit Derek. Because I wasn't sure how Derek was that day, the girls stayed in the car so I could see him before they did. Derek was sitting in a room on his own asleep. I gently woke him up. He looked at me and said, 'Angela.' I was so surprised, as I hadn't heard him call my name in a long while, and the fact he recognised me was a great surprise.

Unfortunately, I cannot say the same for the girls. There was no recognition at all. It was very difficult for Derek to stay awake. Donna commented on the fact that he didn't look as bad as I had said. It seems that she thought he would look a lot worse than I portrayed. I was upset and hurt by this because I could see the change in him but couldn't understand why she couldn't. We stayed for a while, but Derek slept most of the time.

2 June. Phone call from the hospital. With regards the drug Olanzapine, the doctor suggested yet again that they try this drug as Derek had hit out for no reason at a nurse. He also hits other patients. It seems his aggression is more apparent and can happen at any time for no reason. I questioned the doctor about not giving it due to Alzheimer's and the high risk of stroke, and that it wasn't used on the ward. His reply was that all antipsychotics have a risk of stroke and that they hadn't used this drug in a long time. When they gave it to Derek as a sedation prior to the blood test it seemed to have a calming effect on Derek

The doctor said that they would give it in tablet form, first at 5mg twice a day. The maximum dose is 20mg a day. I am very concerned about this drug being used. I told the doctor that the decision is theirs as I do not want to be the one who makes this decision. I can see that it's a very difficult situation, as Derek has become more aggressive, and now without any intervention. I asked the doctor that if on giving this drug he is still aggressive that they will stop it straight away. They said they would.

8 June. Called in to see Derek as I hadn't seen him for a week. As I walked through the door I saw that he was at the far end of the corridor with a member of staff. I was shocked to see what state he was in. He was bent over with both hands on the floor, trying to pick something up that wasn't there. He was very hot to touch and his eyes were puffy, he was on a one-to-one watch as he was at risk of falling. I was told that they were waiting for a doctor. Derek's leg was very red as if burning, and still swollen. I have never seen Derek in this state before, but it reminded me of the time he was on Haloperidol, another antipsychotic drug.

The doctor came and drew a line around Derek's leg so that the next doctor to see him would have some idea as to whether the redness was spreading up his leg. The doctor prescribed antibiotics for the leg infection and hoped it would also bring his temperature down. Derek was holding his head against the wall and on the floor. This had me worried as I had read not so long ago about animals doing this action when they are very sick. It has something to do with the nervous system. I tried to google this information to see if this applied to humans, but sadly I could not find anything.

When I left the hospital Derek was sound asleep on the floor on all fours. I am extremely worried. My gut feeling is that this is the result of his new medication.

9 June. After not a lot of sleep, woke up at about 5am. Decided to give the healing clinic a miss. I am too worried about Derek to be any use to anybody.

Arrived at the hospital at about 10am and came face to face with the psychiatrist, so went straight into a meeting with him. I aired my concerns about Olanzapine with him and asked for Derek to be taken off it. He agreed. It is not known if Derek's deterioration is down to the drug or the leg infection. I asked him about Derek pushing his head against the wall, and if it was anything to do with the breakdown of the nervous system. His answer was he didn't know.

Derek was not as bent over as yesterday, but still on a one-to-one. He is still running a temperature.

For his own safety, Derek was kept in his room. He was trying to dismantle his bed. I noticed that his wardrobe has now been taken out of his room.

Twice in the time I was there Derek had to be changed because of pooing himself, which lands up on the floor and he always seems to tread in it. I witnessed the staff changing him at my choice, and washing him down which is very challenging. I couldn't help but notice how thin he was with no clothes on. It was obvious Derek has lost a lot of weight. I also noticed that his lower abdomen was distended, which is another sign of the enlarged prostate.

I had a second meeting today, this time with the young doctor who has been a godsend to Derek's case. He went over all the details of his case, and he then asked about my thoughts on whether Derek needed IV antibiotics as it would mean him having to go to St Richard's Hospital and being sedated. Apparently Derek has been on all the antibiotics and it may become apparent that they will no longer work for him, so an IV would be the only option, or palliative care.

St Richard's, or indeed any other hospital, is not equipped to deal with Alzheimer's patients, so in my opinion Derek cannot be taken there. The only option would be palliative care. I asked if the psychiatric hospital could IV him there, but unfortunately they can't because they are not properly trained.

10 June. Phoned the hospital in the morning to ask how Derek was. He'd had about two hours sleep and at 12am his temperature had peaked. Not sure exactly what that means.

Phoned again just after teatime. He is standing in a more upright position, and is more smiley. They were just going to give him some paracetamol as his temperature was high. My concern is that it seems there is a problem with his temperature. When brought down it seems to creep back up again, and also Derek never had a temperature with a leg infection before, so this is all new. I am going to visit Derek tomorrow with my friend Jane. Maybe as before when I have visited with a friend he will not be so bad, we will see.

11 June. As predicted, Derek was in a much better state today when I visited with Jane. After a while he did acknowledge me and gave me a kiss.

He was very active, walking around, moving furniture. He only stopped twice to sit down for a couple of minutes. The hospital are monitoring his temperature closely and giving paracetamol when needed. Jane was surprised at how active he was, I think that maybe she thought he would be sitting in a chair wasting away, but that is definitely not the case with Derek. He still has his strength and his mobility. That has never been the problem, Derek's problems are internal, although Jane did say that his leg looked bad, but in all honesty it's the best it's looked for a while.

I am now wondering if I have been overreacting, thinking that maybe Derek hasn't got long left for this world. As much as I don't want to lose him, the thought of him living another few years worries me because I see that he has no real life. It's just an existence and knowing he is in pain and having painkillers to get through the day is just not right.

15 June. Fathers' Day. Myself and the girls went to see Derek. He was in a much better place, asleep but at least not in the place he was a week ago. I started to cut his hair as this is the only time now I can cut it. I managed to cut half of his hair, but then he woke up. I had to wait for him to wander around a bit until he sat down and fell asleep before I could continue the haircut. The ward was very restless, with lots of shouting and one patient kicking off, not the sort of thing you want your daughters to see. Derek was unaware of us being there. He ate a couple of chocolates that the girls gave him but they opened his cards and stuck them on the wall of his bedroom.

17 June. Went to visit Derek with Maz today. She hadn't seen him for at least seven months, so she could see the deterioration in him. There was no acknowledgement from Derek that we were there. He kept wandering the corridors, his head bent over. After a while he started yawning, so I tried to guide him to his room. He got a little angry at me and kind of hit me, then he walked past me, put his head on my shoulder and kissed my shoulder as if to say sorry. We left just after that.

20 June. Phoned the hospital to ask after Derek. He seems to be fine. The leg is getting better and he is still on antibiotics. He had been sleeping, but there's always a but. Derek had hit another patient, so therefore the subject of Derek being put back on Olanzapine has been mentioned, although it will only be administered on a 'as and when basis', not on a continual dose as before. I am not happy with this, but I feel there is no option. Derek can't keep hitting out.

24 June. A visit to the hospital today was not a good one for me. Derek was being washed in his room. I could see that he had pooed himself and clearly had walked in it, as it was between his toes and on his hands. To me Derek has lost all dignity, having to be washed down by two, if not more, nurses, and the fact that he has no idea of the concept of messing himself. This should not be happening.

It wasn't the fact of having to be washed, or the poo, or the fact that his toes were shedding skin that upset me. I think it was the fact that it will not get any better. I hadn't seen Derek for a week and today he looked like an old man; he looked like he had lost more weight, his rib cage was sticking out, his clothes were inside out and still had poo stains on them. I can't blame the staff for this, as I know it's becoming very difficult to change him.

At this point in time I asked god why has he not taken him, hasn't he had enough suffering? I noticed that the leg which is always swollen was still red and had a lump forming by his calf. I also pointed out to one of the staff that the swelling seems to be going up his leg. I guess this is inevitable.

30 June. Called into the hospital today. It was teatime. I don't usually visit at this time of day, but I had an appointment in Chichester so I thought while I am here I'll drop in. I walked onto the ward, then into the dining room expecting to see Derek having tea. But no! A member of staff said he was in his room. I walked down the corridor into Derek's room, and there I just stood for a minute or so, in disgust. Derek had only a shirt on, no pants or trousers to be seen, one of his feet was caked in shit, his hands were not too clean either. One of the nursing staff walked in with Derek's tea, I asked that he not bring it into the room as Derek was dirty and it was unhygienic. The ward nurse then came into Derek's room to wash him. She explained that he was asleep on his bed without his trousers on, so they covered him with a towel which he had taken off. As the nurse washed Derek down, she said that he was back on antibiotics as of today because the swelling and redness in his leg was creeping further up his leg. This I could see quite clearly, in fact I had noticed it last week. Derek was also playing, for want of a better word, with his private parts. I asked the nurse why this was. Her reply was that he had thrush on his genitals. We seem to be going round in circles with him and his reoccurring problems – his leg infection, urine infection, thrush, it's never-ending.

Again today, Derek looked old. He is definitely ageing, he looks gaunt, heavy eyed, clearly not putting on weight. My heart breaks on every visit now, and still even today there was a glimmer in his eyes that said 'I remember who you are'.

July 2014
4 July. Went to visit Derek today. He was in the lounge rearranging the cushions, his t-shirt was on back to front, as were his trousers, and to be honest his clothes were none to clean. I noticed that his other leg looked a little swollen today as well.

Derek walked up to me and placed his hands either side of my face and said, 'I know you.' I asked him, 'What's my name?' but the moment had passed. I stayed and helped him eat his lunch. I also noticed that Derek's lower abdomen was very hard again. I am not sure why this is, and there seemed to be no one around to ask this question.

10 July. Getting ready to go away on holiday on the 12 July. Louise performed an hour-long concert at the day centre where I used to work. It was a great hit and some of the clients were singing along, which was nice to see. We left there on a high.

When we got home Derek's social worker phoned. She wanted me to attend a meeting next week. I told her I was away for a week, so a date has been set for 22 July. I asked the social worker about the meeting and if they were going to move Derek. Her reply was that the meeting is to talk this over, get an update on Derek and discuss the move to the forensic science hospital in Surrey. This was the one place I didn't want him to end up in. I am upset that this is even a possibility, so many reasons why I don't want him moved. I pray he passes before this happens, I feel I have let him down, failed to fight his corner.

11 July. I went to visit Derek before we go away. The girls wanted to visit but I am glad they didn't.

When I arrived Derek was asleep on his bed. I walked into his room – there was faeces on the floor, around the power sockets, smeared in corners of the room, on his pillow, and between his toes. His shirt was ripped where he keeps taking it off, then struggles to put it back on. I was careful where I stood as I didn't want faeces on my clothes or shoes.

After a while Derek woke up, wandered around his room trying to pick up nothing off the floor, and he then laid back on the bed. There was no acknowledgement of me being there. I found this visit very upsetting, wondering how much longer this is going to go on for. Ironically, Derek's leg was not so swollen, but it was very red, almost purple in some parts.

12–19 July. Holiday. The start of the holiday was great – great weather, unusual for us. We visited Cadbury chocolate factory in Birmingham, and looked around Stratford, visiting the museums and going on a river boat.

We then travelled to Bath. I was a little annoyed that we had to pay £10 for two nights' car park at a Travelodge and that the room we were given was in an annex at the back of the hotel. Also one of the beds was a mattress on the floor, not good. After travelling we decided to have a meal at the Travelodge. We sat at a table, decided what to order and we then had to place the order at the bar. I asked Donna to go and place the order, as I would pay, but she refused to do it, so I was annoyed but went to the bar ordered and paid anyway. That seemed to be the beginning of the ruined holiday.

The next day we looked around the Roman baths, but then the girls didn't want to look around the costume museums. We were at a bit of a loss as to what to do. We went back to our room, then everything went downhill from there. Donna packed her case and said she was catching the train home, as we were not talking to her or involving her in anything. Truth is, Donna had her head in her phone all the time, or had her headphones in listening to music. We had a big row, I packed my bag and said we would all leave. I didn't want her to catch the train on her own. Louise got upset, things were said about not having much of a family, I got angry saying Derek is dying by the week, month, year, maybe it would have been better if it was me, and that maybe Derek would have handled this better than me.

The argument destroyed the holiday. I have never wanted to end a holiday early before. We stuck it out till Friday, then came home. I think that I have to realise that the girls are growing up and that a family holiday will no longer be an option. We all want different things from a holiday. I just wanted us to enjoy our time together. I feel annoyed that we didn't get along and that Donna has at least three more holidays booked this year, but Louise and I only have a couple of days booked.

I have never come off holiday feeling like I hadn't been away. I thought our holiday might be shortened because of Derek, not because we had an argument between us.

While away I did phone the hospital to ask how Derek was. Unfortunately, the person who answered spoke with such a foreign accent it was very difficult to understand what he was saying. The gist of the conversation was the same as before, whatever that meant. I phoned again when I got home. Same person answered, same reply, same as before.

I will visit Derek tomorrow, Sunday, then I have this big meeting on Tuesday which I am not looking forward to.

22 July. Arrived at the hospital for the meeting. Derek was still asleep on the settee in the lounge. I couldn't wake him up. This is the third time I have visited and Derek has been asleep. Apparently, Derek hadn't slept at all that night. In the meeting room was the social worker, the psychiatrist and the ward nurse. The nurse started by saying that basically they had done as much as they can for Derek, and it's time for him to move on to the forensic science hospital in Surrey as his needs have become more complex. He is in himself more settled, but on changing his clothes or doing any personal hygiene, he gets aggressive.

The funding has been approved for Derek to move on. When I asked when this was going to happen, the reply was within the next two weeks. It was explained to me that Derek could be moved within the different complexes as his health becomes less complex. I pointed out that I didn't think Derek would improve, as each time I see him he has lost more weight, which suggests to me that there is a bigger problem with his health, and I don't think he has much longer to live. They said I didn't know that. I replied my gut instinct says so. Their reply was he could live much longer.

The hospital were also concerned that because they had no showers, and were not allowed to use the bath with Derek, washing him was very difficult, and therefore it could be classed as neglect, which I totally understand. As I had said before, there were times when his clothes and hands and feet had shit on them, but I would not hold that against them as I know they try their very best with the facilities they have. The blame is with the mental health system, the lack of money, etc.

I brought up the subject of when Derek was first diagnosed we were told that one of the most important things with Alzheimer's is that there is continuity. This has not happened at all in Derek's case, and now he is settled and has some recognition of the staff, it's not OK to move him out of the area and to a place where he will know no one. If I am not feeling well, the first place I want to be is home with people I know – how can it be right to move Derek? Their argument was that he doesn't recognise staff and has limited understanding of his surroundings. Then why does he sometimes recognise me? I believe he knows more than the hospital give him credit for.

Some of the questions I asked at the meeting could not be answered, so a further meeting has been arranged with the forensic science hospital on Friday 25 July.

My friend has offered to come to the meeting with me, as it's better to have two of us asking questions.

25 July. Arrived at the forensic science hospital. The social worker and the ward nurse from the psychiatric hospital were there. We had a long discussion about Derek, then my friend and I were shown around the secure unit. There were only eight patients on the ward that Derek will be on, all closely observed by CCTV.

I was surprised at the layout of the hospital, not at all how I envisioned it. Nicely decorated, lots of room to move around and access to a garden. There was no hint of it being a hospital at all, the staff were all friendly and I didn't feel threatened at all. We also had a meeting with the doctor who had met Derek on Wednesday at the psychiatric hospital. He was very nice and spent lots of time talking to us. He told us that when he visited Derek he went to look at his leg and Derek in one very fast movement hit the doctor. But he said that in a way he was glad because it gave him some indication of how Derek is. The outcome of the meeting was that the hospital were very positive at being able to help Derek to have a better quality of life, by addressing the problem of his leg and to alleviate aggressive behaviour.

One thing I wasn't told before was that Derek would not be there permanently. They hoped to be able to get Derek settled enough to be able to be moved to a care home nearer home. I find it very difficult to believe that Derek would improve. Without sounding negative, I can't seem to get out of my head that Derek hasn't got long left to live. The doctors say otherwise, so why do I feel this way? I just don't know. It was confirmed that I do have to phone up to make an appointment to see Derek. A two-hour visit is allocated, and only two people at a time, but with arrangement the three of us can visit. It's not ideal, but I just have to accept these conditions.

28 July. Myself and the girls went to visit Derek in the psychiatric hospital again. He was asleep. The head nurse called me into the office to confirm that Derek was to be moved on Wednesday 30 July. He was going to be given a drug to calm him down at 9am, then at 10am he would travel in a secure ambulance to the forensic science hospital. The nurse in question was to travel with Derek and help him settle at the other end. I, of course, was very tearful for the psychiatric hospital had become like a second home to me, as Derek had spent the last 14 months out of 24 at this unit. Both myself and Derek had become used to the staff and surroundings.

I thanked the nurse for all that they had done for Derek. She replied that they would miss Derek as they had become attached to him over the period of time. The nurse then offered that if at any time I wanted someone to visit with me to see Derek, to call the ward and they would hopefully be able to send a member of staff with me. I was very touched that they had offered this to me, it meant a great deal.

While I was with the nurse, the girls had noticed that Derek seemed to be in a lot of pain with his back. On several occasions when he moved he would wince at the pain. I am not sure why this is because Derek is on quite a lot of painkillers. I thought I would wait until the transfer, then ask the forensic science hospital why this is so.

29 July. I phoned the forensic science hospital to make an appointment to see Derek. It was arranged that we visit on Thursday 31 July at 1pm. I had bought Derek some new clothes, as most of his clothes from the psychiatric hospital had been ripped by him.

30 July. This day arrived for me with great dread. I was convinced that Derek would not make the journey. In my head, I thought that with the medication they were going to give him it would end his life. Maybe my thoughts are no longer rational, maybe I just wanted him to pass quietly. I just don't know any more.

That afternoon Derek's doctor phoned me to say he had arrived. She chatted for about half an hour, asking various questions about Derek's case. She told me that she would also meet me on Thursday along with the social worker.

31 July. First visit to see Derek in the forensic science hospital. Both girls came with me. I felt they needed to see where Derek was, as they may have had the same idea I had in my mind of a prison-type environment. We left home at 12 noon for our 1pm appointment. Louise said she loved the drive leading up to the hospital, with trees overhanging the road. I must admit it is a very beautiful area, just a bit out of my way and too remote for my liking. We arrived at reception and were asked if we had any ID on us, which of course we didn't. We were asked to look at the list of items we were not allowed to take onto the ward with us. This consisted of keys, keyrings, mobile phones, all sharp items, knives, cans and bottles, illicit drugs, lotions, creams, plastic bags, aftershave, matches, lighters, transport tickets, cheque books, electrical items, digital frames, cigarettes, iPads, tablets, laptops, chewing gum, glass objects, picture frames, cameras, pornography, scissors, razors, alcohol, passports, credit or debit cards, money over £30, medication (including herbal), e-cigarettes, dongles, USB or flash drives. Visitors may retain prescribed medication once this has been checked by a nurse or doctor.

Because we were unaware of this we just handed over our bags. We were escorted into the visitors' room while they went to get Derek.

We waited quite a while for Derek to be escorted to us. They wanted him to look presentable to us so they changed his clothes!

Again, Derek just wandered around, then finally sat down and went to sleep. I honestly think Derek is unaware of his different surroundings. The good thing is he wasn't showing any increased signs of confusion.

Occasionally Derek would stir and at one time he took hold of Louise's hand and held it. This reduced us all to tears. The staff were very attentive, offering us drinks and ice creams All staff – and there were a lot of them – greeted us throughout our visit.

At 3pm our visit was over. Derek was escorted back to his ward, and the girls went and sat back in the car, as I had a meeting with the doctor and social worker. They did not want to attend.

This meeting was to take a further two hours. I was not popular with the girls, as they were fed up waiting with nothing to do and no food.

The difference between NHS and private is very evident. At no point in the meeting did I feel rushed, the doctors took their time to go over every detail in Derek's case, they were very thorough. I was very impressed.

The doctor explained that Derek's presentation (loss of weight) may be due to the cellulitis as this can make people lose weight quite quickly. Also the amount of antibiotics Derek has been on could be a contributing factor. We discussed all the medication Derek had been on. I told them that the doctor at the psychiatric hospital had said that they had scraped the barrel as to what other medication might help him. The doctor agreed that this was the case. She did however suggest that one of the epileptic drugs that Derek was on was such a small dose it would not have made a difference, so she suggested that they increase the dosage. At the moment, this will be the only change in his medication.

We also discussed Derek's cellulitis if another infection occurred, a plan of action. Did I still not want him to be admitted to hospital for IV antibiotics? I explained that not knowing this area, or their local hospital, I did not know how well they could care for Alzheimer's patients, so I left the decision to them.

I was also asked about resuscitation again. I still stand by my last answer – no point. Why would you? I was also asked if I had legal power of attorney and an end of life plan.

The social worker asked what benefits we were on. My reply, none. She said she would look into this for us. The doctor then asked me what my expectations were of them, with regards to Derek. My reply was that without sounding negative, I believe that the best we could hope for was that Derek was no longer in pain. I don't believe that he will sleep at night, I also don't believe that his aggression will subside either.

After all the questions, I asked the doctor to be honest with me. It has often been said we are a kind of unique case, and this may only be true in our area. Had they ever had a patient who had come to this hospital with Derek's presentation, with his aggression, his no sleeping at night, his cellulitis and oedema and lymphoedema, and had a good outcome? Her answer was no. Derek was in the latter stages of his illness. I know this to be true deep down, but still it breaks my heart. I am not sure if I will ever get over this. I am to have another meeting next week with all the team dealing with Derek's case.

August 2014

Five years has now passed since Derek was given the diagnosis of Alzheimer's. I seem to be struggling more. Now that Derek is a long distance away from me, I feel like I have lost control of him, if that makes any sense. I hate the fact that I have to make an appointment to see him, and that it takes an hour to get to the hospital. I know I should accept these conditions, but my body is feeling the stress of it all. I have kept in touch with the hospital via phone. They say Derek is OK, but it's not the same as visiting him.

9 August. Donna and I went to visit Derek. We were shown into the visitors' room. One of the staff came to chat with us saying that Derek was good, but he did hit a member of staff, and went to hit another member of staff, but apparently hit his head on a door frame. He has been checked over and has a small gash on his head to which there is now a plaster. When Derek appeared, he looked at me and gave me a big smile. He then took hold of my hand and said, 'I love you.' So this confirms he still knows who I am. I wish I could say the same for Donna, but unfortunately there was no recognition, although Derek did stare at her for a long while. I can't even begin to imagine how that must feel, that your own dad no longer recognises you. So very heart-breaking. The visitors' room is very stuffy with no air. Derek decided to lie across the settee and fall asleep.

When he did wake up or made any movement toward me, two members of staff stood close by to prevent Derek from, I guess, hitting us, but never do I feel threatened. In fact, when I go to the meeting next Wednesday I will make a point of saying I am not happy with this action. Yet again it makes me feel as though they have taken over Derek.

***

I have made a slip-up with regards the meeting on Wednesday. I am away in Glastonbury so I have had to cancel the meeting. This has now been rescheduled to the following Wednesday.

11 August. Louise, Anna and I went to Glastonbury for a couple of days. I can honestly say for those few days I felt fine, and more like my old self. The down side is now I am back home I feel very low. I want my life to change. I am sick and tired of feeling not right. I want to start anew. It didn't help that an hour after arriving home the hospital phoned to say Derek needed some shoes costing £75. It's not so much the cost of the shoes as to whether they will fit or if he will keep them on, as he hasn't worn shoes for at least 18 months. Also his foot could triple in size within weeks, as at the moment his foot has gone down considerably. Also the fact that Derek destroys everything he wears by picking at it. I feel so mean in questioning the expense of these shoes because his state pension, which at the end of the day is his, would pay for this.

15 August. I guess my emotions are all over the place at the moment. I truly thought that Derek would no longer be with us. Not that I want him to pass, but he has no future with this disease, and as time passes his illness is having a detrimental effect on myself and the girls. I am inwardly screaming for help, but feel I have no one to turn to. I don't ever remember feeling so low and alone. I wish I could see a way out of this nightmare. I want to feel strong and excited about what my future will entail, but at this precise moment I just can't see a way ahead, for that I am scared.

20 August. Today the meeting at the forensic science hospital with the psychiatrist, the GP and the social worker.

The day didn't start off too well. There were roadworks on the road near home, which delayed my journey and I arrived six minutes late. I went to the reception to find out I was in fact one hour early. I wasn't allowed to see Derek in that hour because someone else was using the room, so I went back to the car and sat for an hour. I then went back to reception only to find out I wasn't allowed to take my bag or phone into the meeting. I was a little upset by this, but handed it over anyway.

The meeting was quite traumatic, due to the fact that I was asked questions about what I wanted to happen in the situation of Derek having a heart attack, stroke, needing IV, etc. How would I want treatment to take place and if I wanted treatment to take place. These are decisions I do not want to have to make, not on my own. But guess what, there is no one else to help decide, there is no way I can talk to the girls about this. I found the whole meeting quite traumatic.

I seem to be getting mixed messages about Derek. Today it was mentioned that they hope to get Derek to a better place health-wise so that he can be moved on. To be quite honest I don't think they know any more than I do about Derek's condition. At the end of the day they didn't see him three months ago to be able to make a comparison.

After the meeting, I was allowed to see Derek. I was taken into the visitors room while they got Derek ready to see me, in other words change his clothes. This make me angry as I have seen Derek in some unclean states, so cleaning him up is wasted for my benefit.

When Derek was brought into the room I thought how thin he looked, his face was very drawn and eyes sunken. I hadn't seen him for just over a week. I am sure he didn't look as well as last time. He saw me and gave me a hug and kiss, at least he was more awake this time. He did try and talk, just a shame I couldn't understand what he was saying, although one thing was very clear – a few times he said 'Sorry' to me, a very heart-breaking moment. Was he saying sorry for all that has happened or was it just a random word? I would like to think it was the latter. After a while he did sit down, but he was dropping off to sleep. My cue to leave.

30 August. Went to visit Derek with my friend Maz. I had with me two new pairs of trousers, some chocolate, and scissors and comb so that I could cut his hair. I had checked earlier in the week to ask if this was OK.

When we arrived at the reception of the hospital I was not allowed to take the scissors into the visitors' room until it was checked by the nurse on duty.

Derek was in a good place, but still looked so thin. He came and sat down by me, and yet again there was that acknowledgement that he knew who I was. He also tried to have a conversation with me, but alas this was made difficult because of his lack of speech.

After we had been there a while I asked the staff about cutting Derek's hair. The staff member went and got the nurse. I was not allowed the scissors as it was classed as a risk to both Derek and myself. It was suggested that the hairdresser cut Derek's hair to which there would be a charge. I refused to pay someone else to cut Derek's hair; in fact she would be more at risk as she would be a stranger to Derek.

It's very obvious to me that the hospital think Derek is a violent man. In fact my friend asked how Derek was on the ward. Their reply was OK, until any intervention was required, for example washing, changing clothes, etc. Maz said that Derek was a kind gentle man with no aggression at all before the illness. The staff were very surprised.

We both then questioned the member of staff about the other patients, asking if there were prisoners on the ward Derek was on. That was confirmed. It also came to light that Derek seemed to be the only patient bar one other who does not sleep at night. I questioned if that patient also had Alzheimer's. The answer was no. I get the impression that Derek is the only patient with Alzheimer's on this ward. If this is the case, this is absolutely outrageous. Some idiot who sits in their office with no concept of Alzheimer's should think it was OK to put my husband in a prison-like facility with criminals, just because no one else knows what to do with him. I find this completely out of order and feel ashamed that Derek has been treated this way. OK, so maybe he is unaware of this, but I am aware and I have to live with this fact.

This was my longest visit so far. We were there about two and a half hours. The staff brought Derek's tea into the visitors' room so he could eat with us. He had no problem eating, considering he had eaten a large bar of chocolate beforehand. But still he seems to be losing weight.

September 2014
10 September. Louise and I went to visit Derek, armed with scissors in the hope that this time I will be able to cut Derek's hair. We entered the building as we had the last few times, only to be reprimanded for entering this way. Apparently, they had changed the entrance to the building, but how were we to know about this? Then to top it all we were told we hadn't made an appointment, which was not true. I find these visits with Derek at the hospital trying enough without the hassle I seem to have at every visit.

Derek seemed pleased to see us. I managed to cut his hair while Louise fed him chocolate. I also managed to fit his new slippers on to his feet, to which he said, 'Nice.'

Apparently, Derek has just finished a course of antibiotics, as his leg was looking a bit red according to staff. Both Louise and I thought Derek had lost more weight, to me he also looked pale.

Again I feel very detached from Derek because of the set up at this hospital. We stayed while Derek had lunch, which was fish, mashed potato, broccoli and gravy. Derek ate this with a spoon, followed by some kind of mousse which apparently had his meds in, one of which was morphine. Soon after that, Derek fell asleep.

17 September. I phoned the hospital to ask how Derek was. The hospital said they were just about to phone me. Derek had walked into a glass door and had a bump on his head.

21 September. Donna and I went to visit Derek. When we got to the building we had to phone so they could send a member of staff to unlock the gates and walk us through the building. We were shown into the family room and a member of staff came and told us again about Derek hitting his head on the glass door. When he was escorted into the visitors' room I was shocked at the extent of his bruising. Both eyes were bruised, as was the bridge of his nose, and there was bruising right up to his crown. Also he had a large cut on his left arm. I never expected the bruising to be so bad.

Derek acknowledged both Donna and I which was great. He blew me a kiss, his mood was good, but he was very sleepy. A staff member came to chat to us, saying that they couldn't examine him because he wouldn't let them, but they were keeping a watchful eye on him. They think he may have had two falls, they are also padding his room to prevent any more injury.

22 September. Our twenty-fourth wedding anniversary. I wasn't feeling too happy with the bruising on Derek's head, so I contacted the Alzheimer's Society to ask for advice. They put me in contact with Admiral Nursing who advised that I get a copy of the report and ask questions as to how this happened. I also phoned Derek's social worker at the hospital, who didn't even know about the incident, so I asked her to go and have a look at him to see for herself. I then contacted Derek's GP who visits the hospital once a week. Through the many phone calls, a meeting was set up for Wednesday 24.

24 September. Arrived at 10am for the meeting at the hospital, which was attended by Derek's GP, his psychiatrist, the ward manager, the second-in-charge manager and the social worker. The social worker asked me if she could contact Derek's family, because she was concerned that I had no back-up in dealing with the problems with him. I told her there was no use talking to them, as far as I am concerned they are dead to me. A little harsh maybe, but as far as I am concerned they lost the right to be associated with me a long time ago. The social worker then asked if his family were involved with the girls at all. I told her no. The social worker then said that the situation didn't sit well with her. I swear she had tears in her eyes, as did I. She asked why was this. My reply was that they blame me for his illness.

The meeting was held. I feel more confident that Derek did just walk into the door. The outcome is for him to only wear his shoes outside, as he may have tripped as one foot is bigger than the other due to the lymphoedema. Also his morphine will be reduced by 50ml so he's not so sleepy, and also his one-to-one has been stepped up. I also asked about the large scratch on Derek's arm. It was agreed that this was done in his room, as he fell by his bed. I am quite concerned that Derek seems to be falling a lot.

It has also been agreed that Derek will be moving, maybe as soon as next week, to another unit on the same site, but an 18-bed unit that deals with Alzheimer's patients. Plus we as a family have less restriction on visiting him, and don't have to hand in our bags, so I am quite pleased about that. I was shown around today, and it has a more homely feel then the hospital. Although when I visited this unit a year ago I was adamant Derek wouldn't go there, things have changed and I have to learn to accept these changes.

October 2014

10 October. Derek has been at the unit just over two weeks now. Logistically I haven't managed to visit him until today. I had phoned a couple of times to ask how Derek was. I was told that he had a foot injury and that he had a UTI, otherwise he was OK and sleeping a few hours at night which is good.

Today on my visit, Derek recognised me and seemed to settle well after a few minutes.

The social worker came to have a chat with me, asking questions about his education, family, work, etc., same questions that were asked before. I was also asked if we had a mental health solicitor. Bizarre, I know, but apparently it is advisable that Derek has one.

Another thing that was quite strange was that the social worker told the ward manager that I wanted to see Derek's room. I can't remember having that conversation, but maybe I did. Anyway, I was escorted to his room but was told to only look ahead of me when walking to his room to protect the other patients' privacy.

I feel it's quite strange that I was shown his room and that I was asked about a mental health solicitor, in case of a tribunal. Maybe because I confronted them about Derek's head injury they are being extra careful? Or worried I may kick off?

16 October. I phoned the unit to ask after Derek. The manager answered the phone. I asked how he was and she said he was fine, then a long pause. I was expecting her to elaborate more, so I asked if his urine infection had cleared up. Her reply was that Derek had finished his antibiotics, but his urine was still strong. Maybe he needed more antibiotics, but getting a urine sample from him was very difficult. I replied that he was on a one-to-one, so why couldn't that member of staff get the sample? Her reply was that he was incontinent and that he urinates wherever, which makes it difficult. Also, there's the problem of Derek being immune to antibiotics. I was then asked to bring cranberry juice to my next visit with Derek.

I have to say that the manager seems quite cold and matter of fact about Derek, and again I feel alienated from him and what's really going on. I just wish for once he could speak to me to tell me if things are OK there.

22 October. Today I went to visit Derek. Before I saw him, I had to attend a meeting with his doctor and medical team. It was a long drawn out meeting, most of the time going over old ground about how he became ill, his family life etc. Also at the meeting was a lady from the psychiatric hospital. I had also asked my friend to attend as I feel more comfortable going with someone else. The meeting was about an hour long and I was given lots of paperwork which consisted of a clinical report, social worker report and nursing care report. This is the first time I have received anything like this.

I felt the meeting had a positive spin on it, with reports that Derek has made an improvement. The thing is, at the end of the day he will not get better, so to say there are improvements kind of messes with my head. I wait each day to see if today will be the day I get the final phone call, and to be told of improvements just doesn't make any sense in my head.

After the meeting my friend and I went to see Derek. We were shown into the visitors' room. It clearly wasn't a good day for him, he was very agitated, he wouldn't sit down at all, kept wandering around, talking in his own way to a person unseen. He kept rubbing his hands continuously and spitting on the floor, his leg looked very red and was very hot, he had no colour to his face and just didn't look well at all.

Derek was also trying to move furniture and was getting quite angry. I said to the staff that he must have an infection for him to be acting this way, but they didn't seem to be that concerned.

After the visit, when I got home I phoned the unit to say I thought Derek had an infection. The answer was that it may be he was just constipated. When I mentioned his leg being very red and hot I was told that his leg would not get better than it was, due to the lymphoedema. I was then told that they would ask the doctor to look at him tomorrow if he still seems agitated.

23 October. I have tried phoning the unit several times today, but there is no answer. I will try again later.

Finally someone answered, but they were in a meeting and said they would phone back later.

November 2014

8 November. I haven't seen Derek since 22 October. This is most probably the longest time I haven't seen him, the reason being that after our last meeting I was affected emotionally and it was so bad that it's taken me a while to bounce back. To be quite honest, it scared me. I am emotionally very vulnerable at the moment and very scared what his illness is doing to me. Even my friend who came with me on my last visit said that it had upset her. I have however phoned the unit on several occasions, but I always seem to get the same reply. Derek is eating well, sometimes sleeping, his leg is the best it will ever be. Apparently, he has no infection.

I wish Derek was closer then I could visit more often, even for just a few minutes to make sure he is OK.

9 November. Today Louise is singing in a concert to raise money for Alzheimer's. How proud that would make her dad, just wish he could know this.

14 November. Today I took dad shopping to the local shop. He always insists on going to this shop as he knows where everything is. The shop is in my village. I parked the car, got a trolley and proceeded into the shop with dad's shopping list in my hand.

While approaching the centre of the shop I saw Derek's brother and his wife. The brother just stopped and stared at me. For just a split second I thought he was going to speak. I can only describe the look on Derek's brother's face as hatred. Neither of us spoke, I carried on with dad's shopping, but the overwhelming feeling of anger came across me. I said to my dad that I really hate Derek's family. He quite rightly said I shouldn't hate anyone. I just wanted to go up to him and ask him why he thought it was OK to not bother about his brother who was terminally ill. I said to dad that they were a poor excuse of a family and Derek didn't deserve them.

We happened to be at the checkout at the same time. I couldn't help noticing how chatty and jokey Derek's brother was to the checkout girl, as if he was trying to make some pointless point. I am sure if half the people knew how disgraceful Derek's family have been they would have a different opinion of them. Turns out I had parked next to them in the car park. As the sister-in-law was trying to get into the car, she was on her mobile, personally I think she used this as a prop. It's not the first time she has done this when she has seen me. I moaned for her to get a move on as she was stopping me from getting the shopping into my car. I then went to put the trolley back, but the van next door but one was reversing into a space, then Derek's brother tried to reverse, even though I was standing behind his car. He then proceeded to shout out, 'Fat cow!' to me. What an imbecile. Yes, I have a weight problem, I don't think I am a cow though! If that's the best he can come up with, maybe he needs some vocabulary lessons. I won't lie, it did shake me up a bit, and I did cry, unfortunately in front of my dad, but I don't think I will be taking dad shopping there again.

***

This incident has got me thinking again about when the time comes for Derek's passing and the funeral. I don't want a scene, I don't want them there, but I would never stop them attending. I just don't know what to do for the best. This plays on my mind more than it should, and after today it has made me worried as to what to do.

19 November. Today I went to visit Derek with my friend Susan. We were shown into the visitors' room, which I must say was very cold, not really suitable for Derek as I assumed the unit he is in is warm. Even when Derek walked into the room he said 'Cold'! I was upset on seeing him. I hadn't seen him for a month, the longest time I had not seen him. I could see he had lost more weight, this time it showed around his hips and bottom. At no time throughout the visit did he recognise me at all, which was very sad.

I must say, though, that Derek was a lot calmer. The only thing that was a little upsetting was that after we had been there a while, Derek clearly needed the toilet. He started to wander around, then proceeded to urinate into the corner of the room, so the staff had to take Derek back to the unit to change him.

I had made him a rummage box which I was going to give him for Christmas, but decided to take it with me on this visit. Derek seemed interested in some of the items enclosed, such as the plastic tools.

24 November. This afternoon I received a phone call from Derek's social worker to inform me that his case was going to a tribunal. At that point I just snapped, explaining I was in bed with a bad headache, and previously I had a missed call on my mobile and on the home phone so I had contacted the unit suspecting it was them trying to contact me. So I had tried on several occasions to phone them but no one was answering. I couldn't continue the call. I was upset, I just had had enough of having to deal with issues with Derek. Again I feel alone, angry having nowhere to turn, a true feeling of being lost in a situation I have no control of. I did phone the social worker back to apologise and she explained the tribunal was to do with the Mental Health Act that Derek was sectioned under. It was now time to be reviewed.

27 November. Had a very busy day today. When I got home at about 5.30pm dad had left a message on the answerphone asking me to call him back. Fearing something bad had happened, I phoned him back straightaway. He wanted to know if I could take him to a hospital appointment in two weeks' time. I had previously said that I didn't like doing hospital appointments for obvious reasons. I thought my family would have realised that, but no I don't think they do. They go about their own little lives, never asking how I am or even contacting me. Yet think it's OK for me to do a hospital run. I am afraid I had to say no, but I feel bad about letting my dad down.

29 November. Received a letter from the forensic science hospital asking me to attend a professional clinical review meeting on 11 December at 11am.

December 2014
5th December. My birthday, not that Derek would ever know now, but I felt the need to phone and ask how he was. This time the lady who always answers the phone and says Derek is fine, handed the phone to someone else, who was more willing to give information on how he is.

Derek is back on antibiotics due to a leg infection. If I hadn't phoned, I guess I wouldn't have been told!

9 December. Phoned the unit to ask how Derek's leg was and to see if the antibiotics are working. I asked how Derek's clothes were as he has a tendency to pick and make holes in them. Because I am not allowed on the unit or in his room I have no idea of his clothes situation. I was told that this would be looked into. No sooner had the call ended when the unit phoned back to say that it was discussed at the last meeting that Derek needed more clothes. This is not true. I was then told Derek needed more t-shirts and trousers. I had two days to find suitable clothes and sew in labels.

11 December. Louise wanted to come to visit Derek with me. I didn't want her in the meeting and agreed that she could sit in the car and after the meeting I would see Derek, and if he was OK and not agitated I would text her to come in. She has a big audition for stage school in London on the 15th so I didn't want her upset.

The meeting was attended by a doctor, the social worker and a legal person. The meeting was about taking Derek off section 3 of the Mental Health Act and placing him on a Deprivation of Liberty Safeguards (DoLS) Act. Even though I had said I didn't want to attend that meeting I thought the meeting today was about how Derek's health was. I won't even pretend to understand the legalities of the Mental Health Act. I just agreed with the people there.

The meeting covered how much better Derek was and how he was much less agitated, and more smiley and happy. I was asked if I had any questions, so I brought up the subject of how when I phone to ask how Derek is I don't want to be fobbed off with 'He's fine'. I want to know if there are any problems, infections, etc. It was agreed that I would be informed at all times. It was mentioned that most families do not want to be informed of such things, but I explained I am the opposite. I want to be told, as 'fine' means nothing to me, and in fact I worry more when someone says he's 'fine'.

I was informed that I need to phone the main hospital and ask to be put through to the ward nurse, that way I will be given more details. So we will see if that works! I always end up tearful at any meetings concerning Derek, and I hate that this always happens. I wish I could be a stronger person.

After the meeting I was taken to the conservatory to meet Derek. I had the rummage box with me and scissors and comb to cut his hair. Also, a Christmas card. I think that Derek recognised me, but I can't be sure. He wouldn't sit down. I gave him his card, he opened the envelope, but wouldn't take the card out. No matter how I tried I couldn't get Derek to sit down. He then said the word toilet and got his penis out. I called a member of staff to take him to the toilet, but Derek's face was in pain as though he could not wee. He kept holding his tummy as if to show it hurt. By this time I was very upset. I asked the staff why they hadn't noticed that he was having problems and yet within ten minutes of me seeing him I could see this to be the case.

They took Derek to the toilet, but he didn't go. They brought him back to the conservatory where he was still showing signs of discomfort.
Now I don't know if he was in pain. My gut instinct was that yes he was, after all I have been with Derek for 25 years. I think that it's safe to say I know him well. Having said that, Derek then walked off into another room and was waving to other members of staff, as if all was OK. This is messing with my head big time. I gathered up my things and left.

18 December. Today the hospital phoned to say that the doctor saw Derek the day before and he has reduced his morphine and he is less agitated. This is good news, but

I did ask the hospital to take note if Derek starts to show any signs of pain, because I believe the morphine was given for pain relief for the prostate problem. I told them that a friend of mine's husband has an enlarged prostate and at times when he needs to urinate it was like passing shards of glass, so the staff must be observant of Derek.

22 December. Today all three of us, myself and the girls, have planned to visit Derek with his Christmas gifts. I won't lie, I am not looking forward to this, mainly because I don't know how Derek will be and I don't want the girls to see him agitated. Also I was worried of the effect this visit would have on me, as with each visit it becomes harder to bounce back. On arrival, I could see Louise was a bit apprehensive and gave her the option to sit in the car, but she said she would come in with us.

When we entered the hospital we were told that another family had arrived without booking, so we were shown in to the board room, consisting of a very large long table with dining room chairs, and fancy lamps and ornaments. These were then removed by the staff so only the table and chairs were left.

Today, thank god, was a good visit. I gave Derek his Christmas card, this time without the envelope, but he just threw it across the table, which did upset me a bit. I gave Derek his new jumper, and he said, 'Thank you.' The girls gave their gifts to him, a model of a Ducati bike and some chocolate. He ate quite a bit of the chocolate and seemed to enjoy it. He did however try to eat the bike!

We had taken the rummage box in with us and Derek seemed to enjoy playing with the plastic tools, which was good to see. He eventually fell asleep with the tools on his lap. At this point we left.

I noticed on this visit, and probably on others, when the girls have been with me that Louise does interact with Derek quite well, but Donna holds back. I don't think she knows how to deal with the situation. My heart goes out to her. I don't think I fully understand the full impact this is having on her, as she closes down when the subject of her dad comes up.

This is the last time I will see him this year, unless of course I get called in, who knows.

I have to say that Derek did look well, and it's hard to believe how sick he is on days like today. I can't help but wonder how much longer Derek will fight this evil disease.

2015

January 2015

24 January. Another year has passed. So far this year, life has been uneventful, although I did come home one day to find the social worker had left a voice message on the home phone to say something about a deterioration and needing a wheel chair. I phoned her back, but she clearly didn't believe me that such a message was left and asked if I could get a copy of it. This made me angry, I do not lie. Anyway, all was cleared up – the message was left in error, it was meant for someone else.

I don't think that I mentioned that when we went to see Derek just before Christmas, he had had his haircut which was a surprise as no one had asked if this could happen. Well yesterday I received an invoice for this for £8.40. Now don't get me wrong, it's not about the money, but I have been cutting Derek's hair for as long as I can remember and was still doing so. It's the only thing left that I can still do for him, and now that has been taken away from me. I thought it would have been nice to have been asked if it was OK for him to have a haircut. Common courtesy, I think?

I have not been to visit Derek this year yet. I have made a couple of phone calls to ask how he is. All seems to be well.

I have to admit I have been going through a difficult time in the last few weeks, some days just staying in bed. I think due to the accumulation of Derek's illness, Donna having tummy problems, taking Louise for auditions for stage school in London, and the realisation that at some point I will be left on my own. Plus having to deal with everything on my own with no back-up from family whatsoever. It's taking its toll. I am very close to reaching my rock bottom, to the point that I cannot see a way out, or I can if it wasn't for the girls.

Thank god I have them. They are my rocks, even if they don't realise it.
As I have said before, I used to bounce back, but it's getting harder as each year passes.

If anyone had told me that a member of the family's illness would affect the whole family as much as this, I would find it difficult to believe. But it is with great sadness that this is the case.

31 January. I haven't yet seen Derek this year. The odds are stacked against me, first an inner ear infection, now tonsillitis, with sinus problems. I believe that things happen for a reason, although it's hard to believe what reasons they are at this point in time.

I phoned the hospital to ask how Derek was. I was asked to phone back as they had the ambulance team in. I find it hard to accept that there wasn't anyone else to take my call. Anyway, I phoned back a couple of hours later. Derek is OK!

February 2015

13 February. Today a visit to see Derek. First time this year, due to illness. Not looking forward to it. This has been the longest time I have not seen him, so I guess I will see changes in him. And I wouldn't be surprised if he no longer knows me. I am going with his ex carer, so at least I won't be alone. I hope and pray that this visit doesn't knock me back as other visits have in recent times. I will try and stay positive.

March 2015

16 March. Today is Derek's birthday. Myself and the girls are going to visit Derek, we have presents and cards to give. Derek's presentation is much the same as my last visit. There was no recognition this time of either myself or the girls. When he entered the room, he was handed a glass of coffee-coloured liquid to drink, which was a bit strange as they had already brought in a tray of tea and coffee for us all. Derek was wearing a much too large sweatshirt, clearly not his. I questioned the staff about the sweatshirt not being his, but they seemed to think it was!

Derek had no concept of it being his birthday. He didn't open the cards, even with encouragement, nor did he open his presents, which were items of clothing and a bar of chocolate. It is heart-breaking that we have brought gifts and to Derek it has no meaning. To us it's as though we shouldn't have bothered, but we still do, we still care. But its destroying to see and to experience.

Toward the end of our visit Derek did get angry, maybe because I was trying to get him to hold the gift bag containing his birthday presents to take back to his room. The visit ended abruptly with me getting upset and walking out.

When I got home there was a message on the answerphone asking me to call the hospital. This was to ask me if I had any questions about the up and coming meeting on 22 April. I asked what the meeting entailed. It's an update on Derek's progress and to discuss the possible move to a care home nearer to our home. Also I was asked if I could buy Derek another shaver. My reply was he had only had this one less than a year. Why did he need a new one? Apparently, Derek's shaver is going to be handed back to me at the meeting so I can return it to the manufacturers.

April 2015

14 April. At 8.30am the phone started to ring. I was in bed at the time and didn't bother to answer, as I suspected it was yet another nuisance call.

Later on that day the phone rang again, it was Derek's sister informing me of Derek's mum's death. I thanked her for letting me know. She then asked if Derek was still alive. My reply was what kind of a person do you think I am to think that I would withhold that kind of information from you? She replied that she had been trying to find Derek. She had phoned the care home who told her that Derek had been moved back to the hospital. I asked why she didn't just phone me to ask where he was. Her reply was that I'd told her that I wanted nothing to do with the family. I replied that that still stands, but that didn't mean she couldn't ask where he was. I then said that Derek was so delusional about having a close family and that it has only been myself and the girls who have taken care of everything. Her answer was 'In your opinion', which to be honest did hurt.

Now I have to deal with attending the funeral. The girls obviously want to go, but I question if I should go, as I feel it would be like a lamb to the slaughter. I am not convinced that even though it's a funeral the family may just see a chance to have yet another go at me.

My other dilemma is whether to tell Derek. It would go against all my beliefs not to tell him, and at the end of the day chances are he will have no idea what I am saying to him. My spiritual belief is he will already know, and I fear that it may be not long before he follows. Maybe that was what he was holding on for.

16 April. This morning I received another phone call from Derek's sister telling us the funeral was on Wednesday 29 April at 2.45pm at our local crematorium, which we could attend, but no wake. I asked were they not having a wake? The reply was yes, but we are not invited. Words cannot even describe how angry I am at the moment. How dare they say that my daughters are not invited to their nana's funeral wake. Thank god Derek will never know just how low his family have sunk.

21 April. It has taken me a few days to calm down after being told we are not invited to the wake. It's surprising how time can make things feel better.

But today there was a message on the answerphone ('Oh it's gone to answerphone, I'll phone back'). It was Derek's sister's voice. Later on that evening, another message on the answerphone ('Hello Angela, please, please let me ring you, I need to speak to you, it's really important. I cannot bury mum without speaking to you. Thank you.')

You can imagine I found it very difficult to get to sleep after that, and here I am now at 5am writing this down. I feel on edge, not knowing what's going on with that message.

22 April. Today I have a meeting at the hospital about Derek. Not looking forward to that at all. Yesterday the hospital phoned to ask if I have any questions to ask at the meeting. And to tell me Derek needs more clothes.

Before my friend and I went to see Derek, we stopped off for coffee. I told her of the phone call I'd received the previous day. With some persuasion from her she advised that I make the dreaded phone call to Derek's sister as she was worried of the effect it was having on me. Turns out they really can't bury Derek's mum until I give my permission, due to Derek being in charge of the piece of ground and holding the papers to prove ownership of it. As I have legal power of attorney it is now down to me to say it's OK to go ahead with Derek's mum's ashes being put into the ground. Well what can I say, other than karma does exist. Obviously, I now have to sort out this, as if I didn't have enough on my plate.

Derek was on good form. He ate chocolate and drank tea. I told him of his mum's passing after consulting with the ward matron, who confirmed that it was Derek's right to be told, as I also agree. But sadly when I told him there was no reaction. I don't think for one minute he understood what I had said.

After our visit we went into the meeting, same old same old. Two things that stood out for me were I asked the question what happens if Derek becomes bed bound. Their answer was he would be moved to a nursing home. I asked if, for example, Derek got pneumonia how would this be dealt with regarding me visiting, as I am not allowed in his room. The reply was we would sort that out if this happened. At the moment, Derek is still on a one-to-one and does still have times of aggression, so they agreed that Derek would not be moved at this time.

Secondly the subject of Derek's family came up and they said that they felt that if Derek had contact with his family it could help improve his awareness. I then told them about how the family have treated us over the funeral, and also when Derek was in a local hospital in Chichester for seven months none of his family bothered to visit, so why would they now when it's an hour's drive away? I feel they are pressuring me to get Derek's family involved, but I am the person in the middle of all this and don't know what to do for the best.

I was also told Derek needed more clothes. I explained that we had bought t-shirts and a jumper for him on two of the more recent visits. I now have a list of clothing he needs, which consists of six pairs of jogging bottoms, ten t-shirts, four jumpers and four long-sleeved t-shirts. The matron said Derek had worked hard all his life, as if to say I shouldn't begrudge him more clothes, which I must say was quite hurtful as the only reason I questioned more clothes was because his entire wardrobe is now at the hospital and that's quite a wardrobe full of clothing. I have also been handed back Derek's razor so I can send it back to the manufacturers.

29 April. Today is Derek's mum's funeral. I delivered the flowers to the undertakers and the paperwork to the crematorium. I have signed all responsibility of the plot of ground over to Derek's sister.

Donna and Louise attended the funeral under the caring watchful eye of Derek's cousin. Apparently the service was quite short. Derek's brother greeted the girls with a hug – strange really! After the funeral, the girls were invited back to the wake. After all that was said, obviously it's me they have a problem with. When the girls came home, they were saying that there was a customer from the café, where the girls work, at the funeral who was very upset, but they didn't know who she was. They said she came into the café often, was very friendly towards them and gave them hugs. This got me thinking, surely it wasn't Derek's ex-girlfriend, who had befriended my girls? That would be totally out of order.

May 2015

2 May. Donna and I went to visit Derek. We took with us all the new clothes, plus a new razor. Donna is going travelling very soon and wanted to see her dad before she went.

The visit went OK. There were a few funny moments when Derek had managed to unlock the visitors' room's door leading outside, but obviously was unaware of this as he didn't pursue going outside. He also managed to lift off the windowsill, taking out a couple of bricks whilst doing so. He obviously still has his strength.

Donna had bought Derek a large model of a Ducati bike, but sadly this didn't interest him. We have added it to his memory box which I take with me on every visit. The topic of conversation over the past week has been the mystery lady at the funeral. The girls have been waiting for her to come into the café so they can find out who she is. She has befriended the girls, and both have said how nice she is.

8 May. Today just Louise is working, Donna's out shopping. When Donna returned home she asked if Louise had contacted me. She had managed to find out the mystery lady's name, and yes of course it's Derek's ex-girlfriend. Words at this moment are lost. Yes, I understand she would be at Derek's mum's funeral, after all she was always close to them, but to befriend both my girls is underhand and out of order. I feel sick that she would do that.

***

I made a call to the hospital to enquire after Derek and I was put through to the ward. The person on the other end seemed distracted as though it was inconvenient to be talking to me. Yet again another wasted phone call.

28 May. Got a phone call from the hospital from the trainee social worker asking how I was getting on in getting a replacement shaver for Derek, even though I had brought him a new one along with all the new clothes about a month ago. As you can imagine I was very angry. I was also asked about sorting out an end of life plan, which was done ages ago. This does not give me much confidence in the hospital. As predicted, I was asked again about Derek's family getting involved. I said I was still thinking about it.

June 2015

12 June. Today a visit to see Derek with his ex carer. I have not seen Derek for a few weeks and was surprised at how well he looked. There was an element of recognition from him and he told me that he loved me, which was a nice surprise. The ward nurse came into the room to say she needed to see me after the visit. I asked her why Derek was wearing someone else's clothes. Her reply was that she had given me a list of clothes needed. I told her I had brought everything on that list as requested to the hospital about a month ago. You could see by her expression that she doubted me.

After the ward nurse left the room a member of staff came into the room to ask about Derek's clothes. I explained again that I had brought a large bag of new clothes in for Derek. All had hand-sewn name labels on. I asked that all Derek's clothes be brought up to the visitors' room so I can see what clothing he has. A quarter of the clothing was not Derek's, some t-shirts were missing, but they could have been in the wash. What I was most shocked at was a couple of the t-shirts that were new looked like they had come from a rag bag, they were worn around the neck and the printed picture was almost non-existent. I am now being told that Derek needs about 30 t-shirts as they have to change him up to seven times a day. Apparently, they have to wash his clothes on a very hot wash then tumble dry. I am shocked that new clothes look like this after one month.

Apparently, they need Derek to have some nice clothes, for when they have entertainment come into the hospital and when they take him for a walk. Heaven forbid he wear scruffy clothes then! No matter when his wife comes to visit he wears someone else's clothes.

The visit, however, was a good one, albeit that Derek did fall asleep.
After the visit, I called into the ward nurse's office. I just knew it was going to be about Derek's family involvement, and not to disappoint I was right. I asked what advantage it would be for them to be involved after three years. Her reply was they believe Derek's long term memory is still intact and it could benefit Derek to see his brother and sister. I questioned why after three years?

The reply was that Derek's sister had contacted Derek's care coordinator asking for access. I don't even know who his care coordinator is, so how does she know? I am suspicious of this and need to check this story out, so when I got home I phoned Derek's previous social worker who informed me Derek's care worker is now the second CPN nurse from a few years ago. I am now waiting for her to phone me back so I can check out this story.

18 June. Derek's care coordinator got back to me. I asked about Derek's sister trying to contact Derek. Apparently she had phoned back in March to find out where Derek was, but obviously they were not allowed to give out details. But that was only the one time, and that was just before Derek's mum died, so whether this was connected I am unsure. I still don't know what to do for the best. If Derek's family were not so nasty towards me I would just phone them with the details of his whereabouts, and clearly if they really wanted to see him, why not just phone me and ask?

25 June. The day before Louise and I fly out to Paris to meet up with Donna and her boyfriend after their two months of travelling. I receive a missed call on my mobile from the hospital asking me to phone as soon as I get this message. My heart missed a beat, fearing the worst. I dialled the hospital number to be told that Derek needs medication for his leg and that they need to section him again under section 2. They needed my approval to do this, which obviously I gave. I was then asked yet again about Derek's family getting involved. I am so sick and tired of this persistent asking I gave the hospital Derek's sister's name and said they would have to look up the details of her number. Hopefully this will be the last I hear of this.

July 2015

2 July. Arrived back from a really lovely holiday, a whole week of forgetting home life and all the worries that go with it, only to find three messages from the social worker from the hospital on my answerphone. I returned the call thinking it was urgent. It was only to tell me Derek was re-sectioned and how did I feel about it? Besides pissed off that three messages were left on a matter that was not urgent, I said I knew he was sectioned and why didn't they phone my mobile. Her reply was she didn't know that I had been told or that the hospital had my mobile.

***

Later the same week I received a message from the social worker to say Derek needed more clothes, and could I phone them back, which I didn't of course. This is getting beyond a joke.

11 July. A phone call from the hospital to say that Derek was on antibiotics. I questioned that Derek was put on them a couple of weeks ago which was why he was sectioned. Turns out that the antibiotics did not work and a doctor had to be called out to prescribe more as Derek's leg is not healing.

14 July. Today myself and the girls went to visit Derek. Before we left home I phoned to ask that all Derek's clothing be brought to the visitors' room so I could check it all.

On arrival, we were let into the building then left for a while in the corridor while someone brought Derek into the visitors' room. We had brought more clothes for Derek, 13 t-shirts and four tracksuit bottoms.

Derek was very restless, wandering around the visitors' room not aware of us being there at all. He was agitated and walking with quite a stoop. When he eventually sat down it was to sleep, and that's how he stayed for the hour-and-a- half long visit.

While Derek was asleep I went through all his clothing, mending all rips and removing any cord from waistbands, which has become an issue with him. I also made sure that all name tags were securely fixed so they wouldn't come off.

Yet again Derek was wearing someone else's trousers which had elastic around the legs, even though I have continually told staff that Derek does not own elasticated-legged jogging bottoms, and more to the point should not wear them due to the condition of his legs.

Well no one ever listens, so drastic action was needed and while Derek was asleep I cut around the trouser leg bottoms removing the elastic. I will continue to do this every time he wears this type of trouser, then maybe someone will take notice

August 2015

4 August. I phoned the hospital, this time to speak to the ward nurse in charge because I can understand her speech a little better. I asked how Derek was. She said he was still very restless, but sleeping at night, some nights. She said he was in no pain, but I did detect a kind of 'we don't know what to do with him' kind of attitude.

5 August. Six years ago today we were given the news that would change our lives forever, the diagnosis of Alzheimer's.

The phone conversation yesterday with the hospital was playing on my mind, so I decided to phone the hospital and speak to the doctor to see if she could shed any light on what's going on with Derek. I was informed that she had left the hospital in April so he now has a new doctor.

The hospital took my phone number and said they would ask the new doctor to call me back when he returned to his office. Less than 15 minutes later the doctor did call back. The new doctor was very informative about Derek. He told me that he had been put on a painkiller patch, because they thought that maybe this was the cause of his agitation, and since the patch was applied Derek had been less restless. He told me that Derek was seen every week and sometimes more, because they were concerned about the swelling in his leg. The doctor also told me that Derek was the only patient on his ward who was on a one-to-one 24 hours a day – this I didn't realise – and that because he has been sectioned he will not be moved to a care home until the section was lifted, which I guess will not be anytime soon, if ever.

The doctor explained that they were concerned that Derek keeps falling over and walking into everything and banging his head, so they have ordered a helmet for him to wear. Ironic really, he never wore a safety helmet when climbing on roofs, but he has no choice now. I have to say that this piece of news was very upsetting. I know that the visits will be even more distressing now if he is wearing a helmet. How can I delete this image from my brain?

I now realise that to obtain any information about Derek's welfare I need to speak to the doctor, not the ward nurse who says he's OK.

7 August. Myself and Donna are going to visit Derek. I don't want to go on my own, but I also don't want to make Donna feel she needs to come. I am worried that the visit may be too upsetting for her. Out of our two daughters I fear she is the one who will find Derek's poor health the hardest to deal with.

Our visit to the hospital today was short, about an hour. This was due to the fact that Derek was very agitated. He continually walked back and forth, pacing the visitors' room. He sat for about 30 seconds, then started pacing again. I had taken some chocolate with me wrapped in foil. As I went to unwrap it, Derek tried to grab it off me, grabbing my hand with such force it brought tears to my eyes.

For one second Derek acknowledged Donna which was nice, although I could see how upset this made her, no matter how much she tried to hide it. As well as Derek pacing, he was also chewing his fingers and spitting which was very strange. The nurse said it was just a habit.

28 August. Myself and my friend went to visit Derek. We were shown into the visitors' room then left waiting just over half an hour before Derek was brought in. As Derek was walking down the glass-covered walkway my friend said, 'That's never Derek, surely?' He was bent over and wearing the helmet I was told about. I realised that she hadn't seen Derek for a while so I guess she could see the deterioration.

Yet again on this visit Derek did not sit down. He wandered around the room. We had to have a nurse sit in with us again. Derek wandered over to the conservatory doors then opened them to go outside. By this time, the nurse had pushed the panic button and about three nurses turned up. I made the comment to my friend that it was like being in prison. It only took a piece of chocolate to bring Derek back inside, which my friend and I achieved by ourselves. Derek is very unlikely to do a runner, and even if he was able, he's committed no crime.

The nurse that sat in with us was Italian, and although my friend was trying to have a conversation with him I could only pick out a few words that I could understand. He asked if Derek was from Afghanistan because of his speech/accent. I just turned around and in a sarcastic voice said, 'No, he just picked up that speech along the way.' I was annoyed that yet again no one seems to understand.

Derek is the way he is due to the illness. His speech was normal. He slept at night, he didn't use bad language, he didn't hit out, spit, destroy furniture, he was a very placid man. After a while, the Italian nurse was replaced by another, who quite clearly didn't want to be left in the room with Derek. She was scared, it was written all over her face. By this time I had had enough, so we left. I plan to visit Derek again on the 22 September as it's our silver wedding anniversary.

September 2015
22 September. Today is our silver wedding anniversary. I have planned a visit to see Derek. Louise is coming with me. I am not looking forward to this visit. I am wondering if it was a good idea when emotions are running so high, but part of me wants to see him. We arrive at 11am as booked. As Derek approaches the visiting room I notice he no longer has his helmet on. I asked why. Apparently Derek ripped it to pieces. Our visit went well. Derek actually sat down for almost an hour. We had brought with us some Duplo and he was quite happy putting the bricks together. Then as if his personality changed he jumped up and started to pace the room as before. It was time for us to leave.

We did get a couple of smiles from him, and a chuckle. I guess this is the best we can hope for now.

23 September. I had just got home from a friend's funeral and there was a message on the phone from the hospital to say Derek needed a new helmet. As the hospital funded the first one it would be good if I purchased the next one, and they will be putting in the order, just to let me know. I phoned the hospital to ask how much this was going to cost and they said they would find out and get back to me. I explained that I don't have a job and money is not unlimited. Their answer was that Derek gets a pension. I explained that we needed that money to keep the house going, not to mention Derek's clothing, haircuts and podiatry.

When I hung up I felt so guilty for questioning Derek's needs for funds for his safety. My other concern is how many helmets will he go through, the last one lasted two months. If he's on a one-to-one 24/7, how did he manage to destroy the helmet?

24 September. The helmet is still playing on my mind. I decided to phone Derek's ex social worker to see if she could help. She asked if Derek was still sectioned under section 3. I said he was re-sectioned in July. In that case, I do not have to pay, the hospital needs to apply to the funding panel. Good job someone knows, if I hadn't questioned this I would have landed up with yet another bill. I phoned the hospital social worker back to say they need to apply for funding. I was asked to phone the manager of the hospital. I replied that surely as Derek's social worker it's their job.

October 2015

2 October. Throughout Derek's illness I have had some anger issues, mainly due to frustration of a system that doesn't work. Today was no exception. I received a letter by recorded delivery from the hospital dated 30 September so it was written after my conversation with the hospital social worker.

Dear Mrs Hogarth,

Further to our telephone conversation on 23 September 2015 where I agreed to inform you about the price of a helmet for Derek, I am writing to inform you that we have identified helmets within the price range of £15–70. I can further inform you that the helmet that the multi-disciplinary team have identified as suitable for Derek costs £20.60 with free delivery from Amazon. I have attached a printout of the item should you wish to purchase this yourself. As this is considered necessary, an urgent response is required please.

I phoned to speak to the sender of this letter – she was on a day off. I then phoned Derek's CPN – their day off too. Why does this always happen? No wonder I am angry. The whole system just does not work, why do the hospital not listen to me? I thought I had made it quite clear they need to apply for funding for such items.

12 October. The meeting at the hospital scheduled for tomorrow has been cancelled.

When I received the phone call about the cancelled meeting at the hospital I was also asked again about the helmet Derek needed. I explained again that the hospital needed to apply from the funding panel for this as it's a medical aid.

I then contacted Derek's previous social worker again to ask what I should do. She advised that I email the hospital to say funding would pay for the helmet.

My email:

Hi,

With regards Derek Hogarth needing a new helmet.

I was contacted to ask if I could purchase another helmet for Derek because he had destroyed the last one. I found out that Derek's funding includes medical aids, so I contacted the social worker to explain this. I then receive a recorded letter asking again about the helmet. I was offended that the letter was recorded and still insisting it's my job to fund this item. I have yet again contacted my social worker and it's been confirmed again that Derek's funding pays for medical equipment.

I ask that you please sort this out by contacting Derek's care coordinator from the psychiatric hospital in Chichester.

This is not something I should be dealing with. Also Derek's care package will confirm this.

Many thanks,

Angela Hogarth.

14 October. A reply to my email reads;

Dear Mrs Hogarth
I write further to your email. I am afraid I completely disagree with you. Mr Hogarth is severely demented as you know and requires 24/7 1:1 support from the teams here due to his challenging behaviours.

A helmet is a small provision that prevents potential admission for constant head injuries that may be inflicted by falling and/or spatial awareness difficulties, and is therefore not deemed a medical aid. It is a prevention aid. The same of course goes for his clothes … As a result of the constant incontinence, Mr Hogarth requires a volume of easily washable clothing of which you provide some, but we are supplementing. Clean and ample clothing can be deemed as a preventative measure, to stop urine burns and complications arising from that … but they cannot be considered a medical aid either. Thus far, Mrs Hogarth, we have provided all of your husband's toiletries (numerous) and a high standard of care. Our social workers have offered repeatedly to help you if there are financial hardships, but you have refused their offers and therefore I can only assume that there may be some money available from Mr Hogarth's pension that could buy him something that will help prevent any further distress to him. We are only asking for a very small amount and have sourced the cheapest helmet we can find.

I have brought the second helmet (and indeed the first) on behalf of your husband simply because he needs it and I will be sending you the bill for such. I am afraid that I expect for it to be paid.

As you can imagine not only did this make me angry but it also upset me for many reasons, starting with Derek is 'severely demented' (did I need that pointed out to me?), to the fact I have not supplied much clothing, and I was not told at any point I needed to supply toiletries. Also about Derek being constantly incontinent – he is discontinent, there is a difference. He knows when he wants to go to the toilet, he just doesn't know how to get to the toilet. This I have witnessed myself on many occasions, also Derek wears incontinence pads.

Yet again I contacted our previous social worker who asked me to forward this email to her. She then said to leave it with her for a couple of days so she can sort it out.

When I went to bed last night my head was in such turmoil. I just hate the fact that people think I haven't done enough for Derek. I feel so frustrated, with no one to turn to. I ask myself again and again how much more heartache can there be?

15 October. The last email played on my mind so much I just had to reply, to make my point.

I am sad to hear that Derek's clothes are supplemented by the hospital. I do not understand why this is so. In April this year I purchased eight t-shirts, four jumpers, four tracksuit bottoms and a pair of shorts; in July this year I purchased 13 t-shirts, four tracksuit bottoms, and this on top of all the other clothes he already has at the hospital.

As for toiletries, I have never been told to bring these items in. I will of course bring them on my next visit. I would also like to point out I have not been approached by any social worker from the hospital to discuss hardship. I manage to keep afloat with Derek's state pension and my savings. I do not work at this time due to stress and I receive no benefits. I would never begrudge Derek anything, but the amount of clothing needed seems to me a little excessive.

The hospital's reply to this email.

Dear Mrs Hogarth,
Thank you for the clothes that you brought Derek in July which have been amazing and he is now up to speed. Previously we had supplemented, and to be fair when bearing in mind that he can be changed up to 8–10 times in a 24-hour period it is essential to have a large stock. At present all is good – I was just hoping to give you an example of how head guards are viewed under contracting (which you had mentioned in your earlier e mail). As I understand it the SW department had indeed approached you about discussing help with regards to finances and that you were finding it understandably tough … therefore I have included my colleague in this email who may be able to enlighten me as to the conversation that I understood had taken place. I have also included the CPN and another colleague in the email as they are directly involved in his care so are kept in the loop as to our correspondence.

21 October. As promised, our ex social worker contacted me. Both she and the CPN paid a visit to the hospital to try and sort out the situation with Derek's helmet and the funding. The hospital will not back down, insisting I pay for this piece of safety equipment. The hospital told the social worker that I don't bring clothes for Derek nor do I pay any of the bills associated with his care. This, I hasten to add, is a complete lie. I pay every bill sent to me from the hospital. This includes podiatry and haircuts to which I was never asked if this was OK.

The only thing I am guilty of here is not supplying Derek's toiletries, but I was never asked to. I feel I have been backed into a corner, with the hospital lies. I just have no one to fight my corner. The social worker and nurse are also fighting a losing battle. The only option I have is to pay for the helmet

November 2015

3 November. Today another meeting at the hospital, plus a visit. Sadly my friend cannot make it this time, so Louise has offered to come.

The visit wasn't too bad, although Derek did not sit down for the whole visit, and at one point did hit Louise. Not hard, but the fact he hit out suggests he didn't know who we were. The meeting was a nightmare.

The meeting consisted of the doctor, the ward nurse, the manager, social worker, a lady taking the minutes, Derek's care coordinator from Chichester, Louise, myself and the matron, who I would like to point out turned up late and with her dog (which I thought was quite rude, as she didn't ask if it was OK with us that the dog was in the same room as us – personally I am not keen on dogs).

The doctor spoke first. He was very easy to talk to, explaining about the drugs that Derek is on and how his presentation was. All was OK until the social worker started her little speech about how unapproachable I was about Derek's razor, clothes, how I didn't return her call, the helmet etc. As if someone had taken over my mouth, I began one by one addressing each issue she had with me. I explained the reason I questioned the new razor was because Derek had already had a new razor and it was still under guarantee. The clothes issue – I had purchased this year alone large amounts of clothing and I don't believe Derek gets changed ten times a day. The reply to this was Derek eats five times a day and after food he needs changing to look presentable. I asked why he didn't wear an apron. Their reply was he just rips it off.

I had replied to the phone call, but the social worker had left and was not due back into work for a couple more days. The helmet issue is just never going to go away. I asked why if Derek is on a one-to-one 24 hours a day, how did he manage to destroy the helmet. Turns out that the helmet was washed, so I questioned whether Derek destroyed the helmet. They were uncertain of whether the wash or Derek had caused the damage.

The social worker also mentioned that I had said Derek's pension goes towards the running of the house, apparently because I have lasting power of attorney I have to by law save a portion of Derek's pension for his care needs, otherwise I can be prosecuted. The social worker had kindly photocopied the paper from the government website to prove her point.

The social worker also mentioned Derek's end of life care package. This gets mentioned at every meeting. As far as I know this was done a long time ago, but apparently there is no record of it.

As if this was not enough to deal with, the social worker then had to bring up about Derek's family again. It was said that if the QCC found out that Derek's family was kept away from visiting him they would be in big trouble. If I didn't forward on the information about Derek's brother and sister they would involve the Salvation Army at a cost of £45 to trace them. I am so sick and tired of this ongoing battle I wrote down Derek's brother's address.

I have said it before and I will again, I am totally fed up with the situation. Why does this have to be an ongoing battle? A part of me is crying out to run away, wash my hands of this whole situation. My life with Derek is being tainted with this total anger, resentment and wondering why I ever got involved with such a family. The only good part was having the two girls, everything else is tainted with hate and sadness.

The vibe I got from this meeting, and was mentioned by the matron, was that Derek has had one-to-one care 24/7 for a year for free! Which was uttered under her breath. I guess this all boils down to one fact – money. The only good thing, if it progresses, to come out of the meet was the doctor asked how things could be made better for me. I explained that I was not happy having no dealings with Derek one-to one with visiting his room, checking his clothes, repairing any that are damaged, cutting his hair etc. The matron said that maybe this could be catered for and that I could visit Derek in his room, but the doctor was not too happy with this idea because of my security .

4 November. This morning I phoned the social worker to ask for the end of life plan papers to be sent to me, also to send me the minutes of yesterday's meeting. I need these for back-up in case there is a backlash from Derek's family.

I received what were the end of life papers, but which was in fact just a piece of paper asking name, date of birth, ward, date, followed by seven questions:
Is there someone you would like us to contact to be with you at this time?
Would you like us to contact a religious or spiritual leader? If so who?
Do you have a funeral plan in place?
If yes, who?
If no, do you have a preference?
Would you prefer a burial or a cremation?
Anything else you would like to add?

With this came two examples of other patients' plans with their name and address blacked out. I am not sure that's even allowed.

I had some questions about the end of life plan, so I phoned the hospital's social worker, but she didn't have the answers and said she would phone back. That of course never happened.

11 November. Donna had an appointment through from the hospital for a scan. She had been having women problems for a while and asked for a scan, only the appointment wasn't for that. Donna told me she didn't want to upset me but she had found a lump in her breast and was going to hospital to be checked. My heart just broke. The fact she had kept this a secret because I had enough to deal with made me realise how I had failed as a mum if she felt unable to talk to me about such an important thing.

To say I was worried sick is an understatement. I felt my world was falling apart and I no longer wanted to be in it. I attended the hospital appointment with her. I thank god that all was OK, but I still feel a little shaken by the whole thing.

13 November. So much has happened in such a short space of time. Today my long-awaited log cabin arrived. This is a major deal for me. After much thought, I had decided to try and set up a business with my spiritual healing, working from home. I should have known Friday 13th was not a good day. Turned out that there was no room down either side of the log cabin to treat the wood once erected. This resulted in the log cabin now being stored down the side of the house, to which three fence panels need to be replaced or the wood will get wet. I was so upset that I now have a major problem of sorting this out next year, when the better weather returns.

***

During this same week I phoned the hospital to ask how Derek was. All seems to be OK. I asked if Derek had any visitors. Yes, his brother, sister-in-law and sister came to visit. They were so pleased that they now know where Derek is and will visit often. I could have predicted they would make it sound like I was holding back information on his whereabouts. Let's see if they continue to visit.

21 November. You would think that was enough for one week, but unfortunately not. The week ended with more stressful news.

Both Donna and I received letters from the Office of the Public Guardian. I quote.

Dear Angela Hogarth,
Re: Mr Derek Hogarth
I am an investigating officer with the Office of the Public Guardian. I am investigating concerns raised about how Derek Hogarth's property and financial affairs have been managed, in line with the Mental Capacity Act 2005, section 58, and the Lasting Power of Attorney, Enduring Power of Attorney and Public Guardian Regulations 2007, regulation 46. To help me with my investigation, I need the following

information by 4th December 2015.

1. Details of Mr Hogarth's:

- *Income (including state benefits and private pension)*
- *Expenditure*
- *Assets*
- *Financial liabilities*
- *Bank accounts – copies of bank statements (from all of his accounts) from the registration date of the LPA on 11 th December 2010 until now.*

2. Explanations of any transactions that are not detailed in his financial records.

3. Details of any gifts and loans that have been made to you or anyone else since the registration of the LPA.

4. Details of the financial arrangements you have in place to make sure that Derek Hogarth has enough money for his everyday expenses.

5. Copies of any social services mental capacity and financial assessments for Mr Hogarth.

6.Name of a social worker or a contact from the local authority if Mr Hogarth is a service user.

7. A copy of Mr Hogarth's will.

8. Describe your role and how you work with your co-attorney in making decisions as attorneys for Mr Hogarth.

9. Describe how you consult Mr Hogarth in decisions about his property and financial affairs.

10. Details of any items you have purchased for Mr Hogarth during his residence in the nursing home.

11. Do you have any concerns or any other information you would like to tell me about?

Because I question about the amount of clothes Derek needs and the issue of the helmet, I believe that the hospital have set this in motion. I feel totally betrayed. I have never begrudged Derek anything. Yet again I have been stabbed in the back. The emotional roller coaster we as a family have been on has just got scarier. I know Derek would be very angry at me being accused of taking his money. All this unnecessary stress to an already stressful situation. I don't understand what I did to deserve all this heartache? The girls don't deserve a life of stress. I question again and again why are all these problems thrown at me constantly. I only ever want what's best for Derek, I would never steal from him or anybody else. He's my husband, I love him, but society is taking away from my mind the good times, the happy times, my marriage.

***

I have now received the invoice for Derek's helmet. The cost was more than first quoted, so I phoned the hospital to ask why this was so. First they said it was the postage, but I replied that the letter I received from them said it was postage free, so then the hospital said they add a percentage for handling/admin. When I questioned this they replied that when Derek was first admitted I was told about admin costs. Well I can confirm I never was told about this. I then asked if there was a book of rules they could send me, because so far it seems they make the rules up as they go along.

I have also just received a phone call from Derek's new doctor at the hospital. This is the third doctor in a year, which makes me wonder why the quick change over in doctors. She sounds very nice and asked lots of questions about him.

December 2015

3 December. Early this evening I received a phone call from the hospital to say Derek was unwell. He was not himself and was losing his balance when walking. I asked if I could come and see him in the morning, but the hospital said his brother was visiting. I asked the hospital to phone me day or night if there was any change. I didn't get much sleep. I phoned the hospital at 7am, but Derek was still asleep. I then phoned again at 9.30am and the staff said he was OK today, so I am not sure what's going on. I cancelled the meet-up with my sister, I just can't deal with her at this time. Although she said that she would be there for me, it's too little too late.

4 December. Still no bank statements from Barclays so I made a trip into town, but never is anything easy in my life. The computers went down, so I had to call back later today to get them. I then packaged all the paperwork up and sent it off. It cost me £11 to send, all unnecessary extra expense thanks to the hospital.

22 December. All three of us went to visit Derek to give him his Christmas presents and cards. The visit was about an hour long, but at no point was there any recognition from Derek. All cards and presents were opened by us. Derek did however sit down, but then fell asleep. He had no shoes on as his foot was very swollen, so I assume his shoes or special slippers did not fit. We gave Derek his box of Duplo, but he didn't acknowledge that either.

***

Really not looking forward to Christmas, yet again I am left having dad on Christmas Day. I should be pleased that I still have my dad, but I seem to have him every year since mum died. Only once did he go to my brother's in five years. Because of his illness, I find it very difficult to deal with his negativity.

I had planned to send my sister a Christmas card, all written out, except when I got home from visiting a friend there was a card and parcel on the door mat. It was a Christmas card for Louise and I, and a card and present for Donna from my sister. No present for Louise. I was so annoyed. How dare she segregate the two girls. It always has to be her way, hence her card from me went in the bin.

25 December. Woke up with a bad headache, no surprise there. I had worked myself up into such a state at having dad over for Christmas. Let's just say I have had better Christmases. I found it very difficult with my dad, to the point I was worried about my own sanity. It's a scary thing. I want to support my dad and have sympathy for him, but I am angry that six years down the line of his breakdown he's not much better. I am not sure how much he plays on this, so sad. I cancelled visiting my brother as I was in such a state. I didn't want to be with anyone other than the girls. This makes me so sad, and yet again confirms just how vulnerable I am. Also how all of this is affecting the girls. Donna has had a virus lasting over two weeks, and Louise feels she needs more counselling. My wish for the new year is for us three to find ourselves and start living a better happier life. For Derek, I wish for him to find peace.

2016

January 2016

Another year has passed. With each year, I wonder if this is the year Derek will pass. I seem to live with this thought each day, week, month and year. He doesn't have a life as such, but still he holds on to every day with the inner strength that I know nobody else has.

15 January. I receive a phone call from the hospital to say Derek has been put on antibiotics because of a leg infection. I wonder if this is the point when the antibiotics no longer work and leads to Derek's decline.

Three days later I phone to ask how Derek is. All is well again.

19 January. Received a phone call from Derek's doctor at the hospital – a request for yet another helmet, this time at a cost of £75, plus a shoe needs to be made at a cost of £30. Apparently neither comes under the medical aids description.

***

After the Christmas with dad it's made me realise that something needs to be sorted out with him. He certainly isn't getting any better; still he has issues with the heating not working so keeps turning it off then gets really cold. He is so negative about everything and at the weekend he told my brother he was cold and dying. I phoned up Mind to ask if they could help. When I explained the situation they suggested that I also needed some kind of help. Maybe they are right, but I am not ready yet.

Louise has gone back into counselling. I worry as to how much Derek and dad's illness has affected her. From the age of 13 it's all she has known. Donna has continually got something wrong with her, due to I believe her not being able to open up about the illnesses around her; and me, I just juggle everything.

Louise and I are visiting Derek tomorrow. I have asked the hospital to have all Derek's clothing brought to the visitors' room so I can check it all over.

27 January. Our visit to see Derek went OK. Derek insisted on walking around. When he did finally sit down it was on an ornamental chest, which was not suitable as a seat. Therefore Derek fell asleep but was doubled over as if about to fall. I tried to coax him to move, but he wasn't wanting to move and I could feel his hostility, therefore left him on the chest.

The hospital staff brought two bin bags of clothes for me to check over. Sadly one bag was full of someone else's clothes, the other 80% of the clothing was very damaged. I couldn't believe Derek had caused this much damage to his clothing;, even the jumper Donna had brought him at Christmas was now double the width due to washing. It's an impossible situation trying to understand the reason why so much of Derek's clothing is ruined. I am very upset that while the hospital demand untold amounts of clothing, that no care is taken to look after it.

Because of the extent and quantity of the damaged clothing I decided to bring it home to repair, and in some cases to re-dye it as it looked as though some of the clothes had come into contact with bleach.

When I got home I phoned the hospital to ask to whom I make a complaint about the condition of Derek's clothes. I was told they would find out and contact me. No surprises that I received no such phone call, so I phoned again. I was told to email the CEO with my complaint which I did on 1 February.

On my last visit to see Derek on Wednesday 27th January I asked to see Derek's clothing to check that all name tags are still intact. I was shocked to see the condition of some of the clothing, I would be interested in your view on how Derek s clothing got into such a poor state. I understand that with his aggression he may damage some clothing, i.e. the t-shirts ripped at the neck, but how did the jumpers get damaged under the armpits?

Also the jumper my daughter brought for Derek for Christmas is ruined (double the width) in under one month. As Derek's wife and his lasting power of attorney, to which I take the role most seriously, I would like an explanation for this damage.

Please see enclosed photos to prove my point.

The reply I got back on the same day was:

Dear Angela,
Thank you for your email. I have circulated your photographs to the relevant people and have asked for comments for which I will reply when they have returned answers for me.

February 2016
9 February. Phoned the hospital to ask how Derek was. I am a little concerned that his leg is still red and to me looks infected. With no disrespect to foreign workers, but unless they speak English that I and other members of the public can understand should they hold a position whereby they can advise you on a patient's condition? No word of a lie, I could not understand more than a couple of words of what was being said. I think the gist of the conversation was Derek's leg was itchy, which to me suggests there is an infection.

After the phone call I decided I needed to talk to Derek's GP. I phoned the number I had, but the number was incorrect, so I phoned the hospital to ask for the number. I was told that they would have to find out as they couldn't just hand out the number. I asked if they could just tell me what surgery he was at, but again they said they would phone me back. Guess what, they never did. Good job for the internet. Luckily, I knew the doctor's name and googled surgeries in the area and found the number. I had written the number down wrong by one number.

I explained that I needed to speak to Derek's doctor because I couldn't understand the staff at the hospital. The receptionist was very understanding and put me on a list of phone calls for that day. The doctor explained that Derek was still on antibiotics and that hopefully the leg would become less infected, although it was seeping fluid, but I do remember that happening before. The doctor explained that because Derek hadn't been on antibiotics for a while there was a better chance they would work, with more options of antibiotics if not. All sounds very promising.

10 February. Still no reply from the hospital about Derek's clothes, so I message the CEO again.

Hi.
Still not heard any comeback on Derek's clothes.

The reply:
Oh god sorry … I thought I had, as I got reports from laundry and units straight away! Will get on to it and forward responses today. Apologies, have just surfaced from flu.

The reply:

Dear Angela Hogarth,
Thank you for your email dated 1st Feb. 2016. I do apologise for the delay in response, but as you can see below the housekeeper responded quickly to your query via myself and therefore any delay is entirely my oversight. As I understand on this occasion the care staff and nurses had tidied up Derek's wardrobe and taken bundles of clothes out that were ripped or worn out or (they felt) beyond repair.

They offered you this bag of clothes and you wanted I believe to take it for mending which of course is your prerogative. She also goes on to state that when Derek is restless or agitated he pulls at his clothing with some force, which could well explain the rips and (as you know) Derek can be very challenging to get dressed at times so getting clothes on and off can be very difficult and not always sympathetic to the clothing or the staff in question. It is hugely good to note that you are an excellent seamstress and that you are able to mend at the level that you do. We are grateful that you continue to take such an interest in Derek's continued wellbeing and appearance … it means a lot to the staff I know.

I find this reply quite condescending. Why would I not still take an interest in Derek's wellbeing and clothing? He's my husband, still till death do us part for god's sake. As for the excellent seamstress, how patronising.

The reply from the housekeeper on this matter was:

As my colleague has explained, Mr Hogarth's clothing is changed frequently and placed in red bags, as all wet and soiled items should be in accordance with our infection control policy. When this laundry is brought to our laundry room the red bags are placed in the washing machine unopened, then it is washed at a high temperature. This again is part of our infection control policy. Some garments shrink and some garments become baggy during this process, and if as it would seem to be the case Mr Hogarth's clothing is being processed in this manner daily it will affect the shape and look of his garments.

I replied:

If that's the case, that's very worrying, as some of the clothes in the said bag were in good condition and were returned to the ward!

The hospital's reply:
I have to admit I am totally at a loss. Did the team think that these clothes were worn out or had come to the end of their natural life? I don't know … I have included my colleague in your email and they can respond to you perhaps better than I myself can, as I am unsure what more I can say or indeed what you propose that we do.

Isn't that called passing the buck?

My reply to this was:
Let me explain. I asked to see Derek's clothes to make sure all name tags were still intact. I came with my needle and cotton to re-sew if required. Two black bin liners were brought to the visitors' room, one bag contained some random person's clothes, in the other bag were some of Derek's clothes. I was annoyed that the extent of damage to 80% of Derek's clothing. I am not sure where the rest of his clothing were. I bagged up the good clothing and gave it back to the staff. The remaining items – 12 in total – I have here at home to repair. Hope this is less confusing.

I now wait a reply.

March 2016
1 March. Today the long-awaited letter arrived from the Office of the Public Guardian.

I have now concluded my investigation into the management of Mr Hogarth's property and financial affairs in accordance with the Mental Capacity Act 2005, section 58, and the Lasting Power of Attorney, Enduring Power of Attorney and Public Guardian Regulations 2007, regulation 46. Concerns had been raised regarding the provision of items for Derek Hogarth during his residence at the hospital and whether these were sufficient to meet his needs.

I am pleased to inform you that the concerns raised have not been upheld and that the Office of the Public Guardian will not be taking any further action with regards to this matter.

I feel a great relief that I was cleared, but at the same time very emotional that I was accused at all. I have always only done my best for Derek and I know he would be very angry that this has happened.

16 March. Derek's 70th birthday. All three of us went to visit Derek. Sadly he was unaware of it being his birthday or that we had come to visit. We had brought him two cupcakes which we cut into small pieces and had to put into his mouth.

Derek's leg is clearly infected. Not only is it swollen, but seeping fluid, with skin peeling off. The doctors have prescribed yet another antibiotic, the fourth this year. Hopefully this one will work.

30 March. I have been phoning the hospital more often as Derek's leg seems to be not responding to the antibiotics. When we visited Derek on his birthday I asked if he had MRSA and I was told no.

Today when I phoned I was told he does have MRSA. Although Derek has had this before, it's quite worrying that he is on his fourth antibiotic and now has MRSA.

***

Spent Easter morning in A&E with Louise.

She had been complaining about back/side pain for over a week, but we couldn't get to see a doctor for over a week. The pain was not getting any better. Unfortunately, due to what we three have been living through we always assume the very worst when being unwell. I guess this is only natural. Apparently, it was a pulled muscle and she was told to rest.

I am beginning to realise that we are living in a kind of vortex, trying desperately to climb out to see the light of day, but always there's something trying to pull us to the bottom of despair. How much longer we can go on, I don't know. The feeling of wanting to pack my bags and run away returns once again. The feeling of utter loneliness takes over my mind again. I am not sure how I will cope when Derek passes, but I have to remind myself I have come quite far already.

I need to find a job for my own sanity or I will lose myself in loneliness. Louise will be off to uni in September, Donna is looking for work maybe in London. That leaves me and the cat, not quite how I expected to live my life in my 50s.

April 2016
4 April. At my request, the GP from the village where Derek is in hospital phoned to advise me on what was happening to his leg. He advised that although the antibiotics have not really worked too well up till now, due to swabs being taken and the presence of

MRSA they can now try a different antibiotic. If, however, this doesn't work there may come a time when the best they can do for Derek is to make him comfortable.

6 April. Today I visited Derek with my next-door neighbour, who has known Derek longer then I have. This is the first time she has seen Derek since he has not been living at home.

As before, Derek was wandering around, not wanting to sit down. A tray of tea was brought in for us. Derek made a bee line for the tea pot. It took two of us to stop him from picking it up and burning himself.

On several occasions when calling Derek's name he responded with 'Yes'. This was a very new occurrence, he has not acknowledged his name for a very long time. After we had been there a while Derek looked at my neighbour and gave a smile as if to acknowledge her. Again, this was something new.

Derek still has immense strength. This was evident when I handed him his cup of tea. He went to take the cup from me, but was holding it at an angle so I wouldn't let go, but he just grabbed the cup and most of the contents landed on the leather sofa.

The second incident of the day was quite amusing. In the visitors' room is an oak unit with a drawer. Derek opened the drawer and put his cup inside, but he couldn't close it because the cup was too tall. So Derek laid the cup down full of tea then closed the drawer. Obviously the tea started to trickle through the drawer. It added much amusement to the visit.

Derek's leg is clearly still infected. Although it's no longer seeping out fluid, his leg is very red and clearly he finds it very itchy. I am quite concerned that the infection may not go away this time.

***

Apart from dealing with Derek's illness, day-to-day life can sometimes be very challenging.

Louise has gained a place at university, which I am very proud of. She is the first one in my family to have achieved this. The financial paperwork alone is a challenge for me, made even more difficult by the fact that Derek does not live with us and cannot fill out his side of the paperwork. I contacted the financial people sending my legal power of attorney papers, a letter from the doctors and a handwritten letter explaining the situation.

So far the hospital has received two letters asking Derek to fill in his financial details. I have spent many hours on the phone explaining, but still the system does not recognise our situation, which is very frustrating for me.

Along with one of the letters from the financial services via the hospital was a letter from the social worker saying she still awaits my phone call to discuss setting up a budget for Derek. Well she will have a long wait, that's just never going to happen. I will explain this to her at the hospital meeting next month, not something I am looking forward to. I have already started to write down my speech about how betrayed I feel about being accused of abusing my legal power of attorney.

28 April. At 6.15 I get a phone call from the hospital. Derek has a UTI and has to go on to antibiotics again. He has not long finished taking them for his leg infection. The hospital asks if I still stand by the 'do not resuscitate' on Derek. I ask why are they asking this now. Their answer, to make sure I still agree with this. I find this upsetting; I'm not sure if the hospital are expecting Derek to not react to the antibiotics or if the UTI is worse than others he's had.

I asked the hospital to contact me any time day or night if Derek becomes worse. They said a note would be made. This makes me wonder at what stage would they tell me if Derek became worse, surely I shouldn't have had to tell them to contact me at any time? Last night I went to bed with a heavy feeling in my chest. The phone call has upset my body system, and I feel very unsettled, almost on edge.

29 April. This morning I phoned the hospital to ask after Derek. I was told he was fine, eating, drinking, wandering around. I asked how his infection was. The answer was he's on antibiotics and a five-day course, and it's better. I have absolutely no idea what's going on. The language barrier has always been a problem with this hospital. I hung up not really knowing what's going on. I now wait on tenterhooks to see if the antibiotics will work. I hope if there is a deterioration they will phone me.

May 2016
1 May. Today I was working at the Mind Body Soul Fayre at Hayling Island. At approximately 11.15am I received a text from my brother saying, 'Hi sis, can't get hold of you. Dad has had a bad night hallucinating about your cat and Louise. Had paramedics out to do with his medication. Our sister's been with him since. I am here now, just wondering if you have any time to be with him as it's my wife's birthday and we are out for lunch.'

I was very angry at this text being sent. My thoughts were, who's there to cover my back when I am in need? No one, that's who. Have either my brother or sister been there for me? No. I apologise if this sounds cruel, because at the end of the day this is my dad who's not well, but there's two of them each with a supporting spouse. Previously I would have come running at the drop of a hat, but something inside me has changed.

I feel that my mum may be looking down on me in disgust at the way I behaved towards my dad's illness, and that I am not there to support him. This is something I will just have to live with.

3 May. Meeting at the hospital. My friend came with me. We saw Derek first. He was his usual self, wandering around moving furniture. A couple of times there was recognition of me, which was a nice surprise if not a little upsetting for me.

The usual crowd were around the table. Derek's CPN from Chichester was there along with her replacement, the usual social worker was on holiday so the original one was present. It was noted that there was little change in Derek over the past six months, and the antibiotics given to Derek were still working to some degree, albeit that the infections do seem to come back after a while.

The social worker commented that messages were left for me to contact them about any comments I wanted covered at the meeting, and to discuss budget for Derek. This is true, but I was too annoyed to contact them after the allegations of misuse of my power of attorney.

My reply to the budget was that as I now have to account for every last penny of Derek's money due to being accused of misuse of my legal power of attorney by, I suspect, a member of the hospital team (which they denied), I need receipts for every purchase of items bought for Derek. Also, I am happy to continue to purchase toiletries and anything else Derek requires, for it's the only thing left for me as his wife to do as all other duties have been taken away from me including cutting his hair. All the hospital needs to do is contact me by phone or email to request what Derek needs and I will forward the money. I was then told Derek needs another helmet at a cost of £100, plus a leg support shoe at £100. The budget for Derek is needed to purchase extras such as Derek's favourite foods, ice cream, extra puddings, etc. The suggested amount was £20 a week.

Not only was I lost for words, but this whole ordeal is all about the money as if they are trying to squeeze every last penny out of Derek's pension. I stupidly agreed to £15 pounds a week, but now I have had time to think even that's too much. I cannot think what Derek could possibly buy with £15 a week. I already pay for his haircuts, his podiatry, all of his toiletries, his clothes and helmets. When we visit we always bring sweets. I don't mind giving a small amount of money, but I just can't understand why after two years this is even an issue.

The social worker then went on to say that Derek's family, i.e. his brother and sister, were overjoyed at visiting Derek. They were pleased with the care he's been given, how well presented Derek is and how he always smells nice. This was of course a dig at me, letting me know that his family are involved.

To define 'involved', they do not know half of Derek's story on his path of this illness, only the nice stuff. They only see him at his best. The anger I feel inside is overwhelming, the anger of the illness, of so-called family, of how I feel trapped and unable to move forward with my life.

Today I phoned the previous social worker to ask for help on the money situation. She is going to make a few phone calls to get some advice.

4 May. I have still not heard back from the social worker, but I have received an invoice from the hospital for £100.

13 May. Today is dad's birthday. I phoned him up at lunchtime to wish him a happy birthday. I was going to suggest that we call in after Louise finished work, maybe pick up fish and chips if it's OK with him. Dad's reply was that my brother and sister and their other halves were coming over at six, with a fish and chip supper, so I guess it would be a bit awkward if we turned up at the same time seeing we were not invited.

I don't understand why I was excluded. To have been asked would have been nice. Instead I went to dad's on my own in the afternoon. It seems my brother and sister are now getting along better, me I feel like an outsider. I feel very hurt, I have never had any support from any of my family. It seems they don't understand what my girls and I have been through.

June 2016
9 June. Called round to dad's with my nephew's birthday present as my brother was seeing dad the next day. As I approached dad's, I noticed my sister's camper van and car parked in the drive. At first I drove past, then said to myself, I have just as much right to be here as anyone, so I turned the car round and pulled up in the drive. Dad came out to meet me, which was quite unusual. I walked back into the house with him.

One of the first things dad said was that my sister and husband have moved and asked if I knew. They are storing some of their things here. I asked if she was here. Dad replied, yes she was upstairs. She didn't bother coming downstairs to see me.

I did notice two envelopes on the windowsill, one addressed to my nephew, the other to my brother. I guess it was to advise of the new address. Obviously I didn't get one.

10 June. Today I visited Derek with my friend. Our appointment was booked for 2pm. We were let into the building and sat waiting in the visitors' room for half an hour. I phoned the manager to ask why Derek wasn't here. The first question I was asked, was did anyone know we were there. Quite ironic, really, as you can't get into the building without speaking on the intercom!

Eventually Derek was brought to the room. The excuse for the long wait was that there had been a staff meeting. I had brought some goodies for Derek – nine bars of chocolate, two packets of his favourite shortbread, and some tins of coke. I always bring chocolate for Derek, as it's soft and easy for him to eat. I unwrapped the chocolate and started to feed Derek with it. A member of staff walked in and asked what I was giving him. I replied chocolate. She asked if I had cleared it with staff. I replied that I always give Derek chocolate and that no one has questioned it before. Even in meetings I say I bring chocolate, and nobody has ever questioned this. I was told that the chocolate was a choking hazard. I asked why I wasn't told this before, and asked if they had a list of what I could bring in. They said I could bring in chocolate mousse.

The girls had bought Derek chocolate for Fathers' Day the next week, now they can't give him that. There is no communication between the hospital and myself unless it's to ask for money. A member of staff then came into the room with a chocolate magnum ice cream, and chopped it up into a bowl so I could feed it to Derek. In two years, they have never given this to Derek on a visit.

Derek's presentation was pacing up and down the room, moving furniture. We had been there a good hour and a half before he sat down and became more peaceful. His leg was still swollen, and had a pink/purple look to it. To me it looked as though it might still hold some infection.

As we were leaving the building, Derek's doctor was coming in. We said hello and she asked how my dad was. 'My dad?' I replied, thinking she knew my dad was unwell. I hesitated. She looked at me, waiting for my reply. I said I am Derek's wife. 'Oh sorry, I thought you were someone else,' then she asked me if my daughter had got into stage school. Good recovery.

July 2016

18 July. Received a phone call from the hospital social worker asking if I had any comments to make about Derek's care, or any issues that I want airing at a manager meeting next week. Also, she wanted to know if I had set up a direct debit for Derek, for any extras he may need. I asked what kind of extras. The only two items the social worker could come up with were ice cream and yogurt. I don't think it is possible for Derek to eat £15-worth of ice cream and yogurt in one week. I questioned why after two years I am now being asked to set up a direct debit. I asked was it because I won the case that they filed against me for misuse of Derek's money? Her reply was that they find me difficult to deal with, in getting items for Derek. By that I guess she means I question why Derek needs some items. The social worker then said she had asked for advice from the public guardian about the helmet and they took it upon themselves to investigate. I believe the social worker was the one to ask for the investigation.

I told the social worker that in the eight years Derek has been ill she is the least empathetic person I have had dealings with, that she has no idea what we as a family are going through, how I have to keep things together and support my daughters. Her reply was that my daughters were old enough to support themselves. The conversation got quite heated, the social worker saying Derek's worked hard all his life, he deserves his treats. On reflection, this made me very angry. I am well aware how hard Derek worked, I am his wife. I am not depriving him of anything, I am questioning why the hospital are asking for a direct debit payment of £60 a month for extras.

I have contacted our previous social worker from home. She is looking to see if I can have an advocate. She also mentioned that she had asked the person who decides about funding for the helmets. He said I should not have to pay for them. I also phoned the Office of the Public Guardian to ask for advice, because I am worried that out of spite the social worker will file another case against me. They advised that I email them to get my point across first. This I have now done.

All this agro makes me so sad, and has added more stress to my life. If Derek knew half of what has gone on he would be so upset. I feel that this could all have been avoided if the hospital had given me a book of rules of what's expected of me.

August 2016
After making another phone call to the hospital asking for the list of Derek's requirements, I finally received a letter with a list.
- Rolo mousse
- Cadbury bubbles of joy
- Oykos yogurts
- Aero bubbles mousses, mint and chocolate
- Ski mousses
- Grape boost juice
- Coca-cola
- Tropical juice
- Magnum ice creams

I really do not think that this would cost £15 a week.

I have a visit planned on 12 August so I will be taking these items to the hospital.

5 August. Seven years ago today we received the devastating news that Derek has Alzheimer's.

Today I have a hospital appointment to have a sigmoidoscopy. I didn't want the girls to know, but unfortunately I needed to have someone with me according to the hospital. I had already attended one appointment on my own which was a terrifying ordeal for me. I had hoped that I didn't need a follow-up. The hospital staff were very good, and three hours later the results were given that all was OK. I cried with total relief, I had been so worried. What if I was ill, who would look out for the girls? I always worry about them.

12 August. I visited Derek today with my neighbour. It was a very hot day and Derek was dressed in tracksuit bottoms, a shirt and jumper. As always, he was intent on walking around the visitors' room, trying to move furniture. I had brought with me some 'extra food' that the hospital had asked for. I fed Derek a chocolate mousse and some coke. I had brought my iPod with me so I started playing some sixties music, but Derek seemed unaware of this. Then I played a recording of Louise singing. Derek became more relaxed and proceeded to sit down. Coincidence? Maybe.

The matron came into the visitors' room with some clothes that needing repairing. I gave her the food I had brought, asking that the cool bag be returned as I needed it for my next visit.

After we had been there a while, Derek wanted to go into the garden. Me and my neighbour stayed in the conservatory, as there was no shade outside for us. After a while one of the nurses told us that Derek needed his pad changed and so took him back to the unit through another door, without us being able to say goodbye to him. I thought this was totally out of order. I asked another member of staff if I could have my cool bag back, but they couldn't find it, so phoned the matron. It was handed back to me. I went to get in the car and realised that the cool blocks had been removed, so I had to go back into the hospital, who then had to phone the matron to ask where they were. Talk about disorganised, what would it have taken for the matron to just unpack the cool bag then return it to me, after all I was only in the next room.

When I got home from our visit I had received an invoice from the hospital for yet another helmet. When I checked my cheque stubs I only purchased one in April. Clearly the more expensive ones do not last as long as the cheaper ones. I have now phoned the hospital to say I only want the cheaper helmets purchased from now on.

28 August. Donna and her boyfriend went to the hospital to take Derek's clothes that I had mended. The staff asked if she wanted to see Derek and she said yes. The member of staff went onto the ward, came back and said to her that Derek was asleep, and the manager said that they didn't want to wake him as he would be agitated. So sad that she didn't get to see Derek, also a bit annoyed at the hospital, after all Derek is her dad.

September 2016
1 September. This evening I received a phone call from Derek's doctor from the hospital. Nothing to worry about, Derek's on antibiotics, which I already knew, but what I didn't know was that the infected leg was his good leg. This is quite worrying as the infection has only ever been in one leg. Derek is still on a course of antibiotics but they are not working as well as they could. There is only one other antibiotic to use on Derek, but the doctors are trying not to use this one at the moment.

The doctor also said that they were going to try to get Derek to sleep on a mattress on the floor, because at the moment when Derek falls asleep in a chair, to get him into bed wakes him up, then he wants to walk around. If he was on the floor he would find it difficult to get up. Hopefully they could then elevate his legs.

The doctor also said that Derek needed a new helmet. I told her that I had only just paid for one a couple of weeks ago. She is now going to send me the link so I can purchase the helmets. I again said that I shouldn't have to pay for helmets as they are a medical aid and that the hospital should apply for funding from the funding team. She agreed that this should happen. The doctor also mentioned that next week they will try to do a blood test on Derek, to make sure that his kidneys and liver are OK and that's not what is causing the swollen legs.

2 September. Went to visit Derek with my next-door neighbour. Was a little apprehensive as to how Derek was going to be. I had brought him some new clothes and some chocolate mousse.

I didn't think Derek's leg was as bad as anticipated, but clearly the infection was in both legs. Although Derek didn't acknowledge me he did at one point wink at me. I did however think he had lost weight. My neighbour also thought so. Derek was more subdued and for once he sat down. Towards the end of the visit he was very sleepy. I can't help thinking is this the last time I will see him, surely his body has had enough fighting infections. This may seem very harsh, but it's out of love and not wanting him to suffer any more.

November 2016
8 November. Big meeting at the hospital today. My friend came with me. I had made an appointment to visit Derek at 1pm, and meeting was at 2pm.

We arrived at 1pm, signed in then waited for someone to show us into the visiting room. Derek was then escorted towards the room, then turned around and headed towards the ward. We were told that Derek needed changing and that we couldn't sit in the visitors' room because the dining room was still being used which was not appropriate, so we were shown into the meeting room. Derek was then brought up to the room, which means our visit was only about 20-minutes long.

The meeting was much more relaxed. The matron, and social worker were not present, and there were new faces at the meeting. This was the least stressed meeting I have had. The outcome of the meeting was much the same as six months ago, the only change really was that Derek needs help with eating and drinking.

Yet again at the meeting it was brought up that Derek's brother was pleased with the care and that he would love to visit Derek more, but due to the distance it's not possible. So when Derek was in Chichester six miles down the road they didn't visit because...?!

December 2016
22 December. Our visit didn't go quite to plan. Donna was unwell, so sadly had to stay home. Louise and I visited, but again Derek didn't settle. He walked around the whole of our visit, not once sitting down.

We had all brought items of clothing as Christmas presents for Derek, along with Christmas cards, but as before on other Christmases he was not aware of these gifts.

There didn't seem to be any change in Derek. I have to admit that the visits to see him are not ideal. I feel I have to follow him around the whole time making sure he doesn't trip, walk into the glass doors or destroy the decor. I find myself wishing for the hundredth time that he was in a care home as opposed to a hospital with no comfort or warm feel to it at all.

When Louise and I got back into the car we both had a little cry at the situation we are all in.

24 December. Christmas Eve. We had planned to go to Longleat to see the Festival of Lights, but unfortunately Donna and Louise were unwell so we had to cancel. Donna also had a lump come up on her arm which was very painful. She phoned the doctors who said they would make an appointment for her in the next few days.

25 December. The lump in Donna's arm got bigger and the pain had travelled up her arm into her armpit. She phoned the out-of-hours doctor and I took her to St Richard's Hospital to get it checked out.

Never had I been to hospital on Christmas Day, it was surreal. Again, I felt alone. Here was my daughter unwell, and only me to deal with it. I needed back-up, someone to tell me all will be OK. Thankfully it was, but I feel more and more vulnerable as time goes by. The fear within me for our wellbeing scares me always. I don't think I was like this before, the loneliness won't go away.

I truly think that Derek's illness has affected all three of us in such a way that I only pray that we recover. As we approach yet another year I wonder what 2017 will bring.

2017

January 2017

4 January. Had a phone conversation with the doctor about Derek's care at end of life, This came about after two of my friend's husbands who have similar illnesses passed away just before Christmas. I realised that because we as a family do not have easy access to him or his room, that end of life might be an issue for us as a family.

The doctor said she would look into my concerns about what would happen. I asked if Derek would be moved to the care home for Alzheimer's patients which is next door, but she said that would depend on if there was a bed available. There was already a patient who's been waiting two months to be moved there. The doctor said that arrangements would be made for me to visit Derek on the ward and I would be escorted to his room. I asked how safe would we be, as in normal situations we were not allowed on the ward. She said I would be OK, but it may not be possible for the girls to go onto the ward due to some of the patients not being allowed to have contact with children or teenagers.

This confirmed my suspicion of the type of patients that were at the hospital. I feel sick to the stomach that Derek has been put in this environment. I hope that he never finds out or that he doesn't blame me for him being there. I did not make that decision.

12 January. The doctor phoned to say that she had been in discussions with the hospital and it was decided that when Derek needs palliative care they would move him to the room closest to the entrance to the visitors' room so that we as a family would have 24/7 visitation and the girls would also be able to visit. Another thing off my list of concerns. This situation does not become any easier with time, that's for sure.

I received a letter from my dad's solicitor out of the blue asking if I could be my dad's replacement attorney. I phoned to enquire as to why I was sent this letter. It seems that because I don't get on with my sister, my brother is stepping in. It's all a bit confusing and I am not sure what's going on and I am a bit annoyed that I wasn't contacted by either of my siblings to discuss this. My dad seems to be equally confused when I phoned him up about it.

23 January. I have written to dad's solicitor to say I no longer want to be a named lasting power of attorney. My main reason, let's just say after the major problem, grief, heartache I had with Derek's lasting power, and the accusations made against me, I do not wish to be put in that situation again ever.

31 January. Our first visit to Derek this year. Donna came with me as she couldn't come with us at Christmas due to being unwell. I found the whole experience of the visit unsettling due to Derek's need to walk around the visiting room moving furniture and other loose objects. Our visit was at 2.30pm, so later then my usual visits and I could see that Derek was more unsettled at this time of day.

The whole set-up of the visitors' room is wrong for an Alzheimer's patient such as Derek. The two settees are OK because they are heavy pieces of furniture, but the two coffee tables are movable, as are the two smaller chairs which I had to remove from the room in the end. Derek managed to tip over the oak coffee table and the drawers fell out. The large glass vase with flowers in had to be removed, and the free-standing heater and fan were also a hazard, not to mention the hat boxes which were decor and the mat on the floor a trip hazard to Derek.

I did manage to feed him a chocolate pot, but that was difficult due to the continuous walking around, plus his head is bent over so spooning food into his mouth is not so easy. I think it's fair to say that Derek did not recognise either of us, it was like he was in his own world, a world we no longer exist in. The only highlight of the visit was that the children's mug I brought him was a great success. We were concerned that Derek wouldn't grasp the concept of sucking the outer rim, but he drank the whole contents much to my excitement. I left the mug at the hospital, and hopefully they will use it. Donna is purchasing another mug so we can bring it with us each visit with some juice in it.

February 2017
2 February. I contacted the doctor at the hospital to ask that the conversation we had a few weeks ago about Derek's palliative care could be put in writing. She said she would ask the social worker to contact us to add this to Derek's end of life care plan. This afternoon I received a phone call from the said social worker, who asked about point of contact on Derek's death. I asked that they phone me, whatever time of day or night. Also I asked that it be put in writing about the palliative care. The doctor had, as promised, already put this in the care plan, but with a clause which states that we can have 24/7 contact with Derek at the discretion of the staff. I questioned this and the social worker said that if there was an issue with a patient or a fire we wouldn't be allowed on the ward. I trust that if there was a fire all patients would already be evacuated! The hospital always has to have the last word. Personally, I feel it's unacceptable to not be allowed on the ward if a patient is acting out. Let's hope that this is never an issue.

I don't anticipate this will be a smooth journey. Let's face it, so far it's been far from smooth. It seems every scenario has been put in front of us just to see how far we can be pushed.

March 2017
7 March. Today I received a phone call from the hospital asking if Derek's brother could attend the CPA meeting in May, as they were asking questions about Derek's illness and the hospital thought it a good idea that they attend the meeting. Why do I feel guilty for saying no?

I can't put myself through that again. The last time there was a meeting about Derek it turned into a 'we hate Angela' campaign. Why would I want to put myself through all that stress? The doctor then went on to say that Derek benefits from his brother's visits, and that they sing to him and Derek acknowledges this. Well, all I can say is good for them. When I visit it's stressful, Derek doesn't know me or the girls, he's continually walking the room, moving furniture. I am so angry right now just thinking that they have better communication with Derek, if in fact that's actually true.

11 March. All three of us went to visit Derek, as it was going to be his birthday on Thursday 16th. As with previous visits, Derek did not sit down at any point, he constantly walked the room and moved furniture. We gave him his birthday cards, but as before he didn't open them or acknowledge them or the presents.

Derek's overall appearance was the same, although he was wearing someone else's jumper. You would have thought that with all the clothes we buy him he could at least be dressed in his clothes. Derek also didn't smell too clean either, which was upsetting for me.

***

Two days after the visit both Louise and I were very emotional, unbeknown to each other. It resulted in myself having major anxiety issues.

15 March. Received a phone call from the doctor at the hospital asking when I last saw Derek. I replied four days ago. She asked how I thought Derek was. My reply was the same as the last few visits. She then went on to explain that it had been noted that Derek was sitting down more and was less aggressive on personal care. She then went on to say that the hospital were considering moving Derek. This was a complete shock to me. I certainly have not seen any changes in Derek to make me think he was ready for a nursing home. The doctor said that Derek would still need one-to-one care, which of course no nursing home near us would be able to offer.

The suggestion is to move Derek to one of the units which is part of the forensic science hospital complex. We are now awaiting the assessment from the unit to see if they can manage Derek. This all seems to have arisen after I asked about palliative care and how the hospital would be able to accommodate myself and the girls if Derek should need such care. Like when Derek apparently walked into a glass door, I questioned the fact then Derek was moved. Coincidence?

***

I have since contacted the doctor with some questions about the possible move, one being the fact that moving Alzheimer's patients can cause a decline in the disease, the fact the unit is a mixed ward, and would Derek still have the same doctors. She said that they do recognise that the move could cause upset for Derek, but the transition would be made with the least amount of disruption. The doctor would no longer be involved in Derek's care and Derek would be appointed a new GP.

With regards to the mixed ward, apparently Derek's Alzheimer's is such that a mixed ward would not be a problem. My concern is what if a little old lady sat in her chair fast asleep and Derek comes along, moves the seat and tips her out? I asked that if Derek doesn't settle into the unit, would he be moved back? Her reply was yes, if there is a room still available.

To me that raises more questions. I guess I will have to wait and see what the decision is before I start worrying about the next dilemma.

27 March. I phoned the doctor today to see what was happening about Derek's move or if there was going to be a move, as it's almost two weeks ago I had the phone call. The doctor said that she hadn't been notified yet and was going to chase it up and see what the decision was.

I can't believe that it takes two weeks to come to a decision. Why bother telling me in the first place, adding even more stress to our situation?

April 2017

19 April. My next-door neighbour and I were booked in to see Derek at 2pm. We arrived just after. I could see that there were people in the room adjoining the visitors' room so we waited to see where we could go. We were shown into the conference room and were told that Derek was quite aggressive today, but hopefully he would calm down.

I questioned why the hospital wanted to move him to a nursing home when clearly he can still be aggressive, it just doesn't make sense. No comment. We were kept waiting almost an hour before Derek was brought to the visitors' room. At no point did he know or acknowledge that we were there, he wandered around for a few minutes, resting his head against the wall. Finally the staff got him to sit down, at which point he fell asleep leaning forward and bent in half. I pointed out to the member of staff that Derek may have an infection, as the leaning his head against the wall and more aggressive behaviour indicates this from previous experience. The staff member said that if he had a urine infection that his urine would have an offensive smell, which was not the case.

We left after about ten minutes. It was clear Derek needed sleep, so the staff were hoping to get him to his bed without him waking up too much. My shortest visit yet, hardly worth the hour's drive. Maybe it would have been a good idea if the hospital had contacted me to say Derek was not in a good place for visitors today.

20 April. I phoned the hospital to speak to the doctor, but there was no answer so a message was left to phone me.

21 April. Phoned the doctor, but the hospital informed me that she doesn't work on Fridays. I asked to be transferred to the ward and spoke to the same member of staff that accompanied Derek on our visit. I asked how Derek was and he said the same. I asked if Derek had slept after we had left. Apparently, he was back to his wandering around, so no sleep.

I insisted that Derek had an infection. The staff member said they would be extra vigilant and would try to do some tests.

***

Saturday I am going to see a homeopath again. My anxiety has become a bit more of a problem. I guess after nine years of dealing with Derek's illness it starts to take its toll on all of us.

24 April. Monday morning a phone call from the doctor. I explained the situation with Derek, about how when he has an infection he becomes more aggressive and has a tendency to lean his head against the wall. Her reaction was it's good to know these signposts in Derek's case. He's been at the hospital three years and they hadn't figured that out themselves! Really? It's beyond belief. The doctor said she would ask for extra vigilance and some tests to be done. She also suggested that some of Derek's medication doses be reduced as over a long period of time the body gets used to the medication and it doesn't work. I agreed that this was a good idea.

26 April. What a surprise, a phone call from the hospital informing me that Derek has a urine infection and is now on antibiotics. One week on from my visit, it's taken one whole week! No words can explain how I feel.

***

During this week I receive a letter from the hospital.

Dear Mrs Hogarth,
Re: Mr Derek Hogarth
I am writing to you in my capacity as Mr Hogarth's appointed social worker at the hospital, where I have the opportunity to meet with him on a regular basis. I wish to inform you that I will no longer be the social worker involved with Derek's case and that a colleague of mine will be taking over his social care needs.

That's what I call a result! Hopefully there will be less agro.

May 2017
21 May. I haven't been to see Derek since my last visit. I need to concentrate on me, or I will go downhill. I am seeking help from a homeopath. With constant toothaches and a pending tooth extraction I am getting anxiety attacks. I have been to see the doctor and they suggested antidepressants – no surprise there – and counselling again. So I decided

to see a homeopath instead. It's very surprising how much I have suppressed over the past nine years. No wonder I feel like I do. It hasn't helped that on the 10 May I phoned dad up to see what he was doing for his birthday on the 13th. Oh, would you believe, my brother and sister and their other halves are visiting with a Chinese meal. Nice of them to invite me. I was so upset that I was left out again. I haven't had any contact with my brother for about a year now.

June 2017

I had to text my brother because the floor has gone on the first landing to our stairs. I couldn't find a carpenter to do the repair. So my brother turned up to give me a price. At no point did he ask about Derek.

6 June. A phone call from the hospital at 6.30pm to say there had been an incident. On 27 May Derek had been passing blood for a couple of days, but all is OK now.

I questioned why they hadn't told me straight away. The general feeling I got from the hospital was did I want to know everything about Derek's health, even small things? My reply was yes, he's still my husband. Just because I don't have direct access to him doesn't change that fact.

14 June. A lady phoned me from DoLS, which is put into place when you come off being sectioned. She asked me a lot of questions about Derek's care and explained to me how DoLS works. She was under the impression that Derek at some time would be moved to a nursing home.

20 June. Meeting at the hospital today and visiting Derek first. It's been a while since I last visited him. The visitors' room, a conservatory, was extremely hot, too hot for us to sit in, so we went into the garden, hoping that Derek would sit down with us as the ground is too uneven for him to walk around. Unfortunately, Derek wasn't going to sit down, so we had to go back inside.

The hospital are adapting a room so that they can have a second visitors' room, which sounds good except they have built another unit with more beds so in actual fact the ratio of two visitors' room for 38 residents is still not good.

Anyway we asked to use the new room as it was cooler. Although it was not finished it was a lot cooler. As before with other visits, Derek did not sit down for more than a couple of minutes. His presentation was upsetting, still very much bent over, very thin, and where he was wearing shorts I could see how bad his veins were in his legs.

I gave Derek his Fathers' Day cards, but sadly he's too far gone to recognise what they are. He didn't even acknowledge me. My friend who came with me was very good with Derek. I always feel so useless. I felt quite detached from Derek. I think that the homeopathy treatment has made me like this, in a good way.

The meeting went well, probably the best one so far. There was a good feeling around the table and a new social worker an added bonus. Two people from Chichester came to the meeting, Derek's CPN and social worker because the hospital social worker had informed them that Derek was moving.

This is still an ongoing possibility in maybe six months' time.

I asked the Chichester social worker where they would move Derek. Their answer was the Waterlooville home or one by our home. I have seen the Waterlooville home, and the other one is where Derek's mum was and I haven't heard good reports from there. My answer to the social worker's choice was 'no way'. Derek will go to the unit at the hospital if that's the best they can offer.

When I got home I sat in the garden on my own and cried my heart out. I was starting to feel more like myself. Prior to the visit, I hadn't seen Derek for a while and the sense of finding myself again had begun, until the visit which brought me back to reality. That and the fact that neither of our daughters had asked about dad, or how the meeting went.

I know that they are hurting just as much if not more; this never-ending nightmare still continues. In the meeting the social worker said that Derek was happy in his own world, but is he? How can we possibly know what nightmare he is living in his trapped body; a kind-hearted, hard-working gentleman who loved watching his favourite football team, motor sport, gardening, listening to music from the sixties. Not a day went by without him telling me he loved me. All gone now, just pacing around moving furniture, being spoon-fed and wearing pads. THIS EVIL DISEASE IS SICK.

27 June. After the long conversation about asking the hospital to let me know of any incidences with Derek after he had blood in his poo, I received a phone call from the matron today to say Derek has a blister on this foot! All I can say to this is I am lost for words.

July 2017
2 July. We all went on holiday to Paris for a well-deserved break, a chance to live a normal life of no worries or stresses. On the Tuesday I received a phone call from the hospital to say Derek has a UTI and is now on antibiotics; on the Wednesday another phone call to say Derek had a leg infection and is on another antibiotic. On Sunday I phoned the hospital to ask how Derek was. The reply was that he was responding well to the antibiotics.

I can't seem to get away from this nightmare, even during a one-week holiday there's a problem. Going out of the country, albeit for a week, has done me the world of good. It kind of puts perspective on life. It's made me want to pursue maybe moving abroad in the future.

14 July. A phone call from the social worker at the hospital asking if I could bring some photos of Derek and the family in, and wanting information on Derek pre-illness – hobbies, job, interests. I said it's a bit late for making a memory board for his room, he no longer recognises his children, but the social worker convinced me that it was for the staff's sake as well.

The fact Derek has been there for three years is irrelevant. I don't want to fall out with this social worker as well, so I gave her some info on Derek over the phone and agreed to bring photos on my next visit.

The social worker then asked if I could purchase another helmet for Derek, at a cost of £110. I agreed as I am never going to win the argument of it being a medical aid. That evening I wrote out the cheque and posted it. Prior to my next visit to see Derek I have yet another tooth infection. I believe it's caused by the stress of visiting. I don't look forward to the visits anymore, not only does it upset me but I feel Derek no longer knows who I am. Instead of going to the dentist I am getting help from a homeopath who also feels that my tooth problem is related to stress.

19 July. Both girls and I visit Derek. We go armed with three pairs of jogging bottoms, ten high-calorie desserts, shower gel, shampoo, eight cans of coke, and a collection of photos which consist of an engagement photo, two of Derek as a child, one of his mum and dad, and one of Derek before his illness. No photos of the girls were added because of the environment Derek is in. I didn't feel comfortable having photos of the girls there.

Once signed into the hospital we were asked which room we wanted. We asked to see the new room, but sadly they had ended up putting many movable chairs in which closed the room down and made less room for Derek to walk around in. So we were shown into the old visitors' room. Unfortunately, they had also added new decor to this room – two large oak coffee tables put together to make one large table in the centre of the room with a large glass vase with flowers as decor. Another small coffee table added, with lots more scattered cushions, fur throws over the settees, and another fancy lamp to add to the existing one. New chairs were added along with the two existing settees. All this decor had made the room feel smaller and has given Derek less room to move around and more things for me to stress over on our visit.

Derek was shown into the room, but at no point acknowledged any of us. I managed to feed him one of the desserts I had brought with me, albeit that I fed him while he was walking around. At one point Derek did get aggressive with the carer, and I witnessed Derek hit him. This really upset me as Derek is not a violent man. We noticed that Derek was grinding his teeth quite a bit, something he used to do as a child apparently. He was also chewing his fingers. This was not a new thing, but the grinding of teeth was. We had also noticed that Derek's leg still looked infected. I asked the carer to ask Derek's nurse to come to the visitors' room so I could ask some questions.

Meanwhile the social worker popped into the visitors' room. I gave her the photos and she asked if I had the cheque for the helmet. I told her I had posted it and that she should have received it by now. She said she hadn't and asked why I didn't bring it with me, and then said if there was a problem she would contact me. When she left the room, Donna said exactly what I was thinking. She didn't believe that I posted the cheque. Good to see I am not paranoid.

We had a long and informative talk with Derek's nurse. I explained about the grinding of his teeth, and he suggested that the hospital dentist have a look. I asked how they would achieve this and he explained that they would give Derek a sedative and take a look at his teeth. It may be he has toothache, or it could be just a habit.

I asked about Derek's leg and said it still looked infected. The nurse said they had taken a swab and were awaiting results. Whilst we were talking Derek had sat down and fallen asleep, and as before he was bent forward in half. I commented on how it was almost a foetal position and the nurse explained that when a person is poorly and frail they do take on this position when asleep, something I didn't know. I commented that maybe it was because they were going to be reborn.

20 July. I had an appointment at the doctors today to check a small mark on my face. While there I asked about a small lump on my eye lid which had been there for at least a couple of years. The mark on my face was due to age, however the doctor wants the lump on my eye investigated as he said it might be a tumour. I actually feel physically sick with worry right now. As always, the worst-case scenario is going through my head. I pray to god it's not that.

***

My life has so much stress, there never seems any let up in my worries. I am no longer sure if I am just always worried or that due to Derek's illness my brain is in constant worry mode. I often question the meaning of life.

A week after our visit to see Derek the social worker phoned to inform me that they still had not received the cheque for Derek's new helmet, and that he no longer has a helmet as the old one has disintegrated.

Obviously, the cheque has got lost in the post. Just my luck, now the social worker really believes I didn't send it. I have had to contact the bank and cancel the cheque and reissue a new one. The social worker informed me to address the envelope to our old social worker as she is leaving at the end of the week. I was at a loss as to why the social worker from hell is now Derek's social worker again.
I have sent off the new cheque recorded delivery. See how they like it.

August 2017

10 August. I had to see a consultant at St Richard's about my eye. He has referred me to an eye specialist for a biopsy.

22 August. Phone call from hospital to say Derek has a very sore foot which is close to breaking the skin. It's on the sole of his foot. The hospital want Derek to wear some special socks costing £20 a pair.

29 August. I had to go to Shoreham hospital for a biopsy. The staff there were brilliant, they put me at ease. I now have to wait four weeks for the results.

***

Derek has yet another new social worker, this time a male. I haven't met him yet, but he did phone to say Derek needed another pair of special socks, the last pair only lasting two weeks.

September 2017

25 September. At 4.50pm I received a phone call from the hospital to say they are moving Derek tomorrow to the nursing home on the same grounds as the hospital. To say I was shocked is an understatement.

26 September. Needless to say, I have had little sleep. I am still trying to process the fact that the hospital think it's OK to tell me the day before that they are moving him. I don't know what part, if he will have the same doctor, what the visiting procedure is, if he will be able to accept change, how he will react. Questions, questions, going around in my head.

I phoned the hospital back to ask if I could visit Derek on Thursday. My friend and I are visiting Thursday afternoon. I have no idea what to expect. I am still in shock that I received very little notice of Derek's move.

***

After a night of little sleep, I decided the next morning to try and contact Derek's social worker from Chichester. Luckily she had attended the last CPA meeting so by looking at the minutes I had a name to chase.

Not surprisingly she had not been told of Derek's move, neither had Derek's CPN nurse. The social worker said I had every right to put in a formal complaint, but I said I wouldn't because last time I complained about something I landed up being investigated.

26 September. Just before lunch I received a phone call from the unit to say Derek has now been transferred, followed by a second phone call from the hospital to say that he has been delivered to the unit.

I have since learnt that because I am Derek's representative for DoLS I should have been advised of Derek's forthcoming transfer. Everything should have been discussed, apparently even the funding had not been put into place because the paperwork had not been done.

27 September. The doctor from the hospital phoned. Even she was surprised how quickly Derek had been moved. I am glad she phoned because I needed to know some answers to the questions going around in my head.

I phoned the unit to ask how Derek's first night was. I was told what he had had for breakfast, which was nice, and they said Derek was OK, busy walking around feeling and moving furniture.

28 September. My friend and I made a visit to Derek's new home. The staff were very accommodating and we were shown into a room and offered tea and biscuits. We were told about the home and they explained that it has a waiting list, but because Derek was known to them they gave the place to him.

We were shown around the building, shown his room, which we can bring anything to personalise it if we wish. We walked in the gardens, which were beautiful, and we were even shown the menu of the day. So different from the hospital. I saw Derek for about ten minutes. I was shocked at how thin he looked, and he did not recognise me at all.

I was then shown all the paperwork involving Derek – charts, info, medical notes. I was very surprised, this should have happened three years ago. I was told that I would be very involved in his care and that they would phone me if there were any changes. The staff were very surprised at the amount of clothing he had. The records showed he had 34 jumpers and 55 t-shirts. I told them it was because the hospital kept asking for more clothes.

I was also told that there might be a possibility that they would try a different drug to help him sleep as he only sleeps for a couple of hours. A different story to the hospital. It all seems very positive, I hope this will be the case. We will have more access to Derek in a more homely environment. I need to visit the home again in a couple of weeks to sign the paperwork for Derek's transfer. The funding hadn't been set up either. Let's keep our fingers crossed that this will now be Derek's forever home.

November 2017
23 November. Derek seems to have settled into the unit, although I haven't visited him for a while. One of the reasons being he has MRSA again and the biopsy on my eye lid confirmed it was cancer, therefore I had to go for an operation so coming into contact with MRSA would be stupid. Prior to this I caught a nasty virus which I was trying hard to fight, otherwise it would jeopardise me having the operation.

The operation went ahead as planned. I had a section of my lower eye lid removed, and after a week got the results back of all clear. I just burst out crying, as did Donna when

I got the result. I then went onto explain to the Dr, that my husband had Alzheimer's. I don't even know why I told him. I feel really stupid that I felt the need to tell him, it's not like I was looking for sympathy, I guess it was to justify my crying.

Throughout this scary ordeal my friends have been so good, texting me and keeping in contact with me. Even three of my work places have stayed in contact, plus my healer friends have been sending healing. But the one thing that's been upsetting is not one member of my family, i.e. my brother or sister, have contacted me. I guess I thought that when something like this happens it would bring us together, as I am immediate family.

It saddens me to know that my family are not willing to stand by me in times of turmoil. I should have realised when they were not there when Derek's illness was diagnosed, how stupid of me to think that my diagnosis would be any different. I do not understand; maybe they have had difficult times or illness, and I didn't know about it and that I wasn't there for them. I hope that's not the case. If it is, I am sorry.

I have just phoned the hospital. Today Derek's OK but still has MRSA. I asked if it was catching, they said only if you have an open wound. That rules me out at the moment. I am not willing to take that risk, as much as it hurts me to say he doesn't know me anymore so why risk my health.

27 November. Monday teatime I received a phone call from my brother to say dad was in hospital because he had stomach pains and the doctor said he thought there was a blockage in his pancreas. He said he would keep me informed as he was just going to see him. I was at home on my own as Louise was still at uni and Donna was out. Less than three quarters of an hour later the phone rang again. It was my brother saying dad had taken a turn for the worse and had died.

***

Died. I still can't believe it. It feels like a bad dream. Surely I'll wake up in a while and all will be fine? He died of a heart attack, and part of my heart died too.

In the time that Derek has had Alzheimer's I have lost both my parents. I feel I have been robbed.

Because of dad's sudden death he had to have a post-mortem, so it was a further two weeks before I could see him. I went to the chapel of rest on my own as the two girls didn't want to come. Nothing prepared me for how dad looked. I guess with the two-week delay and the process of a post-mortem he looked scary. It upset me so much that I couldn't stay.

The funeral took place on the 14 December, on what would have been mum's birthday. In my heart I know that dad is where he wanted to be, back with my mum, but it doesn't make it any easier for me to accept because I was expecting it to be Derek who passed first.

2018

January 2018

Yet another year passes. I miss my dad so much. I can't understand why there is so much sadness in my life, I feel so alone and lost. The impact of dad's death has been more then I could have imagined.

Our Christmas was the worst yet. It was just myself and the girls. We all felt low. I think it's time to make some changes in our lives. I can't go on feeling like this, I have even asked for more counselling to try and make sense of this life.

The job I now have which was supposed to be a home help is basically a cleaner, which isn't helping my moral at all.

16 January. Donna and I went to visit Derek, my first visit in three months due to my operation, Derek's MRSA and then the death of my dad.

I was so shocked when I saw him, he was so thin. His shoulder blades were sticking out and I could see his ribs. I got upset and Donna seemed annoyed that I did. I don't understand why. On a positive note, he did sit down for the whole visit which was good, something he hasn't done for a while. He didn't spit at all and seemed to be having a conversation with someone we couldn't see. By some miracle his leg was not so swollen, and he was wearing socks and shoes. I was shown his care plan and we left feeling at ease, as though he had finally found a better place to stay. At long last.

July 2018

1 July. My last entry in my journal. Our last visit to see Derek was 28 May. Derek, as always, was wandering the visitors' room, trying to move furniture and objects around. He was unaware of us and proceeded to walk into a door with a loud bang. He later had a nasty nose bleed which I believed was a result of him jamming his finger up his nose. The nurse had also commented that Derek had MRSA again. I became very protective of Louise who was with me, and said it was time for us to go. I didn't want either of us to pick up this infection. Needless to say we were both in tears when we left.

I have since had two calls to say Derek has had a fall. Both times he was OK, but the home wanted to inform me. Derek has had Alzheimer's now for ten years; nine years ago he was given the diagnosis. We are still living with this evil disease.

There is no end to this story. We still live the nightmare.

As of November 2018
Derek was moved into palliative care.
He has lost the use of his legs due to the evil disease Alzheimer's.
Myself and the girls continue to live in constant fear of the inevitable phone call .